2021

DAWN OF INFAMY

DAWN OF INFAMY

A Sunken Ship,
a Vanished Crew,
and the Final Mystery
of Pearl Harbor

STEPHEN HARDING

DA CAPO PRESS

Designed by Amnet Systems
Set in 10 point Palatino LT Std by Perseus Books

Library of Congress Cataloging-in-Publication Data

Names: Harding, Stephen, 1952- author.
Title: Dawn of infamy : a sunken ship, a vanished crew, and the final mystery
   of Pearl Harbor / Stephen Harding.
Other titles: Voyage to oblivion
Description: Boston, MA : Da Capo Press, 2016. | Original title: Voyage to
   oblivion. Stroud, Gloucestershire : Amberley, 2010. | Includes
   bibliographical references.
Identifiers: LCCN 2016026005 (print) | LCCN 2016031133 (ebook) |
   ISBN 9780306825033 (hardcover) | ISBN 9780306825040 (ebook)
Subjects: LCSH: World War, 1939-1945—Naval operations—Submarine. | World
   War, 1939-1945—Naval operations, Japanese. | Cargo ships—United
   States—History—20th century. | Submarines (Ships)—Japan—History—20th
   century. | Pearl Harbor (Hawaii), Attack on, 1941. | Cynthia Olson (Cargo ship)
Classification: LCC D783.7 .H38 2016 (print) | LCC D783.7 (ebook) |
   DDC 940.54/26—dc23
LC record available at https://lccn.loc.gov/2016026005

Published by Da Capo Press,
an imprint of Perseus Books, LLC, a subsidiary of
Hachette Book Group, Inc.
www.dacapopress.com

Da Capo Press books are available at special discounts for bulk purchases in the U.S.
by corporations, institutions, and other organizations. For more information, please
contact the Special Markets Department at Perseus Books, 2300 Chestnut Street,
Suite 200, Philadelphia, PA 19103, or call (800) 810-4145, ext. 5000,
or e-mail special.markets@perseusbooks.com.

10 9 8 7 6 5 4 3 2 1

As always, for Mari

CONTENTS

Illustrations following page 134

Eternal Father, strong to save,
Whose arm hath bound the restless wave,
Who bidst the mighty ocean deep
Its own appointed limits keep;
O, hear us when we cry to Thee
For those in peril on the sea!

And now, without having wearied my friends,
I hope, with detailed scientific accounts, theories,
or deductions, I will only say that I have
endeavored to tell just the story of the
adventure itself.
—Joshua Slocum

PROLOGUE

ON THE AFTERNOON OF MONDAY, December 1, 1941, Captain Berthel Carlsen leaned over the bridge wing of the steamship *Cynthia Olson* and ordered deckhands to let go the mooring lines holding the small freighter to a pier in Seattle, Washington. Carlsen, a sixty-four-year-old master mariner, then ordered "slow ahead" on the engine-order telegraph. Minutes later, her single screw churning the waters of Elliot Bay, the twenty-two-year-old ship set out on the 135-mile passage up Puget Sound, bound for the Pacific Ocean.

It was a familiar route for both Carlsen and his vessel. Though the ship had sailed the Atlantic and Caribbean in her youth, for the first seven months of 1941, *Cynthia Olson* had plied the waters of the West Coast as a lumber carrier. Homeported in San Francisco, she made regular calls at Olympia, Tacoma, and other Pacific Northwest ports, often with Carlsen in command. Once her decks were covered with stacks of freshly sawn timber and her holds filled with massive rolls of newsprint, she'd sail for Oakland, Los Angeles, or San Diego. It was a fairly mundane routine, but one that had proven dependably profitable for her owner, San Francisco's Oliver J. Olson Steamship Company.

But that routine changed abruptly in early August, when the Olson Company signed a contract with the U.S. Army. That service had launched a hurried military construction effort in Hawaii in response to the increasing threat of war in the Pacific, and *Cynthia Olson* and ships like her were needed to haul the timber that would become the barracks, warehouses, and aircraft hangars of what the War Department hoped would be a newly invigorated Hawaii-defense force.

Cynthia Olson had embarked on her first timber-hauling passage to Pearl Harbor on August 22, completing each leg of the trip in nine and

1

a half days under the command of Captain P. C. Johnson. A second trip, in late September and early October, worked out equally well, and on November 18, the Army chartered the vessel outright. Now, on the first day of December, she was setting out again, with Carlsen as a last-minute substitute for an ailing Johnson. Sharing the bridge was First Mate William Buchtele, himself a last-minute replacement, and together the two men hoped to better the previous total passage time by at least a day.

What neither mariner could know was that their ship and the thirty-five men aboard her were embarking on their final voyage. Even as *Cynthia Olson* chugged slowly toward the sea, events were unfolding that would pit the ship and her crew against a deadly foe, mark the beginning of a new front in a global conflict, and spark one of the most enduring nautical mysteries of World War II.

PART ONE

PART ONE

CHAPTER 1

A SHIP FINE AND STURDY

The vessel Berthel Carlsen and his ill-fated crew took to sea that day in early December 1941 had started life a continent away, and by the time she set out on her last voyage, she'd already spent some two decades plying both the Atlantic and Pacific Oceans. It hadn't been an easy life, and she was starting to show her age.

A product of Wisconsin's Manitowoc Shipbuilding Company, the vessel was laid down in the late summer of 1918 as *Coquina*, one of some 331 oceangoing freighters built for the U.S. Shipping Board (USSB)[1] by firms throughout the Great Lakes. Of essentially identical design, these steel-hulled ships came to be known as Laker-class vessels, both because of where they were built and because many initially bore names beginning with the word "Lake." The ships were similar in layout to the medium-sized, oceangoing "Fredrickstad"[2] freighter design developed early in World War I by neutral Scandinavian shipbuilders, an economical type that was well-suited to prefabrication and mass production. Both attributes were particularly important, given that the first ninety-one Lakers[3] had been contracted for by British companies planning to put them into service in support of the United Kingdom's war effort. When America entered the conflict in April 1917, the U.S. government abrogated the British contracts, and the following month he USSB requisitioned the vessels for wartime cargo duty on behalf of the United States and her allies.[4]

The USSB and, after September 1917, a subordinate agency called the Emergency Fleet Corporation (EFC), ultimately awarded contracts for the construction of 346[5] Laker-class ships. When this number is added to the requisitioned British-ordered vessels, it renders the Laker program the largest standard-type shipbuilding effort undertaken by the United States during World War I.[6] The ships were of six variants, which differed slightly in gross tonnage and overall length. Each variant was given a type number, with the thirty-three examples ultimately manufactured by Manitowoc Shipbuilding being designated Design 1044.

These solidly built and dependable craft had an overall length of 251 feet, a beam of 43 feet 6 inches, and a loaded draft of 23 feet. Each ship weighed in at 3,400 deadweight, 2,800 gross, and approximately 1,280 net tons.[7] Though they differed in small structural details, all featured the standard Laker "three-island" silhouette—raised foc'sle and poop deck, and a large amidships deckhouse with a single funnel set just aft of the bridge. The vessels had two large cargo holds, one forward and one aft of the deckhouse, each of which was accessed through two hatches, one directly behind the other. Each hold was served by two sets of twin booms. Two of the booms for each hold were fixed to kingposts, one set of which was attached to the forward part of the deckhouse and one set to the aft. The other two booms for each hold were attached to taller masts: one set into the foc'sle and one into the poop. Each boom had its own dedicated winch.

The Design 1044 Lakers were built with cellular double bottoms,[8] single-width side-hull plates, and four deck levels. The upper, or main, deck stretched from stem to stern and was the structure upon which the hatch covers rested and from which the amidships deckhouse rose. The bridge deck—the house's first habitable level up from the main deck—contained the main saloon, the engineers' mess, the galley, a small pantry, the radio room, single cabins for the chief engineer and chief steward, and double cabins for the ship's deck and engineering officers.[9] The aft two-thirds of the boat deck, one level higher, were open to the elements and housed two twenty-four-foot wooden lifeboats (each capable of embarking thirty-six people), a sixteen-foot workboat, and davits for each. The forward part of the boat deck was taken up by the structure housing the staterooms for the captain and first officer, each of whom had direct access to the boat deck. Directly above these two cabins was the Laker's wheelhouse, which incorporated two bridge wings, a chart room, and the captain's small day cabin.

Descending through the center portion of the Laker's boat, bridge, and upper decks—all the way to the keel—was a roughly forty-foot-high and twenty-foot-wide space that housed the lower half of the ship's funnel and, just aft of that, the engine-room trunk. The space at the funnel's base was taken up by two Scotch boilers (oil-fired in *Coquina* and her eight sister ships). These fed a single 1,250-hp triple-expansion reciprocating steam engine, just aft of the boilers, that gave the Manitowoc-built Lakers a service speed of about ten knots (roughly 11.5 mph).[10]

The keel of the ship that was to become *Coquina*[11] and, ultimately, *Cynthia Olson*, was laid down in Manitowoc Shipbuilding's extensive works a mile up the Manitowoc River from Lake Michigan. Bearing the company yard number 100, she was one of nine vessels ordered under EFC contract 180227. Like virtually all Lakers, she was assembled from prefabricated sections, a method that greatly speeded her construction. Her hull was launched—sideways—without fanfare on November 30, and within days she was moved downriver to the Manitowoc Boiler Works[12] for installation of her Scotch boilers and further fitting-out. Over the next five months, she was equipped with all those things needed to turn her into a vital part of the United States' massive wartime trans-Atlantic shipping effort.

Over the course of the nineteen months the United States participated in the war, that Herculean effort used Army, Navy, and USSB-owned and requisitioned civilian ships—both American and foreign[13]—to transport more than two million American service members and some 7.5 million tons of materiel to Europe.[14] Yet, ironically, the military need for vessels like *Coquina* had begun winding down literally weeks before the freighter's launching. The November 11, 1918, armistice that ended the fighting had also effectively reversed the flow of shipping; rather than carrying troops and cargo to Europe, vessels had begun returning men and goods to the United States. Given that much of the war materiel carried to the Old World had been used in the ferocious, final battles of the conflict or been passed on to various European governments to aid in their reconstruction, ships already in service were more than capable of handling the tonnage of cargo being returned to North America. And given that even the most homesick Doughboy would draw the line at returning to America huddled in the vast reaches of an unheated cargo hold, most troops were repatriated on dedicated troopships or requisitioned passenger vessels.

As a result, by the time *Coquina* was completed in mid-April 1919 the EFC had determined that she and many of her sister ships were no longer needed on the trans-Atlantic military cargo runs for which they'd been built. Rather than attempt to sell the vessels at a loss on the already glutted secondhand market, the EFC determined that they should be laid up in suitable anchorages until they could either be gainfully employed or sold for a reasonable price. On April 25, *Coquina* was titled in Milwaukee, Wisconsin, as belonging to the USSB,[15] granted the radio call letters WVAA, and, as far as can be determined from surviving records, was laid up in Lake Michigan the following day within sight of where she was built.[16] It was the first of several periods of enforced idleness the freighter would endure over the course of her life.

It is unclear how long *Coquina* sat quietly anchored in the Lake Michigan shallows, but by the end of December 1919 the USSB had chartered her to the Philadelphia-based Earn Line Steamship Company. The firm specialized in hauling goods of all sorts between the U.S. East Coast, the West Indies, Panama, and the east coast of South America, and during the last days of December 1919 the company's directors were finalizing a deal to ship a valuable, and hugely intoxicating, cargo.

That cargo was whiskey, and lots of it. The U.S. Congress's October 1919 passage of the Volstead Act initiating prohibition had caught U.S. distillers with inventories totaling some sixty million gallons of bonded whiskey,[17] none of which could legally be sold in the United States or exported after the Eighteenth Amendment went into effect on January 17, 1920. In an effort to unload their collective backlog of thirty-five million gallons, a consortium of Kentucky distilleries quickly put together a deal to export some thirty thousand barrels of the spirit, primarily to Cuba and other islands in the Caribbean. Two shipping lines received contracts for the first five thousand barrels—the Earn Line would send one thousand to Havana aboard *Coquina*, while International Freighting Corporation's *Western Comet* and *Shamrock* would each load two thousand barrels for the West Indies. All three were to load in, and sail from, Philadelphia, which was the destination of the thirty-car train bearing the first consignment of booze from Kentucky. Given the tenor of the time, the train also carried armed guards to ward off thirsty potential thieves.[18]

All went well with the shipment of the bourbon to Pennsylvania, but once the train pulled onto a Baltimore & Ohio Railroad siding near the Philadelphia docks on January 1, things began to go sour. Six days earlier, the Harbor Boatmen's Union representing the masters, mates, and crewmembers operating the port's harbor and river tugboats had threatened to strike for higher wages and better working conditions, and on the first day of 1920 the union made good its threat. The tug sailors' early morning walkout brought vessel movements at the port and on the Delaware River to a standstill, though longshoremen had finished loading *Coquina* before walking out in a gesture of sympathy for the tug men. For several days it looked as if her cargo of whiskey might have to be offloaded and shipped to another port for onward movement to Havana. However, an interim agreement between the union and Philadelphia's Tugboat Owners Association sent the tug men back to work within days, and *Coquina* and the other "whiskey ships" were able to leave port before the January 17 deadline.

Having successfully offloaded her intoxicating cargo in Cuba, *Coquina* remained on charter to the Earn Line throughout the remainder of 1920, operating on a Philadelphia–Havana–New York–Philadelphia cargo service. On December 1, 1920, her homeport[19] was changed from Milwaukee to Philadelphia, and she soldiered on without interruption well into the summer of 1921. But while the doughty freighter more than earned her keep during this period, the Earn Line's fortunes continued a decline that had been in progress for some time. Indeed, the firm had been doing so poorly as early as October 1913 that a judged placed it in receivership,[20] and only a series of wartime contracts kept the company afloat. By the end of 1921 the Earn Line was in dire financial straits, and in an attempt to trim operating costs the firm terminated its charter agreement for *Coquina* following her mid-December arrival in New York from Havana.

While the Merchant Marine Act of 1920[21] required, among other things, that all goods transported between U.S. ports must be carried on U.S.-built, U.S.-owned, and U.S.-crewed ships, and authorized the USSB to sell government-owned vessels to private firms at extremely advantageous prices, the continuing postwar glut of idle merchant hulls meant that the market for such ships remained decidedly soft. The EFC therefore recommended that *Coquina* join the hundreds of other USSB-owned vessels relegated to lay-up[22] until better times arrived. The Laker subsequently sat idle in New York for nearly four years, tied alongside a Manitowoc-built sister ship, *Corsicana*, which had been constructed under the same EFC contract.

By the fall of 1925 the market for used merchant ships had improved to the point that the EFC's chairman, Elmer E. Crowley, determined that the time was ripe to begin selling off USSB-owned vessels as quickly as possible. Prices for surplus ships were reduced even more to further stimulate sales, and lay-up anchorages around the country began buzzing with activity as newly sold ships were again made ready for sea. In New York, *Coquina* and *Corsicana* joined the parade of departing vessels, both having been sold on November 2 to the noted San Francisco ship-brokers Pillsbury & Curtis.[23] In its bid for the two freighters, the company stated that both would be converted for the West Coast lumber trade and then chartered to coastwise shipping firms. The EFC approved the sale at the bargain-basement price of just $25,000 per ship, and even allowed Pillsbury & Curtis to defer part of the cash payment when the company agreed to take out surety bonds to guarantee completion of proposed alterations to the vessels. Those alterations included the replacement of each ship's two short fore-and-aft kingposts with taller boom-carrying masts intended to facilitate the on- and off-loading of sawn timber.

Having purchased *Coquina* and her sister ship, Pillsbury & Curtis then had to get the vessels to California. The first step was a cursory overhaul for both freighters, conducted over a four-week period at a New York–area shipyard. The vessels were not dry-docked—that could wait until they reached their destination—but they did get a mechanical once-over. Both were in relatively good condition despite four years of enforced idleness, and by early January 1926 they were judged ready for the voyage to California. Always the canny businessmen, the ships' new owners ensured that each vessel departed for the Golden State with a load of miscellaneous cargo.

While no logs of the voyage survive,[24] we can assume that *Coquina* and *Corsicana* made the passage by the usual route: south from New York to Panama, through the Panama Canal, and then north to California. At a steady ten knots, the roughly five-thousand-mile voyage would have taken each ship about twenty days, allowing for the vicissitudes of weather and the waiting period before transiting the canal. We don't know whether the vessels made the trip in company or separately, but both were present in San Pedro—the port of Los Angeles—by the end of February.

At this point, *Coquina's* life story takes another of its many detours. While Pillsbury & Curtis had intended to put her and *Corsicana* into service hauling lumber under charter, by the time the vessels reached California that plan had gone into abeyance. The most likely reason for Pillsbury & Curtis' change of heart was that the Laker's twenty-three-foot loaded design draft was based on the carriage of cargo in her holds; potential operators may have considered her to be too "drafty" to call at many of the smaller timber ports in California and the Pacific Northwest when burdened with both hold cargo and towering stacks of sawn timber atop both well decks. Whatever the reason for their corporate change of heart, Pillsbury & Curtis decided to lay up both *Coquina* and *Corsicana* until they could find gainful employment for them. The vessels were moved to a quiet spot in San Pedro Bay, and *Coquina* entered another period of hibernation.

Surviving records do not give exact dates for the freighter's first California lay-up, but we do know that *Coquina* arrived in San Francisco on April 24, 1930. She may have been completing a charter voyage or Pillsbury & Curtis may have been repositioning her to what they believed to be a better market. If the latter was the case, her owners were misinformed, because the ship does not appear to have found gainful employment for some time. She apparently sat idle in the upper reaches of San Francisco Bay well into 1931 (and was joined there by *Corsicana* on March 29 of that year) before another ship's bad luck presented her with the opportunity to join one of the West Coast's best-known cargo and passenger lines, the Los Angeles Steamship Company.[25]

Founded in 1920 to provide service between Los Angeles and San Francisco, LASSCO, as it was universally known, had later added a Hawaii service. This put the firm in direct competition with the established power on the trans-Pacific routes, the San Francisco–based Matson Navigation Company, and LASSCO was initially able to hold its own. However, the Great Depression and a series of vessel mishaps—including a disastrous fire in May 1930 aboard the 10,680-ton *City of Honolulu* (II), one of two German-built liners[26] upon which the line's U.S.-Hawaii passenger service was based—ultimately forced the October 31, 1930, merger of LASSCO with archcompetitor Matson. While both companies retained their individual identities, they gradually blended their Hawaiian services and LASSCO ultimately was primarily relegated to operating the merged companies' California coastal service.

Built around the pre–World War I passenger-cargo steamers *Yale* and *Harvard*,[27] LASSCO's coastwise passenger-freight service operated in direct competition with the Pacific Steamship Company. The two firms engaged in a series of rate wars in which LASSCO was able to hold its own, until *Harvard* ran aground at Point Arguello, some sixty miles northwest of Santa Barbara, California, on May 30, 1931. There were no fatalities, but the ship had to be abandoned. Her loss put LASSCO at a distinct commercial disadvantage. In an effort to quickly restart the two-ship service, LASSCO chartered the 6,209-GRT *Iroquois*, a passenger-cargo steamer launched in 1926. The ship went into partnership with *Yale* on June 30, 1931, but proved so uneconomical to operate that LASSCO withdrew her from service in early December and canceled her charter agreement.[28]

It was *Iroquois*'s inability to meet LASSCO's needs that ultimately led to the possibility of *Coquina*'s parole from her lay-up in San Francisco. LASSCO needed to quickly acquire several smaller and more economical vessels to maintain its coastwise freight service following *Iroquois*'s withdrawal, and the company settled on *Coquina* and two of her sister ships, *Corsicana* and *Corrales*. The sturdy Lakers were a known quantity—in 1928 LASSCO had chartered *Corrales* for three cargo-only round-trip voyages to Hawaii—and had much to recommend them for the task. They were extremely fuel-efficient in comparison to *Iroquois*, for example, and the replacement of the short fore-and-aft kingposts by two taller, boom-carrying masts fitted to them by Pillsbury & Curtis in 1926 in anticipation of work in the timber trade would prove just as useful in general cargo service. Equally important, however, was the fact that Pillsbury & Curtis was, like LASSCO, a Matson subsidiary. This meant that the financially struggling LASSCO could take advantage of some fancy corporate accounting to acquire the three Lakers at better than bargain-basement prices. Indeed, while it is unclear how much LASSCO "officially" paid for the three ships, *Coquina*'s record of title shows that when she was conveyed from Pillsbury & Curtis to LASSCO on December 1, 1931, the total mortgage amount transferred was $10—by bill of sale, no less.[29]

Unfortunately, even such a sweetheart deal couldn't get *Coquina* back to sea. Though she and *Corsicana* were moved from lay-up and underwent cursory refurbishment in preparation for their new tasking, the nation's worsening economic depression and LASSCO's falling revenues prompted the company to return both ships to inactive status pending an improvement in both the corporate and national economies. The firm's directors chose to employ only the already-proven *Corrales* on a severely pared-down coastwise freight service, and on December 8, she departed from the port of Wilmington[30] on the first of several round-trip voyages to San Francisco and points north.

For *Coquina* and *Timberman*, as LASSCO had renamed *Corsicana*, the period of forced inactivity in San Francisco lasted just over a year and ended as the result of what seems, in retrospect, to have been a fairly poor business decision on the part of Matson Navigation Company. Despite the failure of LASSCO's limited coastwise cargo-only service—*Corrales* had been withdrawn and laid up alongside her two sisters after just four months—Matson's directors seem to have believed with an almost mystic fervor in the commercial potential of a California coastwise freight operation. Their belief persisted despite increasing evidence that the Golden State's highways and railroads were the transportation modes of choice for cost-conscious shippers, and on August 17, 1933, Matson incorporated the California Steamship Company[31] specifically to address a market segment that had already defeated LASSCO.

While the creation of the new coastwise freight firm struck many industry observers as commercial lunacy, Matson's directors were not wholly detached from reality. Realizing that the venture was a gamble, they chose not to increase their downside risk by procuring costly new vessels in the midst of a worldwide depression. Instead, they would base the new service on used vessels that had already proven themselves to be dependable, suited to the task, and relatively economical to operate. And, by happy coincidence, Matson had immediate access to three ideal ships through LASSCO—*Coquina*, *Timberman*, and *Corrales*. Not only did the Lakers meet the performance parameters for the job, they could be had for a song—like both Pillsbury & Curtis and LASSCO, the California Steamship Company was a Matson subsidiary. And as happened when *Coquina* was "sold" into LASSCO service two years earlier, the mortgage amount listed on the bill of sale to her newest employer was $10.[32] The price was likely no higher for her companions.

Coquina's record of title indicates that the California Steamship Company assumed ownership on December 29, 1933, a date that marks the beginning of a somewhat murky period in the Laker's history. While several published sources[33] indicate that she was immediately placed in coastwise service with *Timberman* and *Corrales*, official documents generated by the Collectors of Customs in both San Francisco and San Pedro state that the vessel remained laid up in the former city until late 1934 or early 1935. There is no doubt, however, about the outcome of Matson's ill-fated foray into the coastwise freight trade—the venture failed. By early December 1935 the California Steamship Company was ready to admit defeat, and on December 30, *Coquina* and her two sisters were "sold" directly to Matson Navigation, most likely in an attempt to ameliorate year-end tax complications for the failing subsidiary. As with her two previous transfers of title, *Coquina*'s official sale price was $10.

Though it's unclear whether *Coquina* actually stirred from her lay-up berth while "owned" by the California Steamship Company, we do know that she, *Timberman*, and *Corrales* had all been shifted to San Pedro by the time of their "sale" to Matson. On February 5, 1936, the homeport of all three vessels was changed to Los Angeles. At this point, it seems that Matson decided to employ the vessels in the manner to which they were best suited, for over the next year all three were chartered out to California-based lumber companies for coastwise lumber-transport work. While *Timberman* was sold out of Matson service in December 1937,[34] *Coquina* and *Corrales* were kept on the company's fleet list through the end of the decade, both apparently working infrequent charters interspaced with periods of lay-up in San Pedro.

Chartering *Coquina* and her sisters out for lumber hauling never constituted a major revenue stream for Matson Navigation Company, and the three vessels certainly spent more time laid up than they did underway. But the scarcity of gainful employment for the Lakers while in the service of Matson and the firm's various subsidiaries hardly mattered in the larger corporate scheme of things. Though Matson had entered the 1930s burdened by debt, reduced passenger loads, and all the other ills that grew out of the Great Depression, by the end of the decade the steamship company was in fine shape and poised to do even better.

This progress was the result of several factors. The acquisition of LASSCO, for example, had eliminated Matson's main competitor in the U.S.-Hawaii passenger and cargo trade, and the subsequent rationalization of the combined fleet allowed the parent company to cut costs and improve efficiency. Moreover, the increase in passenger numbers and cargo tonnages that resulted from the steadily improving world economy during the middle of the decade was further enhanced by international events that were not quite as positive. Japanese expansionism in the Far East and the gathering clouds of war in Europe both helped increase Matson's passenger and cargo numbers on its Atlantic, Gulf of Mexico, and Pacific routes as people and companies sought to escape conflict or the threat thereof.[35] The increase in world tension during the years 1936 to 1939 also prompted the U.S. government to begin ramping up military construction in both the continental United States and overseas, and Matson's bottom line benefited from increasingly frequent government transportation contracts, particularly those concerned with the nation's Pacific outposts.

Given all that was happening for Matson as the 1930s came to a close, the continued ownership of two small, aging, and frequently nonprofitable Laker freighters that had been optimized for carrying lumber was not seen as either sensible or desirable. As a result, the company's directors added *Coquina* and *Corrales* to the list of vessels to be disposed of as part of the firm's ongoing fleet rationalization. Again laid up in San Pedro, both ships were officially put up for sale on January 1, 1940, with Matson asking $85,000 per vessel. It was a fairly steep price for World War I–vintage ships with what most shipping companies would consider fairly limited cargo capacities, but the cost did not deter the interest of one firm that knew the Lakers to be ideal for hauling a very specialized form of freight.

The cargo was lumber, and the interested party was the Oliver J. Olson Company.

CHAPTER 2

THE FAMILY BUSINESS

THE COMPANY WHOSE INTEREST *COQUINA* piqued was the creation of one Oliver J. Olson, the scion of a California family whose history is intertwined with that of both the Golden State and the West Coast's maritime development.

While not humble, Olson's origins were certainly not aristocratic, either. His father, born Lars Ollsen Vastvedt in Stavanger, Norway, in 1828, immigrated to the United States in 1849. Eventually making his way to the West Coast, Lewis Olson, as he now called himself, settled in San Francisco and in 1868 married Delia Lacey, an attractive Irish-born lass some eighteen years his junior.[1]

San Francisco in the years just after the Civil War was a place of infinite possibility for a man with ambition and plans, and Lewis Olson had both in abundance. Realizing that rapidly urbanizing Central California desperately needed good, cheap lumber to build homes and businesses for its burgeoning population, Lewis became a junior partner in a small coastal shipping firm specializing in hauling logs and sawn timber to San Francisco from mills in the Pacific Northwest and along the northern California coast. It was a profitable line of work and Lewis prospered—and a good thing, too, for by 1884 Delia had given him two daughters and seven sons. Oliver John Olson, the second child and first son, was born in San Francisco on January 20, 1872.

By the early 1890s, Lewis Olson had branched out on his own, buying the two-masted wooden schooner *Gem* and putting her to work hauling deckloads of lumber from mills in Oregon to the Bay Area. He made a good living, but it was a hard life, and one in which success depended far too much on the vagaries of tide and timber. Wanting better, more stable lives for his sons, he did all he could to dissuade them from following him to sea. It worked—at least initially—with Oliver. When he turned eighteen, Lewis's oldest son took a job as a junior accountant with the San Francisco–based Wempey Brothers Paper Box Company.[2] Long days spent pouring over weighty ledgers didn't seem to bother him, though he was an avid listener to his brother William's sea stories.

Four years younger than Oliver, William had blithely ignored their father's pleas to resist the sea's siren song and at fourteen had shipped out as a cabin boy on *W.W. Case*, a barque trading between San Francisco and Alaska. Wanting his son closer to home, Louis swallowed his misgivings about the sailor's life and offered William a berth aboard *Gem*, starting him out as an assistant cook at the age of fifteen. Diligent effort and a real love for the sea and sailing helped William progress rapidly through the ranks, and by nineteen he was his father's first mate.[3]

Though Oliver had no real desire to follow his brother and father to sea, their stories of the money to be made in the coastwise lumber trade—and of the wide-open, rough-and-tumble nature of the business—intrigued the stool-bound and increasingly ambitious young accountant. In slow moments at work he took to jotting notes in a spare ledger, outlining a coastwise shipping company modeled after his father's, but which Oliver hoped would be far larger, and far more successful, than Lewis's.

Unfortunately, it took a family tragedy to help turn Oliver's musings into a business plan. In April of 1895 Lewis Olson, with son William at his side, took *Gem* north from San Francisco, bound for Coos Bay, Oregon, to take on a load of sawn timber. The largest and deepest port between San Francisco and the mouth of the Columbia River, Coos Bay is fed by the South Fork Coos and Millicoma Rivers. In 1895—before decades of engineering changed its nature for the better—the mouth of the bay was guarded by shifting shoals known collectively as the Coos Bar. Treacherous even in good weather, the bar could be positively vicious in rough seas, and *Gem*, to her captain's great misfortune, arrived off Coos Bay in the teeth of a spring gale.

Anxious to make port on time, Lewis Olson chose to cross the bar despite the challenges. Years of experience helped him avoid the hazards, and despite rough seas *Gem* had actually made it across the bar without so much as kissing the bottom when the ropes connecting her wheel with her rudder snapped. The wheel spun sharply, hitting Lewis in the leg and knocking him to his knees. Fast work by William and other crewmembers got *Gem* safely past Coos Head and into the bay, but Lewis was seriously injured. A small hospital in Marshfield (now the city of Coos Bay) offered some hope, but it took several hours to tack the schooner up around North Bend and lay her alongside the city pier. William and several crewmen got Lewis ashore as quickly as they could, but within days the elder Olson succumbed to blood poisoning.

While Lewis's death was a shock to his entire family, it was William who was most immediately and directly affected. *Gem* was not only his father's sole legacy; it was the sole source of the family's income. William thus swallowed his grief, oversaw the loading of the timber *Gem* had come to Coos Bay to collect, and then took the schooner back to San Francisco. Virtually overnight, the story of the teen-aged first mate who took command of his dead father's vessel and brought her—and her valuable cargo—home despite savage Pacific storms became front-page news.[4] Sold off at San Francisco's bustling wharf-side timber market, the load *Gem* carried through the Golden Gate helped keep the schooner in business—with William as her captain. He kept her working for a number of years, eventually selling the ship at a handsome profit before joining the San Francisco–based shipping firm Hind, Rolph & Co. Still among the youngest masters on the Pacific, he won fame—and considerable fortune—captaining graceful "sugar schooners" between Hawaii and California.[5]

Lewis Olson's death also prompted change in his son Oliver's life. Seeing the accounting job at Wempey Brothers as a financial and professional dead end, and driven by the same ambition that guided his seafaring younger brother, Oliver took a bold step. He dusted off his earlier plans for a lumber-shipping business modeled on his father's and began lobbying friends, coworkers, and family members to buy shares in the proposed Oliver J. Olson Shipping Company. Probably to his own surprise, sixty-four people invested in the new firm. All became part owners of the company's first vessel, a 667-ton, four-masted wooden schooner built by the noted shipbuilder John Lindstrom[6] in Aberdeen, Washington. The young Olson modestly named the ship after himself.

Ironically, the first voyage of *Oliver J. Olson* was not south to California; it was a triangular trans-Pacific passage that began in March 1901 and which was specifically intended to earn the infant shipping company some fast working capital. Loaded to the gunwales with some six hundred thousand board feet of sawn timber,[7] the schooner made a fast passage to Australia, via Honolulu, offloading half of its cargo in each port of call. In Sydney, her decks and holds now clear, *Oliver J. Olson* took on a load of copra (dried coconut meat), tropical hardwoods, and general merchandise and departed for Callao, Peru, where she sold off her cargo and replaced it with goods bound for San Francisco. When she arrived in that city by the bay some weeks later, her owner's gamble had paid off handsomely—the Olson Steamship Company was most definitely in business.[8]

With *Oliver J. Olson*'s maiden commercial voyage such a ringing success, Olson the man quickly ordered a second and almost identical vessel. This schooner, the 680-ton *Sehome*,[9] soon joined her stablemate in service. While the ships mainly operated in the coastwise lumber trade, each made occasional forays as far afield as Honolulu and northern Mexico, carrying lumber on the outbound passages and general merchandise on the way home. Both vessels proved dependable workhorses, and by 1906 the Olson Steamship Company was solidly in the black. Interestingly, when the firm's success prompted investor and Olson family friend Jim Butler to offer to put up the money for another ship, Oliver Olson opted not for another sailing vessel, but for a 642-gross-ton, 174-foot steam schooner built by John Lindstrom.[10]

The new ship—quickly and understandably named *Jim Butler*—was both faster and more dependable than the sailing vessels already in the Olson fleet, and she was soon turning a tidy profit hauling up to seven hundred thousand board feet of sawn timber per voyage. Most of her cargo, like that of her running mates, was destined for the very same Wempey Brothers Paper Box Company from which Oliver Olson had so fervently wished to escape. By supplying his former employer's need for raw materials at a better price than his larger and bulkier competitors, Olson was able to steadily build a very profitable business in a town that at the time boasted almost a dozen major lumber-shipping concerns. Indeed, business was so good that Olson & Co. ordered a second steam schooner. Also a product of John Lindstrom's yards, the 691-gross-ton *Thomas L. Wand* was essentially identical to *Jim Butler*, and together the two vessels kept up a steady and increasingly profitable service between Northern California and Puget Sound.[11] The company's bottom line got a huge boost following the April 18, 1906, San Francisco earthquake, when the Olson Company won several contracts to provide timber for the rebuilding of homes, businesses, and public structures destroyed by the temblor.[12]

Oliver Olson's success in the West Coast's rough-and-tumble, no-holds-barred timber-shipping industry soon attracted one of the more colorful characters to appear in postearthquake San Francisco, Andrew F. Mahony.[13] A former salesman for Levi Strauss & Co.—whose rambling factory had been destroyed in the earthquake—the flamboyant Irishman had won $15,000 in the Louisiana Lottery and was looking for ways to invest it. Though he knew nothing of ships or the sea, he was an astute businessman and was attracted to the tidy quarterly profits being turned by Olson's small but increasingly successful company. With hat—and cashiers' check—firmly in hand, Mahony sought out the thirty-four-year-old budding shipping magnate and offered to buy in as an equal partner in a new firm to be called, logically enough, the Olson & Mahony Steamship Company.[14]

While Mahony's offer was a generous one—his $15,000 in 1906 was equivalent to some $395,000 in 2016 dollars—Oliver Olson didn't immediately accept the former jeans salesman's proposal. After all, Olson had started his business partly to become his own man and determine his own economic destiny, and taking on a partner would of necessity mean giving up his hard-won commercial freedom. Moreover, business was good and getting better, despite—and, indeed, because of—the tragedy that had so recently befallen Olson's beloved San Francisco. What then, he reasoned, would be the benefit of bringing Mahony and his lottery winnings onboard?

The answer, ultimately, was a simple one, and it grew out of the very commercial success the Olson Company was beginning to enjoy. San Francisco's need for Pacific Northwest lumber in the aftermath of the earthquake was so great, and the profits to be made from supplying that lumber potentially so enormous, that the Olson Company needed more vessels if it were to realize what its founder believed to be his firm's rightful share of the windfall profits to be had in the rebuilding of the devastated city. The acquisition of a larger lumber carrier more capable in all respects than the firm's existing hulls would, Olson believed, vastly increase his company's chances of gaining valuable market share in a highly competitive—not to say cut-throat—industry. And while the Oliver J. Olson Company was doing well financially, the cost of building a new and significantly larger vessel was prohibitive—until Mahony and his lottery winnings came through the door.

Having made his decision, Oliver Olson gracefully (and, one imagines, gratefully) accepted Mahony's offer of partnership. The necessary papers were swiftly drawn up, and in late 1906 the Olson & Mahony Steamship Company was duly incorporated in San Francisco, with offices at the foot of Powell Street (though the firm soon thereafter shifted to offices in the Fife Building at One Drumm Street, just across the Embarcadero from the Ferry Building).[15] The ink on the instruments of incorporation was hardly dry when the new firm put Mahony's lottery winnings to work: Harlan & Hollingsworth Shipbuilders of Wilmington, Delaware, was awarded a contract for the construction of the new lumber carrier Oliver Olson believed was essential to the company's success.[16] At 1,497 gross tons, the ship, which carried yard number 383, would have twice the carrying capacity of either *Jim Butler* or *Thomas L. Wand*. Viewing the new vessel as the flagship of what they hoped would ultimately become the West Coast's dominant lumber-shipping firm, the new partners named her, simply, *Olson & Mahony*. Though the ship's October 1907 delivery voyage from the East Coast to California—made via Baltimore and Cape Horn— was interrupted by the loss of her screw off Argentina, once in regular service she more than fulfilled her owners' expectations.[17]

That the new company quickly flourished surprised many who knew both partners, given that from the beginning of their collaboration Olson and Mahony had a famously turbulent relationship. As is frequently the case when intelligent, intractable, and willful people join forces, the two often butted heads over seemingly trivial matters, and their regular shouting matches were legendary. Even when the partners were not arguing, they were often at odds. One of their earliest and most famous rows grew out of Mahony's fondness for bright colors. Ever the quintessential Irishman, he one day unilaterally decided that the hulls of the firm's ships should be painted a rich Kelly green and their upper works white, and he neglected to consult his partner before ordering the work done.

Olson, who believed stylish yet discrete colors were de rigueur for any self-respecting shipping line, was outraged. But rather than initiating yet another window-rattling verbal slugfest, he simply ordered the company's maintenance chief to have a large, white "O" painted on both sides of each vessel's black funnel. When Mahony saw the new stack markings, he could hardly complain about Olson's unannounced design initiative, and thus were the firm's house colors born.[18]

The personality clashes of its partners notwithstanding, the Olson & Mahony Company continued to prosper in its early years. Through canny timber-distribution partnerships with firms such as the San Francisco–based E.K. Wood Lumber Company[19] and by aggressively courting—and occasionally intimidating—smaller lumber suppliers throughout northern California and the Pacific Northwest, Olson & Mahony had within its first five years become a major player in the West Coast lumber trade. This success allowed the firm to add further ships to its fleet—a total of seven by 1913[20]—and to form its own small retail lumber-supply firm, the aptly named Olson-Mahony Lumber Company.[21]

The secretary of that fledgling retail business, an already successful Bay Area entrepreneur named Charles F. Van Damme, also played a role in Olson & Mahony's 1915 establishment of perhaps their most successful corporate spin-off, the Richmond–San Rafael Ferry Transportation Company. With no bridges yet spanning any part of greater San Francisco Bay, ferries were the only convenient way for tens of thousands of people to travel each day among the region's various population centers. Olson and Mahony perceived a need for a ferry line linking Richmond, in Contra Costa County on the east side of the bay, with Point San Quentin to the west across San Pablo Bay in Marin County. While some local observers scoffed at the proposed line, calling it "a ferry to nowhere" and "the prison express,"[22] it proved immediately successful and remained profitable until the 1956 opening of the John F. McCarthy Memorial Bridge.

As his firm grew, so did Oliver Olson's family. By 1910 he and his wife, the former Mary Elizabeth Whitney, had three sons and three daughters. Following a by-now familiar pattern, the elder Olson bestowed his favorite name—his own—on his first-born son. Oliver Jr., born in 1902, grew up with ships, timber, and business in his veins. By the time he was ten years old he was accompanying his father to the Olson & Mahony offices on Drumm Street, and very soon thereafter—according to family legend—could name all of the company's suppliers throughout northern California and the Pacific Northwest, the names and routes of the firm's ships, and even the names of each vessel's primary and relief captains. He was, as his father so proudly put it, "to the business born." Nor was he the only child of an Olson & Mahony partner to be so commercially inclined—Mahony's son, Andrew Jr., also spent much of his childhood in the company offices.

While the Olson & Mahony Company continued to prosper, the long-simmering personality conflicts between its founders ultimately led to an irrevocable break. In 1916 Oliver Olson and Andrew Mahony agreed to dissolve the partnership, with Olson buying out his erstwhile partner's interest in the company's vessels (the hulls of which he immediately ordered painted black). Interestingly, both retained their interests in the Richmond–San Rafael Ferry and Transportation Company, and their sons both ultimately attained senior positions in that firm—Oliver Jr. as president and Andrew Jr. as secretary, posts each held for the life of the company.[23]

Following the dissolution of Olson & Mahony the two partners went widely divergent ways. Andrew Mahony founded his own coastwise shipping company, but it did not do at all well. In 1919 he become a San Francisco police commissioner, a post he held until his death in 1933.[24] Oliver Olson, on the other hand, redoubled his efforts to corner the West Coast lumber-shipping market, a quest in which his firm—once again known as the Oliver J. Olson Steamship Company—was aided considerably by the United States' April 1917 entry into World War I. The government's need to build barracks and other facilities for the rapidly enlarging U.S. Army meant lucrative contracts for those businesses that could both provide timber and ship it quickly and efficiently to ports on the West, Gulf, and East Coasts. The Olson Steamship Company could do both and quickly secured a series of Army contracts that not only ensured the firm's survival but also virtually guaranteed its dominance of its primary market.

The contracts were fulfilled using the seven vessels of the prewar Olson and Olson & Mahony fleets, plus the new-build *Florence Olson*.[25] That ship was something of a departure for the Olson Company in terms of design in that it replaced the previously standard two-masted steam schooner configuration—with deckhouse right aft and timber deck-loaded between the deckhouse and the bow—with an amidships-house silhouette. In this layout, rolls of newsprint or general cargo were stowed in holds fore and aft of the deckhouse, while sawn lumber took up every inch of space on the fore and aft well decks. This arrangement more than doubled the board feet of lumber the vessel could carry and remained the Olson line's basic design standard for the remainder of the firm's existence.

With all of its vessels gainfully employed throughout the nineteen months of America's involvement in World War I, the Oliver J. Olson Steamship Company thrived. And it was the quintessential family business— Oliver was the president and chief executive officer, while his sea-faring brother William (who'd joined the firm after the advent of steamships knocked his beloved sailing vessels out of the U.S.-Hawaii sugar trade) oversaw vessel operations. Another brother, Walter, was the company's port captain in San Pedro.[26] And, despite his youth, Oliver Jr. continued to work in the company offices whenever he wasn't in school.

The November 1918 armistice that ended World War I did nothing to slow the Olson Steamship Company's seemingly inexorable growth. In October 1919, the firm extended its passenger and cargo routes internationally, sending *Florence Olson* to Hawaii and, from 1920 onward, to both Mexico and the Panama Canal Zone. Using the profits earned from the wartime contracts, the company bought four ships between 1921 and 1923. These vessels—the *George L. Olson*, *Whitney Olson*, *Virginia Olson*, and *Florence Olson*[27] (the latter a replacement of the first vessel of the same name, sold in 1923)—joined the hulls already in service, giving the company one of the largest coastwise shipping fleets on the West Coast.[28] And Oliver Olson put the fleet to good—and continuously profitable—use throughout the immediate postwar period. Indeed, the company did so well that in 1926 Olson commissioned one of San Francisco's leading architects to build a suitably distinctive and imposing family home in the city's tremendously exclusive Sea Cliff district. The architect, Earle B. Bertz, crafted a vast, fourteen-room mansion in the ornate Italian Renaissance style, a home that Oliver Olson dearly loved, and which remained in the family for decades.[29]

Fortunately for Oliver Olson and his family, the company continued to do well throughout the remainder of the 1920s and was therefore relatively strong when the Great Depression hit in 1929. The advent of widespread economic hardship necessitated some fairly significant adjustments to the company's business model, of course, given that drastic nationwide reductions in commercial and residential construction caused severe downturns in timber sales. One change was a considerable increase in the firm's transportation of nontimber cargoes, as well as a greater emphasis on carrying passengers. Through canny business dealings and a rigid insistence on ruthless management of expenditures, the Olson Steamship Company managed to survive the sort of financial calamities that drove several competing coastwise shipping firms out of business.

While the Olson line managed to outlive the Great Depression, it was the possibility of world war that would again prove key to the firm's economic viability. Japanese expansionism in the Pacific and Far East throughout the 1930s, coupled with German chancellor Adolf Hitler's March 1935 announcement that his nation would renounce the strictures imposed on it by Part V of the Versailles Treaty and begin a massive and wide-ranging expansion of its armed forces, sparked immediate concern in Washington, DC. U.S. military planners dusted off and updated the existing plans for war in both the Pacific and Europe, each of which included the expansion of existing American bases and the construction of new ones.[30] The plans also included provisions for the shipment of American raw materials to nations the administration of President Franklin D. Roosevelt assumed would be allies in any coming conflict.

By early 1937, the Olson Steamship Company was—like fellow San Francisco–based corporation Matson Navigation—beginning to benefit from America's cautious martial buildup. Initially contracted to carry passengers and general freight along the West Coast, the firm soon began to haul progressively larger cargoes of general goods and sawn timber, virtually all of the latter being intended for use in the War Department's increasingly more important military construction scheme. Indeed, by 1937 Oliver Olson was feeling economically secure enough to purchase his first vessel in fourteen years, albeit a "previously owned" one, the 1918-built, 2,676-ton *Point Bonita*. Renamed *Oliver Olson*,[31] most probably for the son rather than the father, the vessel was put into mixed passenger-cargo service. While operated primarily between San Francisco, Seattle, and Portland, the ship also undertook several War Department contract passages to the Panama Canal Zone as well as at least one voyage to Peru and Costa Rica.[32]

As the company's fortunes improved, its structure also began to change. Having celebrated his sixty-fifth birthday in January 1937, Oliver

J. Olson the elder began turning more of the day-to-day operation of the firm and its subsidiaries over to his sons. Thirty-five-year-old Oliver Jr. remained as president of the Richmond–San Rafael Ferry (and, eventually, as president of the Olson Ocean Towing Company). Twenty-six-year-old Edward Whitney Olson, known as "Whit," took over as president of the steamship company, assisted by his twenty-eight-year-old brother, George, as the firm's vice president. All three siblings had served long apprenticeships at the knees of both their father and uncles William and Walter and were canny businessmen in their own rights.

By early 1940 that business acumen had allowed Whit and George Olson to win several additional government contracts for the transportation of lumber intended for military construction projects within the continental United States. While those contracts covered coastwise voyages from the Pacific Northwest to San Francisco, Los Angeles, and San Diego, the brothers were aware that far greater profits were to be made on the sea-lanes between the West Coast and Honolulu. Since 1937 the War Department had been pouring increasing amounts of money into upgrading Hawaii's air and seacoast defenses, an undertaking that required massive amounts of wood as both a primary building material for barracks and other structures and for such ancillary uses as concrete forms and scaffolding.

The Olson brothers believed their firm—whose ships had often carried lumber to the Hawaiian Islands over the previous thirty years—was ideally suited to bid for Army contracts connected to the Pacific buildup. The only potential difficulty was that the company's current fleet was already fully engaged in meeting the demands of the existing contracts; to take full advantage of what the brothers believed would be an astonishingly valuable opportunity, they'd simply have to buy at least two additional vessels.

And not just any ships would do. If the Olson Company was to make the most of the opportunity offered by the War Department's Hawaiian buildup, the new vessels would have to meet some fairly stringent criteria. First and foremost, the ships would have to be suited to the task. They'd need to be capacious enough to carry a significant load of lumber, sturdy enough to withstand the rigors of frequent trans-Pacific voyages, fast enough to make the round-trip passage in a reasonable time, and economical enough not to incur exorbitant operating costs. Second, they'd need to be cheap enough that the cost of their purchase wouldn't offset any potential profits. And third, they'd need to be readily available. To ensure a decent chance of winning the chance to take part in the West Coast–to–Hawaii contracts, the Olson Company would need to locate, purchase, fit out, and crew the ships in record time.

Sitting in their offices at One Drumm Street in San Francisco, Whit and George Olson must have wondered where—and even if—they'd locate suitable vessels. America's continuing neutrality ensured that increasing numbers of U.S.-flagged ships were fully occupied in ferrying cargo to various ports that were closed to vessels of the combatant nations. Moreover, many West Coast shipping firms were seeking to expand their fleets to win the very same War Department contracts the Olsons sought to secure. As a result, ships that fulfilled all the brothers' requirements were increasingly hard to find.

Fortunately for the Olson Company, the perfect ships for the job did exist, and they were sitting quietly in San Pedro Bay.

CHAPTER 3

TO THE LAND OF ALOHA

ON THE AFTERNOON OF MONDAY, April 22, 1940, Whit and George Olson's search for two vessels upon which to build their hoped-for West Coast–to–Honolulu service ended on a rickety Southern California pier.

The brothers had flown from San Francisco to Los Angeles that morning accompanied by their director of engineering, and the three made the short drive to San Pedro specifically to get a firsthand look at *Coquina* and *Corrales*. The two Lakers were tied side by side to the same pier that had been their home for much of the past four years, and they looked somewhat the worse for wear. Streaks of rust and swathes of chipping paint marred their hulls, and several months' worth of seagull droppings festooned their upper works. But the Olsons weren't interested in how the ships looked; they wanted to know whether they were mechanically sound. Accompanied by a Matson representative, the brothers and their engineering expert clambered over every inch of both vessels. Satisfied that they were in better condition than they appeared to be, the men pored over the ships' engineering and deck logs and finished up with a thorough examination of their maintenance records.

Coquina and *Corrales* apparently passed the inspection with flying colors, for the following day the Oliver J. Olson Company offered to buy both vessels from Matson Navigation. After a series of back-and-forth negotiations the parties agreed to a final price of $75,000 per vessel, with the Olsons financing the purchase through the San Francisco–based Wells Fargo Bank and Union Trust Company. The bill of sale was finalized on April 25, and the following day both ships were underway for the Golden Gate.[1] On April 30 the Olson Company requested that the Commerce Department's Bureau of Marine Inspection and Navigation officially change the homeport of both vessels from Los Angeles to San Francisco. In a letter dated the same day and sent to the same agency, George H. Pitt—a partner in the Thornley & Pitt customs brokerage house acting as the Olsons' attorney of record—requested that *Coquina* and *Corrales* be renamed as *Cynthia Olson* and *Barbara Olson*, respectively.[2] The homeport and name changes were approved on May 4,[3] and within days both ships had been repainted in their new owner's livery.

The Olson Company obviously wanted to get the two Lakers into service as quickly as possible—most probably to meet a vessel-time-in-service requirement established for firms bidding on Army transportation contracts—but the ships first had to undergo government inspection and certification. For *Cynthia Olson* that process took place on May 27, when she was boarded at her San Francisco pier by Commerce Department inspectors John P. Tibbets and Winslow D. Conn. The two gave the ship a thorough going-over, verifying her dimensions and tonnage, checking the condition of her hull and machinery, ensuring the presence of required safety equipment, and validating the seaworthiness of her two nonmotorized, thirty-six-person-capacity lifeboats.[4] The following day the ship was granted a certificate of inspection—valid for one year—that cleared her for "Pacific Ocean Coastwise" operation anywhere between San Diego and Puget Sound.

The coastwise certification was appropriate in that the Olson brothers intended to keep both Lakers gainfully employed on the coastal service until the company could win an Army contract that would take them farther afield. The ships were quickly put to work, with *Cynthia Olson* departing San Francisco for Portland on June 1 to embark her first load of lumber for her new owners. She offloaded that cargo in San Pedro nine days later and her master, P. C. Johnson, reported that the ship had encountered no difficulties during the voyage. Though getting somewhat long in the tooth, *Cynthia Olson* had proved that she could still handle the day-to-day challenges of the coastal lumber trade.

It was a good thing the Laker was up to the task, for the first Army contract on which she was employed kept her working the same coastwise routes. In the fall of 1940 the Army Transport Service (ATS) Office at San Francisco's Fort Mason—a 1,200-acre complex of warehouses, piers, and administrative bureaus that the Army also referred to as the San Francisco Port of Embarkation (SFPOE)—issued a solicitation for bids to carry lumber from various ports in the Pacific Northwest to San Francisco and San Pedro.[5] The wood was destined for military construction projects throughout the continental United States and would be moved onward from the coastal ports by rail. The job was, of course, right up the Olson Company's alley, and the firm was awarded the ATS contract in September 1940.

While several company vessels were put to work on the ATS contract, *Cynthia Olson* and *Barbara Olson* formed the backbone of the effort. For the next eleven months the Lakers routinely plied the coastal shipping lanes, each loading approximately two million board feet of sawn timber in such ports as Astoria, Oregon; Aberdeen, Olympia, Tacoma, or Seattle, Washington; and Eureka, California. The ships carried the lumber south to San Francisco or San Pedro, where the cargo was transshipped to railcars for onward movement. Under the terms of the ATS contract the Olson Company was authorized to carry nongovernment cargoes if and when space was available and if the carriage of such cargo did not interfere with the timely delivery of the Army-owned timber. As a result, *Cynthia Olson* and her sister often filled their holds with commercial goods on the northbound passages, earning their owners a tidy extra income on top of the revenue generated by the ATS contract.

As was common at that time, the Olson Company did not employ full-time crewmembers for its ships. Merchant seamen were booked for each round-trip voyage through the union halls in San Francisco and San Pedro, and while a particular individual might work steadily on one of the Olson vessels, he could also be booked aboard the ships of such other firms as the E.K. Wood Lumber Company. The process was somewhat different for masters, mates, and chief engineers, as the ships' senior officers had to have both the necessary experience and the appropriate licenses for the routes and vessels. As a result, while masters, mates, and engineers were not technically full-time Olson Company employees, the same individuals tend to appear continually on the crew rosters of both *Cynthia Olson* and *Barbara Olson*. And the name of each ship's master rarely differed—Captain P. C. Johnson for the former and Captain Berthel Carlsen for the latter.

Cynthia Olson and her sister proved to be both dependable and capable, and their performance on the first Army contract stood them in good stead when, in July 1940, the ATS solicited bids for a series of U.S.-to-Hawaii lumber voyages. The Army planned to ship increasingly large amounts of sawn timber to Oahu and thus intended to award segments of the contract to a number of shipping lines. The Olson Company was among the first firms to submit a comprehensive bid and was in fact so eager to tender for the job that it overlooked a key point: *Cynthia Olson* and her sister ship were still licensed only for coastwise operation. Should their owners win a portion of the trans-Pacific shipping contract, both vessels would have to quickly be reinspected and certificated for open-ocean operations before they could legally undertake the passage to Hawaii.

This issue became a real concern during the first week of August, when the Olson Company was awarded a portion of the contract. Both *Cynthia Olson* and *Barbara Olson* were on their way south from Puget Sound when the company learned of the contract award, and Whit and George Olson immediately started planning how to get the ships' current cargoes off-loaded as quickly as possible so the vessels could get back to the Pacific Northwest to load the Hawaii-bound timber and make it to Honolulu within the specified timeframe. *Cynthia Olson* arrived in San Pedro on August 4, and over the next four days stevedores relieved her of just over two million board feet of timber. On the afternoon of the August 8 she departed for San Francisco, arriving the following morning. She stayed only long enough to take aboard food, fuel, fresh water, and some additional crewmen and sailed out through the Golden Gate on the morning of August 10.

The ship's departure for the Pacific Northwest, and ultimately for Hawaii, was something of a gamble on her owners' part. *Cynthia Olson* was still certificated as a coastwise vessel and would have to undergo—and pass—a through inspection before she could be reclassified as suitable for "oceans" use. While the ship could have undergone the inspection in San Francisco, the Olsons decided it would be more expedient to have the ship inspected and recertificated in Seattle, even as she was being loaded for the passage to Oahu.

The brothers were betting that *Cynthia Olson* would pass the inspection in Seattle and would thus be several days ahead of schedule. If, however, the ship failed the inspection for mechanical reasons, she'd have to undergo the necessary repairs or corrective actions before she could sail, thus delaying or even preventing her timely arrival in Oahu. This would, in turn, violate the terms of the Army contract and result either in payment penalties or, in the worst case, the Army's cancellation of the Olsons' contract. Her owners were willing to take the gamble, and on August 12 the Olson Company submitted to the Bureau of Inspection and Navigation's San Francisco office applications for both their Lakers' certificates to be extended to "oceans."

In an effort to better the odds on their gamble on *Cynthia Olson*, the brothers sought the assistance of William Fisher, the Bureau of Inspection and Navigation's supervising inspector in San Francisco. At the Olsons' urging, Fisher sent an airmail letter on August 12 asking his agency's local inspectors in Seattle to undertake the necessary inspection.[6] He noted that "the matter of a hospital is involved," meaning that the terms of the Army contract required the Laker to have a dedicated sickbay, something not normally present on coastwise cargo vessels of the day. Fisher added that *Cynthia Olson* was scheduled to load lumber in both Bellingham and Everett, implying that the inspectors should board the ship at whichever port would be most expedient.

Fisher's request for expedited action had the desired effect. On August 14 local inspectors Daniel B. Hutchings and William Campbell boarded *Cynthia Olson* in Bellingham and, accompanied by Captain Johnson, undertook an expedited but apparently comprehensive inspection. That same day, Hutchings and Campbell reported their findings in an airmail letter to Fisher in San Francisco:

> The steamer CYNTHIA OLSON was boarded today in compliance with the instructions given in your letter of the 12th instant. This vessel has boatage on each side, lawfully equipped, for 36 persons and is carrying a total crew of 30. The fuel capacity is 4,715 barrels, consumption 102 barrels per day; water capacity 117 tons plus 20 tons drinking water, consumption 8 tons per day.

Addressing the issue of a sickbay, the inspectors noted the following:

> The vessel has one spare room that the master intends to use as a hospital and which is, in our opinion, suitable for three berths.

And, responding in kind to the urgency of Fisher's original request, Hutchings and Campbell added the following:

> The CYNTHIA OLSON leaves for Honolulu at 5:00 P.M. tomorrow and the master appeared at this office and requested amendment changing vessel's character to oceans. We would appreciate permission by wire if we are to comply with this request.

Oddly enough, Fisher left on a business trip almost as soon as he sent Hutchings and Campbell the initial request for an expedited inspection. When the local inspectors' airmail letter reached San Francisco on the morning of August 15, Fisher's clerk fired off a telegram informing them that the supervising inspector was at that moment in Portland and would be in Seattle the following day. As *Cynthia Olson* was scheduled to sail before Fisher's arrival, the clerk suggested that Hutchings and Campbell try to reach him in Portland. This the two men managed to do, their telegram a model of economical yet suitably urgent prose:

> CYNTHIA OLSON INSPECTED EXTENSION ROUTE OCEANS HAS SPARE ROOM SUITABLE THREE BERTHS AND HOSPITAL MASTER INTENDS EQUIP SAME AT ONCE PERIOD SHIP SAILS FIVE PM TODAY FROM EVERETT REQUESTS AMENDMENT OCEANS MAY WE ISSUE SAME PERIOD.

Fisher's reply, which arrived at the local inspectors' Seattle office just hours before Cynthia Olson was due to sail, was equally terse: "YOU MAY ISSUE AMENDMENT TO CERTIFICATE AS OCEANS." Captain Johnson, who had been pacing anxiously in the inspectors' waiting room, nervously tapped his foot as a clerk typed up the amended certificate. As soon as the document was ready he sprinted to a waiting taxi and sped off to get his ship underway.

Johnson's haste was understandable, given that the ATS contract under which he was now officially operating (having gained the necessary "oceans" certification) required him to land his first load of timber in Honolulu no later than August 24. The most direct route from Puget Sound to Oahu covers some 2,670 miles, and at her best speed of ten knots *Cynthia Olson* would normally require about nine and a half days to make the passage. If he could get his ship to sea before midnight, Johnson would just barely have time to make the first crossing within the contract limit, and then only if the ship encountered neither mechanical problems nor unusually bad weather.

Luck and the elements must have been on Johnson's side, for *Cynthia Olson* completed her inaugural passage to Hawaii with a full day to spare. The ship arrived off Honolulu on the afternoon of Saturday, August 23,[7] and was soon tied to an Army Quartermaster Corps' pier in Kapalama Basin,[8] on the west side of Honolulu's commercial port. Over the following four days civilian longshoremen relieved her of her load of sawn timber, which was transferred to waiting trucks for onward movement to temporary storage at Fort Kamehameha. Located on the east side of the entrance to Pearl Harbor, the post was home to several batteries of large-caliber coast artillery guns, as well as the site of vast tent camps erected to house the increasing number of troops pouring into Hawaii. Much of the lumber *Cynthia Olson* carried from the Pacific Northwest on that first passage to Hawaii eventually was used to build stout, two-storied barracks buildings into which the newly arrived soldiers were more than happy to relocate.

Almost as soon as the last pieces of lumber were cleared from *Cynthia Olson*'s holds and decks, longshoremen began loading her with mixed cargo bound for Fort Mason. The shipment included such things as the crated household goods of Army officers being transferred from the Philippines and Hawaii back to the mainland; containers of empty brass artillery shell casings being returned to stateside arsenals for refilling; and engines and other parts removed from Army aircraft at Wheeler Field and bound for repair depots in California and Washington. Though the Army cargo manifested for the return voyage filled the Laker's holds, her decks remained clear, so Johnson shifted his vessel to a commercial pier to take on a deckload of commercial cargo. The loading was completed by the morning of September 2, and *Cynthia Olson* sailed for California just after noon.

The return voyage passed without incident, and the ship passed through the Golden Gate on the evening of September 11. *Cynthia Olson* didn't stay in San Francisco long, however, for three days after her arrival from Honolulu she departed for Eureka and Astoria. She apparently loaded lumber at each port and reached the entrance to the Strait of Juan de Fuca by September 19. Johnson then took the ship southeast into Puget Sound, Seattle off his port side and Bainbridge and Vashon Islands to starboard. Passing Tacoma, *Cynthia Olson* made her way around Point Defiance, through Nisqually Reach and, eventually, into Budd Inlet and to a loading pier at Olympia.

A bustling timber port as well as the capital of Washington, Olympia was a frequent destination for Olson Line ships. The company's agent had arranged for *Cynthia Olson* to take on some five hundred thousand board feet of prime lumber, which when added to that loaded in Eureka and Astoria gave the Laker a total cargo of just over two million board feet. The loading process stretched through the night, and *Cynthia Olson* left Olympia on the morning of September 20. She retraced her route of the day before and was alongside a Seattle fueling pier by late afternoon. Over the next three days she took on fuel and food—as well as some additional Army cargo trucked up from Fort Lewis, south of Tacoma—and was ready to depart by the morning of September 23. After some last-minute consultations with a group of Quartermaster Corps officers, Johnson ordered the lines cast off, and *Cynthia Olson* set out on her second Army-contracted voyage to Hawaii.

This passage was apparently as uneventful as the first, for the ship arrived off Honolulu on the evening of October 2, nine and a half days out of Seattle. Congestion at the Kapalama piers kept *Cynthia Olson* anchored out until the morning of October 3, when she was able to pick up her tugs and move into the basin. Unloading began within hours of her arrival at her assigned pier and was completed by the afternoon of Tuesday, October 7. As before, the ship was loaded with miscellaneous Army cargo bound for the West Coast, and she sailed on the morning of the October 10.

While *Cynthia Olson*'s second voyage to Hawaii followed the pattern set by the first passage, her return to the West Coast differed in that she would steam straight to Seattle rather than first calling at San Francisco, as she had in early September. Surviving records do not provide a reason for the changed routing, but because she was operating under Army contract we can reasonably assume that the alteration resulted from an Army request—either to transport some high-priority cargo or to hasten her return to Hawaii with her next load of lumber. Circumstantial evidence seems to point to the former possibility, given that *Cynthia Olson* arrived in Seattle on Sunday, October 19, but did not depart for Honolulu until October 27. If she did indeed carry some special cargo to Seattle, no records survive that identify the nature of the goods. We do know, however, that the Laker left for Honolulu carrying her by-now usual load of approximately two million board feet of lumber.

Cynthia Olson's third passage to Hawaii ended on November 5, when the vessel was once again alongside in Kapalama Basin. As on her two previous trips, the offload process began almost as soon as her lines were securely attached to the pier's bollards. But while the Laker's trips to Honolulu were beginning to settle into a comfortable routine, a meeting that had occurred in Washington, DC, three months earlier was about to alter that routine in a small but very significant way.

ON AUGUST 29, 1941, REPRESENTATIVES of the Army, Navy, and the offices of Production Management and Price Administration (both of which were part of the Office for Emergency Management established by the Roosevelt administration in May 1940) met at the headquarters of the U.S. Maritime Commission.[9] The meeting was intended to address what was becoming an increasingly important issue—the allocation of shipping dedicated to the intercoastal transportation of priority military cargoes. Because an increasing number of U.S.-registered coastwise and short-sea[10] cargo vessels were being contracted to carry freight ultimately destined for Great Britain or France, Army and Navy officials feared there would not be enough vessels available to carry their priority cargoes—mainly lumber for the Army and iron and steel products for the Navy—should the United States be drawn into the war.

The Army, represented at the August meeting by the chief of the Quartermaster Corps' Traffic Control Branch, made the point that lumber was an increasingly important strategic resource for a variety of reasons.[11] First, sawn timber was the basic building materiel for the vast numbers of structures going up at military bases across the country and overseas, and hundreds of millions of board feet would ultimately be required for the ongoing military expansion. Second, wood was an integral part of the aircraft and shipbuilding industries; the B-17 and B-24 bombers then entering widespread service, for example, each contained hundreds of wooden components, ranging from floor boards to racks for radios and ammunition boxes. Navy ships of all types needed wood for decking, and some—such as patrol torpedo (PT) boats and minesweepers—were built almost entirely of wood. And, perhaps equally important in the larger scheme of things, vast amounts of lumber would be necessary to build the millions of packing crates, cargo pallets, and other shipping containers in which the American armed forces would transport virtually every piece of equipment shipped anywhere in the world.

From the Traffic Control Branch's point of view, then, the United States' accelerating military buildup—and, indeed, its hopes for eventual victory if drawn into war—demanded an uninterrupted flow of timber from the nation's forests to its military bases and industrial centers. As neither the Army nor the Navy possessed dedicated lumber-carrying vessels, continued use of specialized commercial ships was unavoidable. However, the Army's position was that it would rather "bareboat" charter lumber carriers—meaning the shipping lines would provide the "bare boats" while the Army would provide crew, fuel, stores, and maintenance—than continue to rely on short-term contracts.[12] This would not only ensure the longer-term availability of suitable vessels, it would guarantee that the ships would remain in service even if hostilities broke out.

While the Army did not need the permission of the Intercoastal Shipping Priorities Advisory Committee—the multiagency task force that grew out of the August meeting—to implement the bareboat charter of suitable lumber carriers, the committee in fact agreed that the plan was the most suitable way to prevent a shortage of such vessels. When the Army began soliciting for charters it therefore had the committee's backing, a not inconsequential fact from the point of view of many shipowners. Concerned that if the United States went to war the Maritime Commission could well begin commandeering civilian vessels for military service, some shipping companies saw the Intercoastal Committee's backing of the Army's bareboat charter plan as a tacit agreement that vessels voluntarily chartered to the Army at prewar prices would not later be involuntarily requisitioned at lower wartime rates.

As a leading West Coast lumber-shipping firm, and one already working under contract to the Army, the Olson Company was among the first steamship lines to be approached about the possibility of bareboat charters. In early November, even as *Cynthia Olson* was taking on cargo in Honolulu for her return voyage to the West Coast, Whit and George Olson met at Fort Mason with the superintendent of the Army Transport Service's San Francisco office, Colonel J. H. Mellon. The Army was interested in chartering both *Cynthia Olson* and *Barbara Olson*, but Mellon, for reasons that are unclear, wished to do so under separate agreements.

The terms Mellon proposed for *Cynthia Olson*'s bareboat charter were straightforward. It would commence on November 21 for an initial six-month period, and the ship would undertake as many voyages during that time as the ATS deemed necessary and which they believed the ship capable of completing. The Army would pay the Olson Company $10,260 per month and would provide $200,000 in insurance coverage for the vessel. The ATS pegged the Laker's value at $71,600 and estimated that the cost of an average cargo of about two million board feet of lumber would be $73,000. The Army stated that it would "at its own expense, man, operate, victual, fuel, and supply the vessel and pay all port charges, pilotages, and all other costs and expenses incident to the use and operation of the vessel."[13]

The clause of the proposed contract that covered the manning of the ship in greater detail specified that deck crewmen would be drawn from the ranks of civilians currently employed by the Army Transport Service. The ship's officers, on the other hand, need not be ATS employees; they only had to have the proper licenses, and the Army actually preferred that *Cynthia Olson*'s officers be drawn from the company's pool of experienced senior mariners. This made sense, given that men like captains Johnson and Carlsen were not only highly experienced in the intricacies of lumber transport, they knew their ships inside and out. And, finally, the Army would provide a radio operator and a medic on each voyage, both of whom would be enlisted soldiers drawn from SFPOE subordinate units.

AFTER TWO WEEKS OF NEGOTIATIONS and scrutiny of the charter terms by attorneys on both sides, the Olson Company and the ATS reached final agreement on Contract No. W928 QM-40989. The document was signed on November 18 by Whit Olson and Mellon and witnessed by George Olson, and as of that date the ship in question officially became USAT (United States Army Transport) *Cynthia Olson*.[14] There was no ceremony aboard the Laker to mark the occasion, however, because she was still inbound from Honolulu. When the phlegmatic Johnson was informed of the charter terms by radio and asked if he would agree to stay on as

Cynthia Olson's master, he reportedly asked only two questions: would he be able to pick his own officers, and would there be an increase in his salary? When both queries were answered in the affirmative, he simply said, "Fine." What he didn't add was that he'd been feeling ill for several days and wasn't sure he'd be able to make the first charter voyage.

That trip was scheduled to begin in San Francisco on November 22, two days after *Cynthia Olson* arrived from Honolulu. According to the itinerary sketched out by the ATS planners at Fort Mason, the Laker would stay in port only long enough to receive and settle her new crewmembers. She'd then depart for Tacoma to load her cargo, then shift to Seattle to take aboard fuel, food, and fresh water for the run to Honolulu. Her departure for Hawaii was tentatively set for December 1, and she was expected to be alongside the Kapalama Basin pier nine days later. It was in most respects exactly the same type of voyage *Cynthia Olson* had been undertaking for the previous few months, and neither her owners nor the Army planners at Fort Mason anticipated any difficulties on this first of what was intended to be at least six trips the Laker would undertake to Hawaii during the charter period.

USAT *Cynthia Olson* passed beneath the Golden Gate Bridge at 12:15 a.m. on November 20, having made the passage from Honolulu in the by-now usual nine and a half days. Though again bearing what her cargo manifest listed as "Army materiel"—the exact nature of which is lost to history—the Laker did not tie up at Fort Mason but continued past that installation and the commercial cargo piers fronting the Embarcadero. Turning to starboard, she passed under the Oakland Bay Bridge and, with Yerba Buena Island off her port side, made her way past the entrance to Oakland's inner harbor. Turning slightly to port, she then did something out of the ordinary; with a Navy yard tug in attendance, *Cynthia Olson* tied up to a pier at Alameda Naval Air Station.[15]

Why the diminutive freighter visited the naval station, and whether the "Army materiel" on her cargo manifest should have instead been labeled "Navy materiel," is unknown. It's possible that *Cynthia Olson* could have been carrying Navy aircraft parts destined for repair at Alameda; it was certainly not unknown for Army-owned, -chartered, or -contracted vessels to carry cargo belonging to the Navy, Marine Corps, or Coast Guard, especially if the ship was homeward bound with little or no Army freight. Or perhaps the reason for *Cynthia Olson's* brief call at Alameda was simply to disembark Navy personnel who'd caught a convenient lift back from Hawaii.[16] Unfortunately, as with many other aspects of *Cynthia Olson*'s brief Army career, we will never know for certain.

We do know, however, that the Laker didn't stay long in Alameda. By the afternoon of November 21 she was back across the bay, tied up to a Fort Mason pier. Given that the ship was scheduled to sail for Seattle the next day and that she would be undertaking her first outbound passage under Army charter, her pier was probably a scene of controlled chaos. The tasks that had to be accomplished before her departure included the paying off of most of her crew and their replacement by civilian ATS mariners; filling the ship's fuel and freshwater tanks; loading enough food to sustain thirty-five men for two weeks; stocking her rather basic sick bay with Army-provided medicines and supplies; and replacing the Laker's existing and decidedly primitive radio with a standard Army high-frequency set that could be manually operated under normal circumstances and set to broadcast an automatic distress signal if necessary.

Soon after the ship tied up at Fort Mason, her master headed off to the SFPOE headquarters building for a meeting with Mellon and his staff. Because *Cynthia Olson* was now under direct ATS control, Johnson needed to be briefed on those Army-specific issues to which he had not been privy while his ship was merely under contract. These would include a review of the Army regulations governing the management of ATS civilian mariners; the handing over of the ship's official sailing orders; and, finally, a briefing on the current military situation in the North Pacific. Interestingly, this would not focus on Japanese forces but on the known or suspected locations of the German surface raiders and submarines that had been active against British and Commonwealth ships for more than a year.[17] While America was still officially neutral, events in the North Atlantic and South Pacific had shown that neutrality was not a sure defense against German torpedoes or mines.[18]

Upon arrival at the ATS headquarters building, Johnson imparted some news of his own: he would not be on *Cynthia Olson*'s bridge for the first charter voyage to Hawaii. The master mariner had been feeling increasingly ill over the preceding few days and didn't think it wise to make the trip. Moreover, his first mate had chosen not to sign on for the voyage, so the two top members of the Laker's crew would have to be replaced, and quickly. It was not the sort of news Mellon wanted to hear with barely twelve hours remaining before *Cynthia Olson* was scheduled to sail.

Fortunately, Johnson also had a solution for the problem. He'd been in radio contact with company headquarters even before bringing his ship into port and had told the Olson brothers of both his illness and his first mate's decision not to sign on for the first charter trip. The news wasn't as bad as it might have been, however, for the ideal replacements for Johnson and the mate were literally sitting in front of Olson's desk when Johnson's radio call came in. Berthel Carlsen had brought *Barbara Olson* into San Francisco from Honolulu on November 4, and he and his usual first mate, William Petersen Buchtele, had then turned the vessel over to another master and mate as part of a normal crew rotation. Carlsen and Buchtele had spent the intervening weeks at their homes in San Pedro but had returned to San Francisco on November 19 to meet with the Olson brothers regarding the Army's pending charter of *Barbara Olson*.

When Johnson announced that he'd be unable to make the impending voyage, Whit Olson immediately asked Carlsen to take command of *Cynthia Olson* for the important first charter trip. The master mariner in turn asked Buchtele if he'd be willing to make the passage as first mate and, when the latter agreed, Carlsen turned back to Olson and in his lilting Norwegian accent said, "Ja, why not?"

It was a decision that was to have consequences Carlsen could not have foreseen, and one that would forever alter the lives of every man in the room.

CHAPTER 4

CAPTAIN AND CREW

WHIT OLSON COULD NOT HAVE chosen a better-qualified man to take P. C. Johnson's place on *Cynthia Olson's* bridge. At sixty-four, Carl Berthel "Bert" Carlsen was at the pinnacle of a long, varied, and successful career; indeed, so experienced a seaman was Carlsen that the title "master mariner" seems a totally inadequate description of the man's relationship to ships and the sea.

Born in Bergen, Norway,[1] on March 19, 1877, he told friends throughout his life that he came from a long line of seafarers.[2] While we don't know the details of Carlsen's childhood—or, indeed, his ancestry—we do know that by the time he reached seventeen he'd apparently had enough of life in Bergen. In the spring of 1894 he boarded an immigrant ship bound for the New World. Traveling on a vessel packed with other Scandinavians who, like him, sought new lives in America, he ultimately landed in New York. While it seems likely that the strapping six foot one, 160-pound Carlsen quickly found work as a seaman in that bustling port city, the eastern seaboard apparently didn't suit him, since by the winter of 1898 he was in San Francisco. America obviously agreed with the young Norwegian, for on December 2 of that year he became a naturalized U.S. citizen.

The following eighteen years of Bert Carlsen's life are something of a mystery, given that surviving records give no clear indication of where he lived or whether he'd started a family. However, his name does occasionally appear on crew manifests of ships sailing both in the California coastwise passenger and cargo trades and on international passages from Pacific and Atlantic ports. In other words, he seems to have followed the normal career pattern for a merchant seaman of his day, taking what work he could wherever it was to be found and steadily advancing in his chosen profession. He passed the required licensure requirements at each level, and in 1916 he received his master's license. Not only did it authorize him to captain any vessel of any size on any ocean, it designated him a

> first-class pilot on San Pedro Bay and tributaries, [the] Bay of San Diego and Bay of San Francisco . . . Gray's Harbor and Willapa Harbor [Washington] and Astoria [Oregon], each to [the] sea; and between Tacoma, Everett, Bellingham and Dungeness [Washington].

The year 1916 was also important in an emotional sense, for at the ripe age of thirty-nine Carlsen apparently decided to settle down, at least somewhat. On September 16 he married twenty-nine-year-old Thyra Oveda Knudsen, the American-born daughter of Norwegian immigrants, in Portland, Oregon. The fact that their courtship and marriage took place in one of the key ports of the Pacific Northwest timber industry implies that Carlsen was probably already working steadily in the coastwise lumber-shipping trade. It would have been a busy and, presumably, profitable time for Carlsen, no matter what type of ship he was sailing on, because the war that had by that point been raging in Europe for two years had proven to be a bonanza for the still-neutral American Merchant Marine. Cargoes of strategic raw materials—including lumber—competed with foodstuffs for space in the holds and on the decks of ships bound for European, South American, and Pacific Rim ports. An experienced ship captain willing to travel, and to spend time away from a new wife, would have been virtually guaranteed all the work he could handle.

How many commercial voyages Carlsen signed on for over the seven months between the time of his marriage and America's April 6, 1917, entry into World War I is unclear. We do know, however, that in the wake of President Woodrow Wilson's declaration of war against Germany, Carlsen the merchant ship captain became Lieutenant Carlsen of the U.S. Naval Reserve Force (USNRF). Created in March 1915—largely through the efforts of Secretary of the Navy Josephus Daniels and his assistant, Franklin D. Roosevelt—the USNRF was intended to be a pool of highly qualified mariners, aircraft pilots, and other specialists who could be quickly called up for service without lengthy training. Bert Carlsen was exactly the kind of man the USNRF sought to recruit, and for the first year of his service, he captained a series of Navy-owned cargo vessels on voyages between ports on the Pacific, Gulf, and Atlantic Coasts.

By July 1918 Carlsen was a San Francisco–based lieutenant commander tasked with overseeing the construction of several ships being built in West Coast yards for the U.S. Shipping Board. One of these vessels—a 410-foot, 5,650 GRT, single-screw cargo ship under construction by the Bay Area firm Western Pipe & Steel Company—was of particular interest because Carlsen had been tapped to command her. Launched on July 4, 1918, as *Nantahala*, she spent four months fitting out and on Saturday, November 16, she was officially taken over by the Navy. She was commissioned the same day as USS *Nantahala*, with Bert Carlsen as her plank-owning skipper, and assigned to the Naval Overseas Transportation Service (NOTS).[3]

The fact that World War I had ended five days before *Nantahala* joined the fleet did not lessen the Navy's need for her. The United States had already committed itself to a massive humanitarian-relief effort aimed at feeding the millions of Europeans displaced by the conflict, and both NOTS and Carlsen's new command were to play roles in that noble endeavor. The day after her commissioning *Nantahala* got underway on her first, admittedly short, voyage, shifting some four miles from Western Pipe's Richmond shipyard on the northeast side of San Francisco Bay to a Navy pier in Oakland. Over the following nineteen days she took on fuel, additional crewmembers, and a mixed cargo of flour, cooking oil, medicines, and several hundred large military tents, and on December 5 she sailed through the Golden Gate bound for New York.

Traveling at her best speed of eleven knots, *Nantahala* took twenty-six days to make the passage. On her December 31 arrival in New York Carlsen was called to a captains' meeting at the Brooklyn Navy Yard, where he and the senior officers of some twenty vessels assigned to the relief effort were briefed on their departure dates and destinations. *Nantahala*'s tasking was among the more interesting and potentially challenging, in that she was ordered to make for Fiume, a formerly Austro-Hungarian port city at the northern end of the Adriatic Sea, on the Kvarner Gulf just east of the Istrian

Peninsula. Inhabited largely by ethnic Italians and long coveted by Rome, the city was often the scene of violent clashes between groups supporting the region's annexation by Italy and those who felt the area's future lay with the new state being advocated by Slavic nationalists. Soon after the November 11 armistice ending World War I, Fiume had been occupied by a combined force of American, British, and French troops, whose brief was to maintain order until the city's ultimate fate was decided at the Paris Peace Conference.

The convoluted politics of postwar Europe were the least of Bert Carlsen's worries, however, for *Nantahala*'s voyage to Fiume would be almost as dangerous in peacetime as it would have been a year before the armistice. The German, Austro-Hungarian, British, and Italian navies had all laid numerous mine barrages in the eastern Mediterranean, Ionian, and Adriatic Seas, with special attention on the narrow Strait of Otronto separating the "heel" of the Italian boot from Albania and around the southern tip of the Istrian Peninsula near the sprawling military port at Pola. Few of the mines had yet been removed, and *Nantahala* would be transiting areas in which other ships had been damaged or sunk since the end of hostilities.

With the risks of the coming voyage undoubtedly firmly in mind, Carlsen took *Nantahala* and her seventy-two-man crew to sea on January 9, 1919. He shaped a course for Gibraltar, with an intermediate stop in the Azores, and passed from the North Atlantic into the Mediterranean during the first week of February. Over the following weeks—often traveling in company with other relief vessels—*Nantahala* made her way steadily east, finally turning north into the Ionian Sea on February 11. Four days later, after an often-tense passage through areas where rogue mines[4] were actually visible on the surface, Carlsen and his mercy ship arrived safely in Fiume. Unloading began almost immediately and with Allied troops standing guard on the pier to prevent rioting, the medicines, flour, and other cargo were quickly put ashore.

Her holds now empty, *Nantahala* went to work shuttling people and materiel around the Adriatic and Central Mediterranean. The passengers often included military personnel and Red Cross and other aid workers, and the materiel ran the gamut from damaged vehicles being carried to rear-area repair facilities to stocks of unused ammunition destined for disposal. It was exactly the sort of mundane yet ultimately important transport work for which the ship had been designed, and Carlsen and his crew ensured that every passage went off without a hitch. By mid-March their work was done, and *Nantahala* sailed for the United States via Gibraltar, reaching New York on April 10. The ship was formally decommissioned on the April 17, and thirteen days later was returned to the USSB. She would go on to other work, as would her newly discharged captain.[5]

For Carlsen, that work would prove amazingly similar to the task he'd just completed. After taking several months off to return to Oregon for a long-delayed reunion with his wife, the now forty-three-year-old mariner signed on as master of the 5,730-GRT *Western Spirit*, a USSB-owned vessel built in Portland in the summer of 1918. She, like *Nantahala*, had been commissioned into the Navy and made two voyages to Europe, one before the armistice and one after. Returned to USSB control in April 1919, *Western Spirit* had been chartered to the New York–based Moore & McCormack Line for use on that firm's European cargo and passenger service. Outward-bound from New York, she would carry a mixed load of relief supplies and general merchandise to various ports, and on the return would embark both immigrants and European goods destined for U.S. markets.

It was the ideal command for Bert Carlsen: *Western Spirit* was similar to *Nantahala* in design and capability, and her planned service was virtually identical to that of the master mariner's previous ship. We don't know whether Carlsen's decision to take the job was influenced by the fact that *Western Spirit* had been built in his adopted hometown of Portland— where his wife still maintained their home at 127 East Twentieth Street— but it would undoubtedly have struck him as an interesting coincidence. Whatever other motivations might have played a role in his decision to take command of *Western Spirit*, it's quite likely the deciding factor was the simple need to earn a living. The end of World War I had put many sailors, both naval and merchant, out of work, and the possibility of several months' gainful employment could not be ignored.

Carlsen took *Western Spirit* out of New York Harbor during the last days of January 1920, bound first for England. Her Atlantic crossing was apparently uneventful, and she offloaded her foodstuffs and manufactured goods in Liverpool before taking on other cargo bound for ports in Italy, France, Holland, and Denmark. By late April, she was in Copenhagen, where she embarked twenty-seven Scandinavian immigrants bound for America. She made a brief stop in Dartmouth, England, and on May 4 departed for New York. Exactly two weeks later she was alongside Brooklyn's Pier 33, where Carlsen signed off as master and headed home.[6]

As he'd done after leaving *Nantahala*, he spent several months in Oregon, presumably readjusting to married life and quite possibly taking the occasional piloting job or coastwise berth. By January 1921 he was ready for the open sea again, though this time he found a ship closer to home. Another Moore & McCormack–owned vessel, *Osage* (ironically, a Laker of virtually identical layout to the Olson Line ships that still lay in Carlsen's future) was lying in Seattle, preparing for much the same type of trans-Atlantic trading sojourn as *Western Spirit* had undertaken.[7] *Osage*'s voyage would potentially be more challenging, however, in that her planned itinerary would take her first to New York, and from there on several round-trip passages to Irish ports. Those ports, like the rest of Ireland, were at that moment engulfed in the final throes of a conflict that within a year would result in the creation of the Irish Free State.

Bert Carlsen signed aboard *Osage* on January 25 and a week later took the ship to sea. After a brief call in San Francisco he shaped a course for New York, and over the following ten months Carlsen and his crew made three round-trips between there and the embattled Emerald Isle. *Osage*'s ports of call differed on each voyage: she visited Limerick, at the head of the River Shannon, on the first trip; the sprawling northern port of Belfast on the second; and Londonderry, also in the north, on the third. While offloading cargo in predominantly Catholic and nationalist Limerick the ship's crewmembers would almost certainly have heard gunfire as British troops battled IRA units in and around the city, and at one point a wildcat strike by dockworkers sympathetic to the Irish nationalist cause resulted in a several-day delay in loading cargo.

Despite the delays and potential dangers *Osage* completed her series of Irish voyages without serious incident, and on Monday, November 7, 1921, Bert Carlsen brought the ship alongside a Seattle pier and rang up "finished with engines" on her engine-order telegraph. It had been a successful but obviously challenging trip, and when Carlsen walked off the ship the following day it seems he'd decided that long-distance international voyaging was not where his future lay. Whether for personal reasons—he had, after all, thus far spent much of his married life away from wife and home—or because he was simply looking for other challenges, he apparently decided to return to the coastal lumber trade.

Surviving records indicate that in the twenty years following *Osage's* return from her Irish odyssey Carlsen's only international ports of call were such British Columbia timber towns as New Westminster, Ocean Falls, and Port McNeill.

Fortunately, his decision to concentrate on coastwise work was an economically sound one. The Pacific Northwest timber industry continued to expand throughout the early and mid-1920s, and Carlsen's proven skills as both sea captain and coastal pilot were much in demand. While he seems to have sailed for several firms, including the Olsons, by 1927 he was working almost exclusively for the San Francisco–based E.K. Wood Lumber Company. The following year he and Thyra moved from Portland to San Pedro—the site of Wood's largest port operation—and were doing well enough financially to contract for a custom-built home on a hillside overlooking the harbor. Though the 1,306-square foot, two-bedroom, cottage-style structure was significantly smaller than several of the other homes on Le Grande Terrace, it was ideal for the childless couple. It was also beautifully crafted and made extensive use of custom details,[8] and at a total cost of $11,000 it was certainly a major investment for the now fifty-two-year-old sea captain and his forty-two-year-old wife.[9]

The Carlsens were able to weather the economic turmoil that followed the collapse of the stock market in the fall of 1929, largely because Bert was able to work steadily. His usual ship through most of the 1930s was E.K. Wood's *Cascade*, a Laker built in 1918 as *War Rifle* by Ohio's Toledo Shipbuilding Company. The vessel made monthly round-trips between San Pedro and the Pacific Northwest lumber ports, usually returning with mixed loads of sawn timber and rolls of newsprint. It was exactly the same sort of work on which the Olson Company ships were then engaged, and the fact that the two shipping lines were headquartered in the same building at One Drumm Street in San Francisco may indicate that they were more collaborators than competitors.[10]

Whatever the relationship between the two firms, by 1939 Bert Carlsen was routinely captaining vessels for both.[11] It was a busy time for the companies and the master mariner, and by the time the Olsons acquired *Coquina* and *Corrales* in the spring of 1940 few captains on the West Coast had as much experience with Lakers, especially those rigged as lumber schooners, as did Carlsen. He went on to further that experience by captaining *Barbara Olson* for much of 1941, and when on November 19 he made the fateful decision to take Johnson's place aboard *Cynthia Olson*, his employers could only have heaved a huge, if ultimately premature, sigh of relief. Carlsen, for his part, was almost certainly equally relieved that he'd be assisted on the trip by a first mate in whom he had both great trust and deep respect—Bill Buchtele.

———

THE MAN WHO AGREED TO join Berthel Carlsen on *Cynthia Olson*'s first Army charter voyage was born in Vordingborg, Denmark, on April 6, 1902. His name at birth was Wilhelm Buchtele Petersen, he had a sister, and he was the son of a well-known musician and academician, Rasmus N. Petersen.[12] Unfortunately, that is virtually all we know of his early life. Among the details that remain obscure are when and on what vessel he immigrated to the United States, but like many Scandinavians he ultimately gravitated to the West Coast.[13] We know that he stood five feet ten inches tall and weighed 165 pounds, that he first became a merchant seaman in 1923, and that he was naturalized in San Francisco on December 21, 1929. For reasons of his own, he used the latter occasion to officially change his name to William Petersen Buchtele.[14]

While the purpose of the name change has been lost to history, we know that the newly "Americanized" Bill Buchtele continued to go to sea. By December 1934 he was steadily employed by the Kingsley Navigation Company, a Vancouver, British Columbia–based firm specializing in the coastwise shipping of lime. He was initially hired through the firm's San Francisco office, and during the first half of 1935 he made seven passages between Canada and various West Coast ports. All of his trips were aboard *Texada*—a Laker laid down in 1917 as *Lake Dunmore*—though work aboard the lime carrier must not have agreed with him. In August 1935 he left Kingsley for a job as third mate aboard the Olson brothers' *Florence Olson*. Like Bert Carlsen, whom he probably met for the first time at about this period, Buchtele chose to make his home in San Pedro.

Though he lived in Southern California he was, of course, a frequent visitor to San Francisco. That allowed him to carry on his courtship with Katherine Johnson Beck, a thirty-five-year-old divorcée whom he'd met under interesting circumstances sometime in 1934. During a brief layover in the City by the Bay, Buchtele and several crewmates did what sailors have long done when they have a free evening on their hands—they got roaring drunk. When the sailors returned to their small hotel on Market Street, Buchtele was too inebriated to put himself to bed so he was assisted by a crewmate and Beck, who was working as a housemaid and night desk clerk to make ends meet. When Buchtele awoke the next morning and discovered what had transpired, he was mortified and was so charmingly apologetic that Beck could not refuse his request to take her to dinner in atonement for his boorish behavior. Their romance blossomed during subsequent visits, and they were married in San Francisco on May 18, 1936.

Bill Buchtele and his new bride set up housekeeping at a rented house on South Grand Street in San Pedro, where they were ultimately joined by Katherine's preteen daughter, Eleanor.[15] Though by all accounts delighted with his new "instant" family, Buchtele still had to make a living, and that meant continuing to go to sea. He worked aboard ships of both the Oliver Olson and E.K. Wood fleets, steadily working his way up to second mate.[16] He often sailed with Bert Carlsen, usually aboard *Cascade*, and the two Scandinavian Americans became good friends.

And it was that friendship, perhaps more than any other factor, that prompted Bill Buchtele to make what ultimately became the worst decision of his life.

———

BERT CARLSEN AND BILL BUCHTELE were not the only people, of course, who would take *Cynthia Olson* to sea. She would make the voyage toward Hawaii bearing thirty-five merchant mariners—Carlsen and his three mates; an eleven-member Deck Department; an eleven-man Engineering Department; a seven-man Mess Department; and two enlisted soldiers. In keeping with the terms of the Army charter, most of the ship's previous crewmen were paid off when the ship tied up at Fort Mason. Even as they walked down the gangplank, the twenty-three ATS contract mariners—many of the Filipinos—tapped to replace them were arriving on the pier.

When Carlsen and Buchtele boarded *Cynthia Olson* late on November 21—following, of course, their lengthy briefings at the ATS office—among the first things they did was muster the ship's crew. Standing on the as-yet uncrowded forward deck, they were grouped by operating departments.

Here, in brief, is what we know of the men who joined Carlsen and Buchtele aboard USAT *Cynthia Olson*:[17]

SENIOR OFFICERS

Carl "Cad" Johnstad, fifty-nine, second officer (ATS preferred the term "officer" to "mate"), was born July 13, 1882, in Norway. He worked for many years for the Wapama Steamship Company, which, like both the Olson and E.K. Wood firms, had its main offices at One Drumm Street in San Francisco. Unmarried, he'd lived in California since at least 1910 and his listed next of kin was his brother, J. Johnstad, of Alameda. He was an Olson Company employee.[18]

James Wood Mills, thirty-six, third officer, was born July 21, 1905, in Galesburg, Illinois, but was raised in Seattle. He served aboard several Matson Line vessels, including *Liloa*, and had thus visited Hawaii on several occasions. Unmarried, his listed next of kin was his aunt, Miss Arra J. Woods of Seattle. He was an Olson Company employee.

ENGINEERING DEPARTMENT

Konrad Harald "Harry" Lofving, sixty-three, chief engineer, was a native Scandinavian, like Carlsen, Buchtele, and Johnstad. Lofving was born November 12, 1878, in Stockholm, Sweden, the son of a cabinetmaker. He immigrated to the United States in 1903 aboard the liner RMS *Celtic* of Great Britain's White Star Line. He was naturalized in New York in April 1906 and had lived in California since before World War I. Initially employed as a machinist for Bethlehem Shipbuilding's San Francisco yard, he apparently first went to sea in the early 1920s. By the late 1930s he was regularly employed by the Olson Company and had served aboard *George Olson*. Married, he and his wife, Hulda, and their daughter, Olga, lived in Oakland, California. He was an Olson Company employee.

Thomas Muirhead Jr., sixty-one, first assistant engineer, was born July 3, 1880, in Dallas, Texas. Had worked aboard a variety of ships, including the Associated Oil Company's tanker *Paul Shoup*. Married, he and his wife, Theresa, lived in Berkeley. He was an Olson Company employee.

Charles H. Taylor, forty-nine, second assistant engineer, was born in Texas around 1892. He had served on at least one ATS vessel, the transport USAT *Leonard Wood*. Married, he and his wife, Mabel, lived in Oakland. He was an Olson Company employee.

Thomas Grier Moore, twenty-seven, third assistant engineer, was born December 18, 1914, in Ilwaco, Washington. Though his application for license renewal was rejected in December 1935 by a marine surgeon in Portland, Oregon, it seems not to have inhibited his career. He had served on at least one other Olson Company vessel—possibly *Barbara Olson*. Single, he had no next of kin listed. He was an Olson Company employee.

Anastacio M. Atad, fifty-two, oiler, was born in the Philippines around 1889.[19] He had served on the Army transport USAT *Republic* 1936–1940. Married, his wife lived in Manila. Like virtually all the Filipinos who served as ATS contract mariners, he remained a citizen of the Philippines.

Maximo Ankot Basbas, forty-three, oiler, was born June 5, 1898, in the Philippines. He had served aboard the American President Lines' *President Jefferson*. His listed next of kin was his brother, Philmyoita, in the Philippines. He was an ATS contract mariner.

Victoriano Tabayay Pedro, age unknown, oiler, had as his listed next of kin his sister, Macaria T. Pedro, in the Philippines. He was an ATS contract mariner.

Sotero Vequilla Cabigas, age unknown, fireman, had his listed next of kin as his cousin, M. Vequilla, in the Philippines. He was an ATS contract mariner.

Isidro Espejo Montegrejo, thirty-four, fireman, was born in the Philippines around 1907. He had served aboard the Army transport USAT *Chateau Thierry* in 1935. His listed next of kin was his father, Agapito Montegrejo, who at the time of *Cynthia Olson*'s departure on the first charter voyage was serving aboard the Army transport USAT *Holbrook*. He was an ATS contract mariner.

Benito Rodriguez, forty-five, fireman, was born around 1896 in the Philippines. He had served aboard the American President Lines' *President Jefferson* in the mid-1920s. His listed next of kin was a cousin, D. L. Cipriano, of San Francisco. He was an ATS contract mariner.

Maximo Terro, age unknown, wiper, was born in the Philippines. His listed next of kin was a brother, Johnie Terro, in the Philippines. He was an ATS contract mariner.

DECK DEPARTMENT

Roland Joseph Dodd, forty, quartermaster, was born May 1, 1901, in Atlanta, Georgia. He had served in the Army during World War I and later worked as an embalmer. At the time *Cynthia Olson* sailed, his ex-wife was living in Los Angeles, and his listed next of kin was a brother, C. M. Dodd Jr., in Corpus Christi, Texas. He was an Army civilian employee.

Joaquin Daguison, thirty-nine, bosun, was born around 1902 in the Philippines. He had served on the Army transport USAT *U. S. Grant* 1937–1940. Married, his wife, Adelina, lived in the Philippines. He was an ATS contract mariner.

Jose L. Buta, age unknown, able-bodied seaman, was born in the Philippines. His listed next of kin was an uncle, Tibrosio Burila, in Sacramento, California. He was an ATS contract mariner.

Claro Maagma, forty-two, able-bodied seaman, was born in the Philippines around 1894. He had served aboard the Swain & Hoyt Line's *Point Reyes* in the 1930s. His listed next of kin was his mother, Adriana Castillo, in San Francisco. He was an ATS contract mariner.

Pio J. Perales, forty-three, able-bodied seaman, was born in the Philippines around 1898. He had served aboard the China Mail Steamship Line's *Nanking* in the 1920s. His listed next of kin was a brother, Tony Perales, in Turlock, California. He was an ATS contract mariner.

August S. D. Santiago, twenty-four, able-bodied seaman, was born in the Philippines around 1917. He had served aboard the Army-operated *President Cleveland* in 1940. His wife, Julita, lived in the Philippines. He was an ATS contract mariner.

Pedro Torres Soliman, twenty-nine, able-bodied seaman, was born in the Philippines around 1911. He initially arrived in the United States in 1929 as a stowaway aboard the Dutch-owned cargo vessel *Siantar*, which landed him in San Pedro. His clandestine arrival apparently didn't keep him from becoming a merchant mariner, for within a few years he was steadily employed aboard the A.H. Bull Company's *Dorothy*. His listed next of kin was a sister, Cristina Soliman, in the Philippines. He was an ATS contract mariner.

Raymond Timtiman Villa, twenty-five, able-bodied seaman, was born in the Philippines around 1916. His listed next of kin was a sister, Mrs. Pedro T. Ramos, in the Philippines. He was an ATS contract mariner.

Sopromio Polohang Bajo, age unknown, ordinary seaman, was born in the Philippines. His listed next of kin was his father, Nacanor Bajo, in the Philippines. He was an ATS contract mariner.

Conrado Melanio Jalocon, age unknown, ordinary seaman, was born in the Philippines. His listed next of kin was his father, Rufino Jalocon, in the Philippines. He was an ATS contract mariner.

Leodegario Tejano Kaay, age unknown, ordinary seaman, was born in the Philippines. His listed next of kin was a friend, Pacifico Pacolba, at the Mare Island Navy Yard in Vallejo, California. He was an ATS contract mariner.

MESS DEPARTMENT

Anthony Gabriel Bushka, twenty-nine, chief steward, was born January 10, 1912, in Chicago. A baker by trade, he apparently went to sea for the first time in late 1939, when he joined the mess staff of the Army transport USAT *Leonard Wood*. He made several voyages aboard that vessel, sailing out of San Francisco, and was transferred from it to *Cynthia Olson*. He and his wife, Della Marie Bushka, had welcomed their first child, a son, in October 1941. He was an ATS contract mariner.

Domingo Lurista Mananita, forty-one, senior cook, was born in the Philippines around 1900. His listed next of kin was a cousin, Badong Rosales, in Sacramento. He was an ATS contract mariner.

Guillermo Osmena Velez, thirty-seven, junior cook, was born in the Philippines around 1904. His listed next of kin was a sister, Januaria Tamay, in the Philippines. He was an ATS contract mariner.

Zacarias Arceno Baes, thirty, messman, was born in the Philippines around 1911. He had served on the Army transports USAT *Leonard Wood* and USAT *St. Mihiel* from 1937 through early 1941. His listed next of kin was a brother, Victor Baes, in the Philippines. He was an ATS contract mariner.

Alfred Morente Basilio, thirty-five, messman, was born in the Philippines around 1906. His listed next of kin was a friend, Moises Evangalista, in San Francisco. He was an ATS contract mariner.

Fred Cabaltera Cadag, age unknown, messman, had his listed next of kin as a brother, Ben C. Cadag, in Seattle. He was an ATS contract mariner.

Leo Misoles Escalante, age unknown, messman, had his listed next of kin as a son, Leo M. Escalante Jr., in San Francisco. He was an ATS contract mariner.

———

THE FINAL TWO MEMBERS OF *Cynthia Olson*'s cosmopolitan crew stood out from the rest during the late-evening muster, mainly because they wore Army uniforms. Twenty-four-year-old medic Private Ernest Jeston Davenport would have dominion over the ship's four-bed sickbay, while twenty-five-year-old radio operator Private Samuel J. Ziskind would be responsible for keeping the vessel in touch with the world at large. Although they wore the same uniform, the young soldiers had arrived on the Laker's deck from decidedly different places.

Born in Creswell, North Carolina, on July 28, 1917, Davenport was the scion of a family that had lived in the same rural area along the southern shore of Albemarle Sound since at least 1684. One ancestor, Daniel Davenport, had been a well-to-do landowner who served in the state senate from 1800 to 1807, and members of the extended clan were scattered throughout what in 1799 had become Washington County. While Ernest Davenport's immediate family had a lineage to be proud of, to be sure, what they didn't have was wealth. His father, Alexander, was killed in a railway accident when Ernest was only two years old, and his mother, Pauline, struggled to make ends meet for herself and her five children. Things got marginally better when in 1921 she married farmer Ausher L. Clifton, whom Ernest—known to family and friends as "Dee"—grew up considering his father. The Cliftons had two daughters, and young Dee was closer to them than he was to his older siblings, who had been dispersed among area relatives.

Dee Davenport's early life was relatively normal, with his time divided between school and farmwork. Things changed dramatically, however, when he was in the eighth grade. His stepfather's farm was not doing well, so Dee dropped out of school to work on the land full-time. He labored away until he reached twenty-two, at which point he decided to join the Army to be able to send money home and, one suspects, to get away from rural North Carolina. He enlisted on June 23, 1939, and was tapped to become a medic. Whether this was his choice or the service's is unclear, but he graduated from training at Walter Reed Army Hospital in Washington, DC, with flying colors. He then moved on to his first post of assignment, which rather ironically turned out to be on the Hawaiian island of Oahu.

One can hardly imagine a place farther removed geographically or culturally from rural North Carolina than Hawaii, especially in early 1940. Though the freewheeling and frequently excessive lifestyles lived by soldiers and sailors on Oahu throughout the 1920s and 1930s had begun to moderate in the face of America's preparations for war, Honolulu's notorious Hotel Street was still the place for young men with a few dollars in their pockets to have an extremely good time. Assigned to the 11th Medical Regiment at Schofield Barracks, some seven miles northwest of Pearl Harbor, Davenport almost certainly enjoyed all the distractions Honolulu had to offer.

He didn't get to enjoy them for long, however, for in October 1941 he was transferred to Fort McDowell, California. Located on Angel Island in San Francisco Bay, the post was (among other things) a processing center for soldiers about to be discharged from the service or who were transferring to the National Guard. Davenport family records indicate that Dee was scheduled to leave active duty in November 1940—possibly by transfer to the North Carolina Guard—and his movement from Hawaii to California most probably was the result of his impending separation.[20] Higher powers must have prevailed, however, for rather than being separated from the Army, Davenport was transferred in mid-November to the SFPOE Port Surgeon's Office at Fort Mason.

The young soldier initially believed the transfer was only temporary. In a letter written to his stepsister Olean during the third week of November, Davenport indicated he'd be returning to North Carolina soon, and for good. He also added a tantalizing bit of emotional news: "By the way, your Bud [another of his family nicknames] might bring home a wife very soon, I would love for you to meet her."[21] Davenport didn't reveal the woman's identity, nor did he disclose how and where he'd met her.

The young medic soon had other, less happy news to impart. Within days of his assignment to the Port Surgeon's Office he learned that his release from active duty had been postponed by a period not to exceed 180 days "for the good of the service," and that he'd been assigned as the sole medical provider aboard a merchant ship being chartered to carry lumber to the island from which he'd returned only weeks earlier.

We can only assume that the news of his delayed discharge did not please Dee Davenport, who from all indications was looking forward to leaving the Army, getting married, and settling down to civilian life in North Carolina. Moreover, his assignment to a chartered lumber freighter must have also come as a fairly significant surprise, given that Davenport's only previous open-sea voyages were his trips as a passenger aboard an Army troopship carrying him to, and from, Honolulu. The thought of being solely responsible for the medical care of an entire ship's crew must have been more than a little frightening, especially as merchant mariners were widely perceived as rough-and-tumble types who tended to routinely encounter both sickness and accident in the course of their work. The news that *Cynthia Olson* had a reasonably well-equipped four-bed sick bay may not have been especially comforting, given that the filling of those beds by seriously ill or injured mariners would result in Davenport having to expend a tremendous amount of energy and would require him to display a level of medical proficiency he may well not have believed himself to possess.

Fortunately, soon after arriving at Fort Mason the young medic met someone who was in an excellent position to fill him in on the realities of a soldier's life among merchant sailors. That person was an irreverent and witty New Yorker named Sam Ziskind.

IF DEE DAVENPORT WAS THE quintessential farm boy, Sam Ziskind was the epitome of the worldly and street-savvy urbanite. Born in 1916 in Brooklyn, he was the second of three children of Russian immigrants Harry and Lena. Like his older sister, Susan, and younger brother, Moses, he grew up speaking both Yiddish and Hebrew in addition to English. While proud of his Jewish heritage he, like many young Jews of his generation, was not particularly observant.[22]

Sam also grew up with a love of jazz, pretty girls, and nice clothes, and throughout his teenage years worked both at his parents' grocery store and at a variety of odd jobs to earn the pocket money that allowed him to indulge his interests. He didn't spend all his time in idle pursuits, however, for he was an excellent student whose grades were good enough to ultimately win him admission to St. John's University, a Roman Catholic college in nearby Queens. He graduated with a liberal arts degree in the spring of 1938 and, having long been fascinated by the technical side of commercial broadcasting, set about finding a job in radio.

His quest was easier planned than achieved, however, for he found it tremendously difficult to break into the highly competitive world of professional radio. The few technical positions that came open went to experienced individuals who'd "paid their dues," and Sam Ziskind had neither the experience nor the connections. He was thus forced to take whatever jobs he could find, and by the summer of 1939 was working as the boy's swimming coach at a Jewish summer camp in Pennsylvania. While he didn't find the job all that stimulating the camp turned out to be one of the most important places in life, for there he met the woman who would become his wife.

Bernice Lerner—pert, vivacious, and at twenty-two a year younger than Sam—hailed from Jersey City, New Jersey.[23] She was as interested in music as he was and, like him, also excelled academically. She was at that point completing a degree at a New Jersey teacher's college and was in the running to get one of the few teaching jobs then available in the state. Bernice and Sam quickly realized that their meeting had changed both of their plans, for within weeks they had decided that marriage was in their future. Partly because of that decision, and because odd jobs would neither allow him to support a wife or break into professional radio, Sam Ziskind made a momentous decision. He would enlist in the Army for two years as a radio technician, a period that would provide steady (if not stellar) income while at the same time giving him the training and experience he'd need to snag his dream job as a technician for NBC in New York City.

We can only wonder whether Sam Ziskind fully understood the possible ramifications of his actions. The war then raging in Europe seemed likely to force the United States to take sides, and the sinking or capture of several still-neutral U.S. merchant vessels by German surface ships and submarines had already begun pushing American public opinion away from isolationism. Did Sam realize that his country could well be involved in a global war before his term of service ended?

The possible consequences apparently didn't dissuade the young New Yorker, because on September 25, 1940, he enlisted in the Army at Fort Monmouth, New Jersey. Within days he was undergoing basic training at the same post, and remained there for schooling as a radio operator and technician. That instruction included Morse code and covered the range of equipment then in Army use—small field units, larger vehicle-mounted gear, and the complex high-frequency sets used for long-range transmissions. Successful completion of the training won him the Federal Communications Commission's first-class radio-telephone operator's license he so coveted and which he believed would open many career doors for him, though he had to complete his two-year enlistment before setting out on his chosen civilian path.

Why the Army chose the San Francisco Port of Embarkation as Sam's first post-training duty station is unclear; it might even have been by the young soldier's own request. Whatever the reason, he arrived at Fort Mason in late March of 1941, and within weeks Bernice moved to California to be with him. They were married in San Francisco on June 7 and set up housekeeping in a tiny apartment in the city's Marina District. Sam didn't have much time to get used to married life, however. After a few weeks of familiarization training with the standard marine radios then in widespread use aboard merchant ships he was assigned to a pool of radio operators tasked for service aboard Army-owned and chartered vessels homeported in San Francisco. He left on his first voyage—aboard a troopship bound for Honolulu—barely a month after his wedding.

Over the next four months Sam Ziskind made at least two additional round-trips to Hawaii, each time returning with small gifts for Bernice and family members back East.[24] Though he lamented the time away from his bride, he apparently enjoyed the trips, and he often talked of showing Bernice his favorite parts of Oahu on some future joint trip. The newlyweds also made a point of exploring their adopted hometown and the surrounding areas when Sam was not at sea, and at one point took a train to Los Angeles for a long weekend.

While we don't know exactly when Sam Ziskind and Dee Davenport met for the first time, it seems the two young men from radically different backgrounds had already struck up a friendship by the time both were assigned to *Cynthia Olson*. As the two young soldiers stood on the ship's deck listening to Berthel Carlsen's predeparture remarks they may well have compared notes on their favorite Honolulu nightspots, anticipating a few days ashore before starting the return trip. What they could not have foreseen, of course, was that in the most literal sense the trip across the Pacific would be the voyage of their lifetimes.

EARLY ON THE MORNING OF November 22 Army harbor tugs nudged *Cynthia Olson* away from her Fort Mason pier. With her decks as yet unencumbered by timber and her holds empty she rode high in the water, though that condition would change dramatically once she'd taken on her cargo up north. Bert Carlsen and Bill Buchtele stood on opposite bridge wings, each closely watching the movements of the tugs and listening to the commands being given to the helmsman by the San Francisco Bay pilot whose job it was to get their vessel safely out of the busy port. Once beyond the Golden Gate *Cynthia Olson* would pause briefly to transfer the pilot, and then her master would turn her north for the forty-eight-hour coastwise run toward Puget Sound.

Carlsen's sailing orders required him to load timber at Olympia, Tacoma, and Seattle and to sail for Honolulu by December 1. He saw no reason why that schedule could not be maintained; his ship was old but dependable, and the merchant mariners who manned her were experienced and capable. While his ATS briefing had mentioned the possibility that German raiders or submarines might be operating along *Cynthia Olson*'s route across the Pacific, Carlsen thought it unlikely any Nazi warship would bother to expend valuable ordnance on a humble lumber schooner.

Unfortunately, he was only half right.

CHAPTER 5

A PREDATOR AT LARGE

EVEN AS *CYNTHIA OLSON* WAS departing San Francisco for the Pacific Northwest, a vastly more lethal vessel—the Imperial Japanese Navy (IJN) submarine *I-26*—was plowing its way eastward through heavy seas toward the Gulf of Alaska.

Laid down at Kure Naval Dockyard on June 7, 1939, *I-26* was a B1-type fleet boat.[1] She and the other nineteen vessels of her class had been designed for worldwide operations and *I-26* was among the largest and most advanced submarines in the world when commissioned on November 6, 1941. Just over 356 feet long and displacing more than 3,600 tons when submerged, the vessel was powered by two diesel engines that produced a total of 12,400 horsepower and gave her a surfaced speed of 23.5 knots. Electric motors propelled her at about 8 knots underwater, and she could dive to a maximum of 330 feet.

While her six torpedo tubes and 5.5-inch "Third Year Type" rapid-fire deck gun made her a formidable seagoing predator, *I-26* was also intended to be a globe-encircling reconnaissance platform. Her range of more than fourteen thousand nautical miles meant she could easily operate off the west coasts of both North and South America and throughout Australasia, and a watertight hangar just forward of her conning tower allowed her to embark a small Yokosuka E14Y1[2] floatplane capable of undertaking over-the-horizon reconnaissance flights. It was this ability to range far and wide and report on enemy movements that led Admiral Isoroku Yamamoto,[3] commander in chief of the IJN's Combined Fleet, to task *I-26* and the other vessels of her class with key roles in Operation Hawaii—the Japanese attack on Pearl Harbor.[4]

In all, twenty-seven submarines were to support the assault, with eleven of them carrying reconnaissance aircraft and five others transporting midget subs that were to infiltrate Pearl Harbor in advance of the planned aerial attack. *I-26*'s role in the strike against the United States Pacific Fleet was initially to be a supporting one.[5] Assigned to Submarine Squadron One of the IJN's 6th Fleet, she would reconnoiter American naval forces and installations in and around the Aleutian Islands. After reporting her findings to IJN headquarters, *I-26* was to sail for a point midway between San Francisco and Honolulu to locate, report on and, if possible, attack any American warships steaming for Hawaii in the wake of Japan's assault. Given the distance she was expected to cover, her hangar was to carry food and extra fuel rather than a seaplane.

It would be a challenging and dangerous voyage for the submarine and her ninety-four-man crew. Fortunately, *I-26* was to be captained by one of Japan's ablest submariners, Commander Minoru Yokota.

LIKE MANY WHO ULTIMATELY TAKE to the sea, Minoru Yokota was born far from saltwater.[6] In his case, it was in a small house in the Chugoku Mountains of Okayama Prefecture in western Honshu, about as distant from the ocean as one can be in Japan. Born in 1903 to Buddhist parents, he lost both his mother and grandfather at the age of eight. He later said that "seeing those two coffins within such a short time [was] a great shock to the child I was, and they led me to recite sutras in front of the family . . . altar every night." Being raised by a father and grandmother who themselves were very devout had a huge effect on the young Minoru. In words that would come to have a different meaning later in his life, he said he "was so devout that a Buddhist priest from a nearby temple asked my father if he would let me become a disciple."[7] As it happened, Yakota's interests changed with age. His adolescence was spent alternating between school and farmwork, and at the age of seventeen he applied for admission to the *Kaigun Heigakko*, the Imperial Japanese Naval Academy.

At first glance, Yokota's decision to seek acceptance to what at the time was arguably the most prestigious of Japan's two military academies seems naively optimistic.[8] He was, in essence, a fairly pious farm boy from the hinterland who had no previous experience with boats or the sea. Moreover, he did not, so far as we now know, have the family connections that were often required to secure admission to the school. What he did have, however, was a passionate desire to escape the confines of rural Okayama Prefecture and see the world. He also had the native intelligence and quick-wittedness that the academy looked for in officer candidates. These attributes, combined with impressively high scores on the entrance examinations, helped him overcome his background and secured his admission into the school's Class 51.

Officer candidate Yokota found himself entering an institution steeped in tradition, despite having existed for less than sixty years. Founded in Nagasaki in 1866—two years before the actual establishment of the IJN— the academy had moved to Yokohama in 1866 and to Tokyo in 1869, but since 1888 had been located on Etajima, an island in Hiroshima Bay.[9] Though created primarily to help educate Japanese naval officers in the strategies, tactics, and technologies then current in the "modern" Western navies the IJN so wished to emulate, the institution was also a bastion of Bushido. Even as they were schooled in the latest trends in naval architecture and engineering, cadets were imbued with the values, beliefs, and attitudes of the traditional Japanese warrior class. The academy thus produced technically competent and tactically innovative officers who, paradoxically, tended toward rigid nationalism and an almost mystical belief in Japan's political, spiritual, and military superiority.

How Minoru Yokota, a young man by all accounts still firmly attached to his Buddhist roots, reacted to the nationalistic and xenophobic subtexts of his naval education at Etajima we simply do not know. We do know, however, that during the three years he was at the school he proved himself to be an excellent student. He did very well on the rigorous final examinations—in navigation, engineering, seamanship, gunnery, and what was then termed "torpedo science"—and was one of only seventeen cadets out of an initial thirty-five to make it to graduation on July 14, 1923.

Some months before that event the twenty-year-old soon-to-be midshipman had applied for follow-on training as a naval aviator.[10] Achieving a posting to flight school was even more difficult, and prestigious, than gaining entrance to the naval academy. Yokota therefore set about preparing for the necessary examinations with his usual determination, but he ran into unaccustomed and completely unexpected difficulties:

> When I was at Etajima I was full of ambition and dearly wanted to [fly]. I took the test, but there were many more applicants who had better instincts than I and, unfortunately, I failed to pass. A person who had intended to fly in the sky was assigned to submarines, which he had not expected at all.[11]

Much to his initial chagrin, in August 1923 Yokota received orders assigning him to the IJN's submarine school. Located at the sprawling Kure Navy Yard, on the mainland of Hiroshima Prefecture just opposite Etajima Island, the facility was barely three years old. In addition to classroom work, Yokota and his fellow students in the Basic Submarine Officer Course undertook practical training on the three Type L3 boats assigned to the Kure-based 6th Submarine Division. Based on the L-Type vessels designed by Great Britain's Vickers Company for the Royal Navy, the Mitsubishi-built *RO-57*, *RO-58*, and *RO-59* were at that time among the IJN's newest and most advanced warships. Realizing that he had been handed a far better opportunity than he'd first thought and vowing not to let his disappointment affect his performance in the field chosen for him, Yokota threw himself into learning all he could about his new trade. He turned out to have a natural aptitude for undersea warfare and ultimately graduated near the top of his class.

Once in the operational fleet Yokota rose steadily through the ranks, in the process attending—and excelling in—the Advanced Submarine Officer and Submarine Command courses. He chose to remain unmarried to concentrate all his energies on his career, and his personal sacrifices were not in vain; he continued developing his technical knowledge and leadership skills in a series of increasingly responsible positions both ashore and afloat.

One of those positions, interestingly, took Yokota to both California and Hawaii. In early 1936 the young naval officer was covertly assigned to a Japanese commercial ship that would be voyaging to North America. This was a common practice in the IJN, and one whose purpose was twofold. First, the passages were intended to sharpen the young officers' navigation and engineering skills by allowing them to stand watches aboard vessels whose officers and crewmen usually had vastly more time at sea—and thus far more practical experience—than their naval counterparts. Second, and perhaps more important from a military point of view, the sub-rosa visits gave the IJN officers the opportunity to experience firsthand the cultures and values of nations that Japan might one day face in battle.[12] Yokota was assigned to a tanker, serving as both navigator and watch officer. The ship called first at Los Angeles and then Honolulu, and while the future commander of I-26 left no written account of his impressions of California, he later recalled his several weeks in Hawaii— especially in and around Hilo, on the Big Island—quite fondly.[13]

On December 1, 1936, as a lieutenant commander, Yokota assumed his first command, that of the mine-laying submarine I-22.[14] He apparently acquitted himself well in that initial billet, for in 1937 he was promoted to commander and went on to captain three other boats, RO-63, I-165, and I-154.[15] He proved himself to be a rising star and gained a widespread reputation for intelligence, skill, and dogged determination. Perhaps because of his early religious bent, he was also known as a fair and relatively humane officer in a service whose unyielding Bushido code fostered strict discipline and harsh punishment for even minor infractions.

Indeed, as author Dan Kurzman has pointed out,[16] Yokota's status as one of the IJN's premier submarine officers was especially unusual, given that he did not fit the typical mold:

> Yokota did not give the impression of someone who could successfully wield authority. . . . He was shorter than most of his men and of slighter build. And his placid, rather gentle countenance . . . made him more like a benign schoolmaster than a tough taskmaster.

In the summer of 1939 Yokota's renown within the IJN won him the plum assignment of equipping officer for I-26. In that capacity, he oversaw all aspects of the vessel's construction and fitting-out, getting to know every inch of the massive and state-of-the-art submarine literally from the keel up. As I-26 neared completion, Yokota was selected to be her first commander, and he was allowed to choose several of his key subordinates. These men, all of whom he had served with on other vessels or in shore assignments, included Lieutenant Sakuma Satô as first officer,

Warrant Officer Saburo Hayashi as chief gunner, Warrant Officer Takaji Komaba as chief torpedoman, and Warrant Officer Yukio Oka as diving officer.[17]

I-26 was officially commissioned on November 6. Early the next day, Yokota took her to sea, shaping a course for the sprawling naval base at Yokosuka on Tokyo Bay. The six-hundred-mile voyage gave the skipper and his crew a chance to put their new ship through her paces; Yokota ordered repeated crash-dives to ensure *I-26* would be ready to evade any searching enemy, and the gun and torpedo crews spent hours on loading and firing drills. He even conducted mock attacks on several passing merchant ships, submerging and stealthily approaching to within torpedo range of the unsuspecting vessels. By the time the submarine arrived at Yokosuka on November 12, Yokota was satisfied that his ship and her crew were ready for whatever awaited them.

It wasn't until November 15, however, that Yokota found out exactly what was in store for *I-26*. That morning he and the commanders of all the 6th Fleet's submarines were summoned to the light cruiser *Katori*, flagship of Vice Admiral Mitsumi Shimizu. The fleet commander and his chief of staff, Captain Hisashi Mito, outlined the general plan of the attack on Pearl Harbor and the role to be played in it by both the large subs and the midgets. The senior officers then surprised Yokota by transferring *I-26* from Rear Admiral Shigeaki Yamazaki's 2nd Submarine Squadron to Commander Yasuchika Kashihara's Submarine Reconnaissance Unit (SRU). Yokota and the captain of the other sub assigned to the SRU, Commander Yasuchika Kayabara of *I-10*, then joined Kashihara for a detailed briefing on their boats' roles in what Shimizu had called "the glorious effort."

Though of different classes, *I-10* and *I-26* were of comparable size and capability and would undertake similar missions.[18] While Yokota would take his boat north to the Aleutians, Kayabara would head south to reconnoiter Fiji and Samoa for the presence of British, Australian, or Dutch warships. Unlike *I-26*, *I-10* would be able to refuel from support vessels during the voyage and would therefore be able to carry, and deploy, her floatplane. Both submarines were to search their assigned areas for enemy activity and report before the scheduled December 8 (Tokyo time) attack on Pearl Harbor.

At the conclusion of the meeting with Kayabara and Kashihara, Yokota hurried back to *I-26*. The pier was already a beehive of activity, as trucks carrying food, fresh water, spare parts, and a hundred other necessary items rolled up in a seemingly endless procession. The loading continued over the following three days, and all went smoothly until the afternoon of November 18. At that point, *I-26* shifted to an ordnance-loading pier to take on torpedoes and ammunition for both her deck gun and twin 25 millimeter antiaircraft mount. As yard workers started the arduous process of loading the torpedoes, Takaji Komaba quickly identified the weapons as being of the obsolescent "Sixth Year" type.[19] In service since 1917, the torpedoes had a maximum range of 7,700 yards and a top speed of thirty-seven knots with a 451-pound warhead, meaning they were shorter-legged, far slower, and significantly less deadly than the Type 95 weapon *I-26* was intended to carry.[20] Perhaps more importantly, the older torpedo's compressed-air-based propulsion system left a telltale bubble trail that pointed directly back to the submerged submarine that had launched the weapon, certainly not a desirable attribute in battle.

Not only were the torpedoes of an inferior type, they'd been in a warehouse for more than a decade.[21] And worse, there were only ten of them. *I-26* was capable of carrying up to seventeen Type 95s, and the thought of setting out on what would ultimately be a combat patrol with too few torpedoes, inferior or not, seriously upset both Yokota and his chief torpedoman. Their protests to the naval yard's senior supply officer fell on sympathetic ears, but the man could not offer either newer weapons or even more of the obsolescent ones. Virtually the entire Imperial Japanese Navy was about to sortie on the service's first major naval action since the Russo-Japanese War of 1904–1905, and torpedoes were in demand for nearly every surface ship, aircraft, and submarine in the fleet. Given that *I-26*'s mission was primarily one of reconnaissance, planners had decided she'd just have to make do with whatever was left over after the first-line vessels—those most likely to engage major enemy surface ships—had received their full combat loads. Though Yokota was not happy with this turn of events, he had no alternative but to continue preparing *I-26* for her imminent departure.

Those preparations were complete by the early morning of November 19. After spending several hours aboard *Katori* for last-minute intelligence updates, Yokota returned to *I-26* just after noon, and by 3:00 p.m. he and his ship were ready for sea. With crewmembers in dress white uniforms solemnly lining her forward deck and the rising sun naval ensign snapping from her stern jackstaff, the submarine slipped her mooring lines and was nudged away from her pier by a harbor tug. Inside the semienclosed forward section of the conning tower Yokota ordered "slow ahead," and *I-26* moved cautiously out into Tokyo Bay. Once clear of the port, the submarine picked up speed and turned south into Uraga Channel and, after rounding Nojimazaki Point at the southern tip of the Boso Peninsula, turned her bow northeast into the vast Pacific Ocean.

The two-thousand-mile passage to the Aleutians was not a pleasant one for Yokota and his crew. The collision of the warm, northeastward-flowing Kuroshio Current with the cold, southeastward-flowing Oyashio Current occurs just off the east coast of central Japan, turning what is a volatile body of water at the best of times into a place of seemingly endless winter gales and riotous seas. Traveling on the surface to make best speed, within hours of leaving port *I-26* was being pounded by mountainous waves that threatened to wash away the two lookouts huddled atop either side of the periscope casing at the aft end of her conning tower. Nor did things improve as the vessel moved farther north; her course took her directly into the Aleutian Current, and conditions that had been merely extremely difficult quickly became potentially lethal. Indeed, disaster was narrowly averted when, during one lookout change, the main hatch leading into the hull—forward on the starboard side of the conning tower's semienclosed bridge—briefly jammed. Though the opening was barely two inches wide, in the time it took for frantically working crewmen to close it, hundreds of gallons of near-freezing water had poured in.

Much to the relief of everyone aboard *I-26*, Yokota's orders directed him to run submerged during daylight hours once his vessel was within six hundred miles of her first objective, the Aleutian island of Attu. That milestone was reached on November 25, and the crew's comfort level improved dramatically. Yet even as his sailors' morale went up, Yokota's already elevated anxiety level almost certainly increased even further. He was taking an armed warship on a covert mission into an area believed to be a stronghold of a hugely powerful soon-to-be enemy, and he had to assume that discovery by American naval forces would lead to immediate attack by both surface vessels and aircraft.

Yokota did not have to be quite so concerned about running into the U.S. Navy, however, for *I-26* was operating in an area that was literally at the end of the world as far as American military planners were concerned.

The Aleutian Islands extend westward into the Bering Sea in a curving arc from the Alaskan mainland, and Attu—the westernmost of a group known, paradoxically, as the Near Islands—is more than 1,700 sea miles from Anchorage. While the United States was aware of possible Japanese designs on the Aleutians, the sheer distances involved ensured that Coast Guard cutters and Navy ships were infrequent visitors to Attu. The closest island with any significant U.S. military presence at the time was Unalaska, about 850 sea miles due east. The United States had completed a new Army post, Navy base, and military airfield at Unalaska's Dutch Harbor in the fall of 1941, but those installations were still far enough from Attu that Yokota's chances of encountering American ships or aircraft were so slim as to be virtually nonexistent.

Of course, the Japanese weren't aware of the scarcity of U.S. military power in the far-western Aleutians; a large part of Yokota's mission was to ascertain the true extent of the American presence. As he took his submerged submarine in close to Attu for the first periscopic observations, on the afternoon of November 26, Yokota therefore ensured that his crew was ready to react to any threat that might suddenly present itself. None did, probably to the secret relief of most members of *I-26*'s crew, and Yokota was able to thoroughly examine the island by periscope. As directed, he paid particular attention to those sections of shoreline that might offer suitable landing areas for an amphibious assault. He did the same when surveying Kiska, a smaller island some 190 miles to the southeast, on November 27.[22] The following day Yokota also reconnoitered Adak, about 260 miles farther east, and again detected no American military presence.

Things changed considerably when *I-26* arrived off Dutch Harbor on November 29. Though Yokota could not know it, of course, the United States had accelerated the construction of naval and military installations on Unalaska, and by the time of *I-26*'s arrival offshore there were some 5,700 Army troops—and several hundred Navy personnel—on the island.[23] While Yokota did not see any major warships in the port, he did note many obviously military structures around the harbor and on the nearby hillsides. These were part of the Army's Fort Mears and included troop barracks, warehouses, and oil tanks. The Japanese sub captain also apparently discovered the presence of American aircraft, though unintentionally; he later recalled that as he was peering intently through the periscope in the direction of the port, the sudden appearance of a twin-engine aircraft caused him to order a crash dive. Though no attack ensued, the incident prompted even greater caution on Yokota's part. He took his ship back out to sea and spent several hours performing intricate evasive maneuvers in case he'd been detected. Only when he was sure he hadn't been did he take *I-26* back toward the island to continue his observations.[24]

Upon completion of his Dutch Harbor reconnaissance Yokota shaped a course to the southeast, running on the surface and aiming to cross the Gulf of Alaska with all dispatch to be in his assigned position when the attack on Pearl Harbor commenced. Even as *I-26* turned her stern to the Aleutians, the force assigned to destroy the U.S. Pacific Fleet was itself on the move.

———

ON THE SAME DAY THAT *I-26* began her reconnaissance of Attu, the ships assigned to the aerial attack on Pearl Harbor sortied from Hitokappu Bay on Iturup, the largest of the South Kurile Islands. Collectively known as *Kido Butai*,[25] the strike force was built around the aircraft carriers *Akagi*, *Hiryu*, *Kaga*, *Soryu*, *Shokaku*, and *Zuikaku*, and their collective total of more than four hundred embarked fighter and strike aircraft. Escorting the vital carriers were the battleships *Hiei* and *Kirishima*; the heavy cruisers *Tone* and *Chikuma*; the light cruiser *Abukuma*; ten destroyers; a screen of three boats from the 2nd Submarine Division; and supporting oilers and impressed merchantmen.[26] It was arguably the single most powerful naval fleet then in existence, and it was aimed like a giant dagger at the heart of American naval power in the Pacific.

Assembling the *Kido Butai* in one of Japan's most remote anchorages was part of a larger plan to elude detection by any American fleet units that might be operating to the west of the Hawaiian Islands. After leaving Hitokappu Bay, Vice Admiral Chuichi Nagumo, tactical commander of the assault force, took his ships almost directly east. He intended to essentially run parallel to the fortieth degree of latitude until north of Hawaii, then turn south and steam to within roughly two hundred miles of Oahu. The attack itself was to consist of several consecutive waves of Nakajima B5N torpedo planes, Aichi D3A dive-bombers, and Mitsubishi A6M fighters, with the latter tasked to both provide cover against American interceptors and undertake their own strafing attacks against ground targets.

Nine A6Ms were assigned to provide a combat air patrol over the fleet to deal with any American aircraft that might appear.

Alerting the *Kido Butai* to the presence of patrolling U.S. warships was one of the tasks assigned to the three Type B-1 fleet boats—*I-19*, *I-21*, and *I-23*—of Captain Kijiro Imaizumi's Submarine Advance Force.[27] Imaizumi had chosen to command his small flotilla from aboard *I-19*, skippered by Commander Shogo Narahara. Though a member of Etajima's forty-eighth graduating class and some five years older than Minoru Yokota, Narahara and *I-26*'s captain were good friends. Both had commanded the Type KD3a sub *I-54* in the late 1930s and had spent time in some of the same administrative positions.[28] That the two men were friends was something of a puzzlement to others who knew both. Though they followed similar career tracks Narahara and Yokota were radically different in personality; the former was a ferocious proponent of the rigid and fiercely militaristic Bushido code popular among many IJN officers, while the latter took a more Western (and perhaps Buddhist-inspired) view of military leadership and discipline.

Though he had served on several surface combatants and commanded three destroyers over the course of his career, Narahara was firmly convinced that submarines had the potential to become the IJN's most cost-effective weapons in the coming war against the United States. He understood the value of subs as long-range reconnaissance platforms but felt that the vessels' true value lay in their ability to stalk and kill enemy warships and merchant vessels without warning and without mercy, anywhere in the world. He was a staunch advocate of the type of unrestricted submarine warfare practiced by German U-boats in World War I and thus far in the current fight against Great Britain and her Commonwealth allies, and felt that the only way Japan could hope to prevail in any drawn-out conflict was by immediately instituting a wide-ranging and pitiless campaign against the naval and commercial fleets of America and any nation allied with her.

It was most probably this fervent attitude that led senior IJN planners to give Narahara a secondary mission to undertake following the Pearl Harbor attack. Once the *Kido Butai* had completed the destruction of the Pacific Fleet and was en route back to Japan, *I-19* was to move at best speed to a position roughly halfway between San Francisco and Honolulu. There, Narahara was to join his old friend Minoru Yokota in interdicting any U.S. naval or commercial vessels bound for Hawaii. It was undoubtedly a job the piratical Narahara anticipated with wolfish delight.

Before he could put his ideas of unrestricted submarine warfare to the test, however, *I-19*'s captain had to complete his current mission of helping protect the *Kido Butai* against American interference. And while the Japanese didn't yet realize it, there were two powerful U.S. forces—one already at sea and one preparing to sortie from Pearl Harbor—whose mere existence could potentially wreak havoc with the planned attack. Ironically, both were built around vessels the Japanese fervently hoped to destroy—aircraft carriers.

On November 28, the same day that Yokota and *I-26* scouted Adak, U.S. Pacific Fleet commander-in-chief Admiral Husband E. Kimmel had dispatched Vice Admiral William F. Halsey and his Task Force 8 to Wake Island. The flotilla was built around the carrier USS *Enterprise*—which was transporting twelve F4F-3 Wildcat fighters of Marine Corps fighter squadron VMF-211 to Wake—and included the heavy cruisers *Chester*, *Northampton*, and *Salt Lake City*, as well as nine destroyers. While TF-8's outbound course from Oahu would take it southwest and away from the *Kido Butai*, the second American battle group might conceivably detect the Japanese attack force. Rear Admiral John H. Newton's TF-12, then assembling in Pearl Harbor and due to sail on December 5, was bound for Midway, an island some 1,500 nautical miles northwest of Hawaii. Newton's task force was based on USS *Lexington*, which was ferrying eighteen Vought SB2U-3 Vindicators of Marine Scout Bombing Squadron 231. Escorting the carrier were the heavy cruisers *Astoria*, *Chicago*, and *Portland*, as well as five destroyers.

———

AS THE THREE BOATS OF Imaizumi's Submarine Advance Force plowed on, leading the *Kido Butai* toward Pearl Harbor, Minoru Yokota and the men of the surfaced *I-26* were again being battered by heavy seas as they raced to reach their assigned guard station. That point was some 1,600 miles southeast of Dutch Harbor, and their course took them across several of the major North Pacific shipping lanes. *I-26* encountered no other vessels, however, and except for sending a brief, coded report of his Aleutian observations, Yokota maintained strict radio silence.

The fact that *I-26* was not broadcasting did not mean she'd stopped listening, however. Yokota's radio operators maintained a constant watch, searching the airwaves for any sign that the sub had been detected. While there was no such indication, as the vessel drove on there was much else to hear. Interspersed among the routine voice and Morse traffic of merchant vessels plying the nearby sea-lanes were occasional snatches of music from commercial stations in British Columbia and the Northwestern United States. At one point, *I-26* even picked up part of a broadcast from KGMB, an AM station in Honolulu.

But there was a far more important message to be heard, one that Yokota and every vessel commander in the IJN had been anxiously awaiting. It was finally broadcast on Admiral Yamamoto's orders from the radio room of his flagship, the battleship *Nagato*, which was lying in the fleet anchorage at Hajirashima, some twenty miles south of Kure in Japan's Inland Sea. Sent at precisely 5:30 p.m. on December 2, signal number 676 consisted of one terse sentence: *"Niitakayama nobore* (Climb Mt. Niitaka) 1208."[29] Innocuous as the code phrase may have sounded, its meaning was clear; the attack on Pearl Harbor would commence as planned at 3:30 a.m. on December 8, Tokyo time, 8:00 a.m. on Sunday December 7, Honolulu time.

Because *I-26* was several time zones to the east of Kure and on the opposite side of the international date line, the submarine's radio operators logged *Nagato*'s message in at 12:30 on the early morning of December 2. After decoding the terse signal, the senior radio officer rushed to notify Yokota. The sub's commander came instantly awake when the sailor knocked on the door of the tiny private sleeping area to which Yokota's rank and position entitled him and then directed the young man to gather the sub's senior officers in the small wardroom. There was much to discuss, now that war with America was a certainty.

And hundreds of miles farther to the east, another captain was preparing to retire to his bunk after a first, very long day at sea. Bert Carlsen took one final look at the maps spread across the low wooden desk in the chartroom at the left rear of *Cynthia Olson*'s small wheelhouse, said a few words to Bill Buchtele and the man at the ship's wheel, and then took the narrow ladder leading down one level to his own stateroom. Despite his exhaustion he likely found it difficult to sleep, for he well knew that the seas ahead of him were in all probability filled with menace.

He had no idea how right he was.

CHAPTER 6

A TARGET FOUND

WHILE GETTING *CYNTHIA OLSON* OUT of San Francisco on schedule had taken frenzied effort, once the doughty steamer passed under the Golden Gate Bridge on November 22 her captain and crew had been able to settle into the less hectic routines of life underway.

The first hours at sea were undoubtedly a time for the vessel's newly assembled crew to get acquainted with both the ship and each other. While Bert Carlsen, Bill Buchtele, and most of *Cynthia Olson*'s senior officers had sailed on her or similar ships before, as far as we know none of her Army Transport Service civilian crewmen had ever shipped aboard a lumber schooner. Moreover, most of them had probably never served on so small a vessel; they were used to passenger liners, troopships, tankers, and freighters easily twice her size. Yet there would not have been a huge learning curve for the new men—aside from getting used to *Cynthia Olson*'s somewhat cramped quarters, of course—as the nature of their jobs and the machinery and systems with which they'd need to work were not significantly different from the ones they were used to aboard larger or more modern vessels.

While the entire crew would have been involved in getting the vessel to sea, once underway the ship's company adopted the standard watch system. Soon after leaving San Francisco, Carlsen, Buchtele, Chief Engineer Harry Lofving, Chief Steward Anthony Bushka, and Roland Dodd,

77

the ATS-provided quartermaster, would have met to divide the officers and men into the four-hours-on, eight-hours-off shifts necessary to ensure proper round-the-clock manning. As on most merchant vessels of the period, *Cynthia Olson* would have observed the first watch from 8:00 p.m. to midnight; the middle watch from midnight to 4:00 a.m.; the morning watch from 4:00–8:00 a.m.; the forenoon watch from 8:00 a.m. to noon; and the afternoon watch from noon to 4:00 p.m. Two additional periods—the first "dog watch" from 4:00–6:00 p.m. and the second from 6:00–8:00 p.m.—ensured that crewmen didn't stand the same watches every day at sea.

Buchtele, Second Officer Carl Johnstad, and Third Officer James Mills would each command a watch from the bridge with, respectively, First Assistant Engineer Thomas Muirhead, Second Assistant Engineer Charles Taylor, and Third Assistant Engineer Thomas Moore on duty in the engine room. Able-bodied and ordinary seamen of the Deck Department and cooks and messmen of Bushka's Mess Department filled out each watch. While Carlsen and Lofving would normally work eight-hour day shifts, the many duties of their respective positions and the need for each man to remain on call at all times ensured that their workdays at sea were often far longer than those of their juniors.

With the watch bills posted and his crewmen settling into their routines, Carlsen turned his attention to the short passage ahead. The route his ATS sailing instructions laid out for him was a familiar one. Indeed, he had made the trip from San Francisco to Tacoma so many times over the previous thirty-five years he probably could have navigated the route in his sleep, though as a master mariner who'd seen too many friends perish at sea the thought would doubtless never have occurred to him. After clearing the Golden Gate he turned *Cynthia Olson* to the northwest, steering a course between the Farallon Islands and Marin County's Point Reyes Peninsula. Having doubled the point, he turned slightly inshore to avoid the shallows around Cordell Bank, then took up a generally north-northwest heading until he had Cape Mendocino off his starboard side. From there his track was basically north, and Carlsen kept his ship about twenty miles offshore unless forced to alter course by natural obstacles or other vessels.

While the West Coast of the United States has more than its share of the former—including dense fogbanks, rocky headlands, and ship-eating shallows—it is the latter that presented the greatest threat to *Cynthia Olson*'s safe passage to Tacoma. By 1941 the coastal shipping lanes off

California, Oregon, and Washington were among the busiest sections of ocean in the world. Warships, passenger liners, oil tankers, fishing boats, and freighters of every description plied the waters within forty miles of the coast, arriving and departing from ports both large and small. In those days, before the widespread commercial use of radar, collision avoidance was largely a matter of eyesight and precise navigation, and we can be sure that Bert Carlsen spent many a tense hour on his ship's bridge as she plowed her way north.

Fortunately, the passage was uneventful and by the morning of November 24, *Cynthia Olson* was rounding Cape Flattery and turning east into the twelve-mile-wide and ninety-five-mile-long Strait of Juan de Fuca. The center of the waterway marks the international border between Canada and the United States, and in that second year of the British Commonwealth's war against Germany and Italy the Royal Canadian Navy's (RCN) sprawling base at Esquimalt—just east of Victoria on the southeast tip of Vancouver Island—was assumed to be a prime target of German submarines or armed merchant cruisers. As a result, every vessel entering or leaving the strait was treated to a close-up visual inspection by the crews of heavily armed Canadian patrol boats. Those craft that were in any way suspicious and were within Canadian waters were detained by the RCN, while questionable vessels on the American side of the international boundary were boarded by U.S. Navy personnel and directed into Port Angeles, Washington. While technically a possible violation of U.S. neutrality, this close cooperation had been established at the highest levels of the Canadian and U.S. governments.[1]

Cynthia Olson aroused no suspicion on either side of the border. By the early afternoon she was turning south toward Puget Sound, taking Port Townsend off her starboard side and Whidbey Island's Admiralty Head to port. As a licensed Sound pilot Carlsen didn't have to take on another to guide him through the busy waters of Admiralty Inlet and into the Sound proper, though his expertise couldn't thin the traffic that slowed his progress past Seattle and the busy docks of Elliott Bay. Things improved significantly once *Cynthia Olson* moved south into the East Passage, and by early evening she was turning into Tacoma's Commencement Bay. Tugs helped guide her alongside the lumber pier at the end of the port's Oriental Dock, and by just after 8:00 p.m. Carlsen was able to ring up "Finished With Engines."

The Army Transport Service had allocated five days for *Cynthia Olson*'s loading, with three days in Tacoma and two in Seattle. Stevedores began putting sawn lumber and logs aboard the ship on the morning of November 25, using the vessel's own cargo booms, and by November 28 had loaded 2,327,259 board feet. The cargo had an estimated total value of between $63,021 and $75,000 (sources vary on the exact amount), and the Port of Tacoma charged the Army $5,000 in stevedore fees.[2] Loading was completed by the evening of Friday, November 28, and the following morning Carlsen shifted his vessel north from Tacoma to Elliott Bay. There, at one of the piers that made up the newly established Seattle Sub-Port of Embarkation, *Cynthia Olson* began taking on fuel, food, and fresh water.[3]

While the ship was being provisioned, Carlsen, Buchtele, and Dodd spent most of Sunday, November 30, attending an extensive predeparture briefing at the Seattle ATS office. Though much of the discussion centered on such relatively mundane topics as weather forecasts, routes, radio frequencies, and the like, the mariners were also treated to a comprehensive briefing on the prevailing military situation in the Pacific. They were told of the possible presence of German surface raiders in the sea-lanes between Hawaii and the West Coast and of the chance that U-boats might be hunting Canadian and British vessels in the approaches to the Strait of Juan de Fuca.[4]

While no American vessel had yet been attacked by German warships in the Pacific, Hitler's *Kriegsmarine* had already shown that it had no compunctions about sinking U.S.-flagged ships despite America's official neutrality. Indeed, between September 1939 and November 1941 at least twenty-two American vessels had been seized, damaged, or sunk by German submarines or surface combatants in the Atlantic and Indian Oceans, resulting in the deaths of some 210 U.S. merchant mariners.[5] The fact that the sides of *Cynthia Olson*'s hull were not painted with the high-visibility U.S. flag neutrality markings common to vessels plying the dangerous Atlantic meant that she might well be mistaken for a British or Canadian ship.

That the threat of attack by German forces dominated the discussion during the predeparture briefing is understandable, yet we can safely assume that the possibility of hostile action by the Japanese was also discussed. While the U.S. military and naval intelligence organizations were as yet unaware of the *Kido Butai*'s existence and mission,[6] the rapid decline of diplomatic relations between Washington and Tokyo had already prompted both the Army and Navy to issue war warnings to all Pacific commands.[7] Sent in late November, the warnings did not specify a threat to Pearl Harbor, but they did require local commanders to brief the captains of outbound naval and military-chartered vessels about the possibility of attack by Japanese forces.

Having captained merchant ships across the Atlantic during World War I as a member of the U.S. Naval Reserve Force, Bert Carlsen was no stranger to the threat of enemy attack and would have taken the possibility seriously. Indeed, even before leaving San Francisco he and Bill Buchtele had talked about the possibility of imminent hostilities, and in their last telephone calls with their wives both men apparently spoke about the probable outbreak of war with Japan.[8] Carlsen thus would have had no difficulty in adhering to the sailing orders handed to him at the end of the briefing. Those orders did not require him to take such overt wartime measures as sailing a zigzag course, but they did specify that he maintain extreme vigilance on the passage to Honolulu and that he observe radio silence except in an emergency.

So it was that as *Cynthia Olson* moved away from her Seattle berth on December 1 and started for the open sea, her master knew that for the first time in almost a quarter-century he was commanding a vessel that was in all likelihood standing into danger of a man-made kind. What Bert Carlsen couldn't have known, however, was that at that same moment, thousands of miles to the west, the captains of three other vessels were also thinking about war. For one of the men, it was already a reality; for the second, it was something to be outrun; and for the third, it was a foregone conclusion. Though Carlsen would never know any of the three men, all would soon play roles in the final act of the master mariner's life story.

————

THE MAN FOR WHOM WAR was already a reality was Commander Frederick Gordon Hart of the Royal Canadian Navy. And as *Cynthia Olson* was chugging her way up Puget Sound toward Cape Flattery, Hart's vessel—His Majesty's Canadian Ship *Prince Robert*—was pounding its way eastward toward the same goal from the opposite side of the planet.

While the forty-one-year-old Hart was a professional naval officer who'd enjoyed a fairly conventional career since being commissioned in the early 1920s, his ship had led a more unusual life. Completed in 1930 by Cammell & Laird Shipbuilders in Birkenhead, England, *Prince Robert* was one of three identical coastal passenger liners ordered by the Canadian National Railways (CNR) for its Canadian National Steamships subsidiary. She and her sisters *Prince Henry* and *Prince David* were intended to help CNR break the Canadian Pacific Railways' longstanding dominance on the lucrative Vancouver-Victoria-Seattle passenger route. At 366 feet and 6,983 gross tons, the twin-screw, triple-funnel liners were ideally suited to the service for which they'd been designed, and each was capable of carrying some 375 passengers in both comfort and style. Unfortunately, the Great Depression killed off CNR's tri-city service, and *Prince Robert* spent the remainder of the 1930s alternating between lay-up, cruising in the Caribbean, and on tourist runs from British Columbia to Alaska.

When World War II broke out in September 1939 *Prince Robert* and her two sisters were requisitioned for military service as armed merchant cruisers (AMC).[9] The decision to use them as AMCs rather than as troopships was made by the British Admiralty and was fairly controversial in Canadian naval circles because the RCN had virtually no trooping capability. *Prince Henry* and *Prince David* were tapped for Atlantic service, while *Prince Robert* was to be assigned to the Pacific.[10] In early February 1940 she was put into Vancouver's Burrard Drydock for modifications that can only be described as extensive: her entire two top decks were removed and replaced with the superstructure of a light cruiser; her hull and decks were reinforced; and she was fitted with four 6-inch and two 3-inch guns.[11]

Prince Robert was commissioned into the RCN with the pennant number F56 on July 31, 1940. Soon thereafter, Commander Charles Taschereau Beard took her out of Esquimalt to join a small flotilla of British vessels charged with preventing the escape of German ships that had taken refuge in Central and South American ports.[12] On September 25, 1940, *Prince Robert* captured the 9,472–gross ton German supply vessel *Weser* in international waters off the Mexican port city of Manzanillo. Beard put a prize crew aboard the seized merchantman—which was the main supply ship for the German raider *Orion*—and she was taken to Esquimalt.[13]

Ill health forced Beard into retirement just days after the *Weser* affair, and command of *Prince Robert* passed to Hart on November 8, 1940. For the next few months the AMC patrolled the Pacific coasts of Central and South America and at one point raced to Easter Island in an unsuccessful search for a reported German raider. During the spring of 1941 *Prince Robert* was dispatched to Auckland to escort back to Canada merchant vessels carrying Royal New Zealand Air Force personnel destined for flight instruction under the British Commonwealth Air Training Plan. All her dashing about took a mechanical toll on the ship, and in the summer of 1941 she returned to British Columbia for an extensive and much-needed refit. At the conclusion of that Esquimalt yard period *Prince Robert* received the orders that would ultimately allow her to play a vital role in the *Cynthia Olson* story.

In mid-October Hart was told that his ship had been tapped for an important mission. The task was to escort the 13,500-ton New Zealand passenger liner-turned-troopship *Awatea*, which was to transport 1,973 Canadian infantrymen from Esquimalt to Hong Kong.[14] The troops, one battalion each from the Winnipeg Grenadiers and the Royal Rifles of Canada, were collectively known as "C" Force and were intended to bolster the British colony's defenses in anticipation of a Japanese attack should Tokyo choose to launch a general Pacific war.[15] While London was happy to accept the offer of troops made by the Canadian government of Prime Minister William Mackenzie King, the mandatory sailing date established by the British allowed little time to assemble the troops and their materiel. Preparations were thus rushed and incomplete, and when *Awatea* and *Prince Robert* sailed on October 27, most of "C" Force's 212 vehicles and much of its equipment remained on Esquimalt's piers. Scheduled to sail for Hong Kong on the chartered freighters *Don Jose* and *Fernplant*, the vehicles and materiel would never arrive in the British colony.

Both fast ships, *Awatea* and *Prince Robert* fairly raced across the Pacific.[16] They paused briefly in both Honolulu and Manila for fuel and fresh water, and at the latter port, they were joined by the aging British light cruiser HMS *Danae*. The three vessels arrived in Hong Kong on November 16, and the offloading of the ill-fated "C" Force commenced almost immediately.[17] Debarkation was completed by the afternoon of November 19, and at 8:00 that night *Prince Robert* sailed alone from Hong Kong. After another brief stop in Manila she shaped a course for Honolulu, initially traveling south through the Sibuyan Sea and then turning east to pass through the San Bernardino Strait separating the islands of Luzon and Samar. The ship ran into strong winds and heavy seas almost as soon as she passed through the strait into the open Pacific, and Hart ordered her speed increased to seventeen knots to reach Honolulu by the scheduled date of December 3.

Though heavy weather continued to dog the ship the passage to Hawaii was uneventful, with the only excitement being provided by the sudden appearance on November 30 of a Midway Island–based U.S. Navy patrol aircraft. Lookouts sighted the islands of Niihau and Kauai to port on the morning of December 3, and by 12:45 p.m. *Prince Robert* was securely tied to Pier 8 in Honolulu's commercial harbor. While the reason for the ship's call in Hawaii was to take on fuel and fresh water her crewmen had other, more pleasurable activities in mind. Hart's sailing orders didn't allow much time for recreation, but good captain that he was he granted the ship's company shore leave from 1:30 p.m. to midnight. Determined to make the most of the few hours available to them, the Canadian sailors made a mad rush ashore. Though some undoubtedly sought out culturally uplifting entertainment, we can be certain that others (if not most) headed directly for the morally dubious delights of Honolulu's Hotel Street.

Prince Robert's crewmen must have been an unusually disciplined lot, however, for all except one were back aboard ship by the midnight deadline, though more than a few had to be helped up the gangplank by shipmates. The missing man had not turned up by the time the ship sailed just after noon on December 4, and Hart noted that the man "is considered to have deserted; His Britannic Majesty's Consul [in Honolulu] was accordingly informed." *Prince Robert*'s captain had more on his mind than missing crewmembers, however, for his sailing orders required him to be in Esquimalt no later than midnight on December 9. The ship had quite a distance to travel, and Hart was mindful that bad weather was not the only thing that could delay him. There was still the very real possibility of encountering German surface raiders or submarines, and he ordered extra lookouts to be added to every watch.

Though Hart didn't know it at the time, a submarine and a surface ship would indeed delay *Prince Robert*, but not in the way her captain expected.

———

THE MAN FOR WHOM WAR was something to be outrun was taking his ship toward Honolulu even as *Prince Robert* was racing away from Oahu.

That man was Commodore Charles A. Berndtson of the Matson Navigation Company, and the ship whose bridge he paced on the afternoon of
December 2 was the firm's 18,163-GRT passenger liner *Lurline*.

The stately white ship, a fixture on the California-to-Hawaii route since
soon after her 1933 maiden voyage, had left Los Angeles on November 29
carrying far fewer than her usual 715 passengers.[18] Widespread press speculation over the previous month about the possibility of war in the Pacific
had severely curtailed the Hawaii tourist trade, and about the only people
taking ship for Honolulu were military and government personnel or civilian employees of firms working on defense-related projects in the islands.
Berndtson, a Swedish-born master mariner and U.S. Naval Reserve officer,
was well aware of the looming threat of war. Before sailing, he and his senior
staff had been extensively briefed about the deteriorating political situation,
and strange radio transmissions picked up on the outbound voyage served
only to reinforce the atmosphere of impending danger that prevailed on
Lurline's bridge. While their exact nature, meaning, and source remain controversial even seven decades later, the signals undoubtedly influenced Berndtson's desire to remain in Honolulu for as short a time as possible.

The transmissions were apparently first picked up either late on November 30 or early on December 1, and the man who first heard them was
Lurline's first assistant radio officer, Leslie E. Grogan. In a report he prepared
and signed upon the liner's December 10 return to San Francisco—a report
he titled "Record for Posterity"—he stated that during one of his four-hour
radio watches he heard faint Japanese radio transmissions that grew increasingly more audible as time passed.[19] As he recorded in his journal,

> The Japanese are blasting away on the lower Marine Radio Frequency—
> it is all in the Japanese code, and continues for several hours. Some of
> the signals are loud and others weak. . . . It appears to me that the Jap-
> anese are not using any deception of signal detection and boldly blast
> away, using the call letters JCS and JOS. . . . I have crossed the Pacific
> for 30 years, and I have never heard JCS Yokohama . . . before 9 p.m.
> our time. . . . If anyone should ask me, I would say it's the Japanese
> Mobilization Battle Order.[20]

Grogan reported the transmissions to his supervisor, forty-year-
old Chief Radio Officer Rudolph Asplund, who, according to Grogan,

informed Berndtson. Asplund and Grogan continued to listen for the Japanese signals, which they reported hearing again the following night:

> Again Rudy and I picked up—without any trouble—all the Japanese-coded wireless signals. It went on for two hours like before, and we are now making a concise record to turn into Naval Intelligence when we arrive in Honolulu.[21]

According to Grogan, the resulting report was indeed turned over to the Navy when *Lurline* docked on December 3, though its reception by Lieutenant George W. Pease, the 14th Naval District's assistant director of naval intelligence, was apparently somewhat low-key:

> We handed . . . Pease all the data we had compiled with regard to this Jap [sic] intercepted stuff. He was a good listener, and showed little outward reflection as to what we felt was a mighty serious situation, but nevertheless, Rudy and I felt relieved in our avowed duty to pass the vital information on to the Navy for whatever value they could derive from it.[22]

While Grogan's report of the mysterious radio messages later helped stoke revisionist theories about the Roosevelt administration's purported foreknowledge of the Japanese attack on Pearl Harbor and sparked decades of controversy among World War II historians, both professional and amateur, detailed analysis of the issue by such experts as former Navy cryptologist Philip H. Jacobsen have dismissed the transmissions and Grogan's interpretation of them.[23] Jacobsen points out, among other salient points, that Grogan knew neither Japanese nor cryptology and that much of the information contained in the report Grogan penned following *Lurline*'s December 10 return to California changed repeatedly in accounts written over the following decades.[24] Jacobsen ultimately concluded that

> Grogan did not hear signals from the Pearl Harbor Strike Force, but, at best, he heard the greatly increased volume of Japanese commercial shipping messages that were then traversing the airwaves of the Pacific, apparently enhanced by some unusually good short-term radio propagation conditions. This increased radio traffic was the result of

the concentration of the huge worldwide Japanese maritime merchant shipping fleet into the relatively small space in and around Japan due to their recent recall from throughout the world, as well as their urgent preparations for new military assignments just prior to the initiation of hostilities.[25]

The actual nature of the transmissions, and what they may or may not have indicated regarding the Pearl Harbor attack, are beyond the scope of this volume. So, too, is the issue of whether Grogan's propensity to muddle facts and give differing accounts of the transmissions in his later years was a case of failing memory or a self-serving desire to present a hugely inflated account of his own small participation in one of the most important military actions in American history.

It is extremely important, however, that we determine Grogan's expertise as a maritime radio officer, given the role he was destined to play in the *Cynthia Olson* story. And on that count the California-born veteran of World War I seems to stand on much firmer ground. Though considered by some coworkers to be almost a caricature of the expansive, not to say garrulous, Irish American, no one had apparently ever questioned the depth or breadth of his technical skills. While his expertise certainly did not extend to even a rudimentary knowledge of either the Japanese language or the codes used by Japan's merchant fleet or navy, the forty-seven-year-old Grogan was considered by the Matson Line to be one of its most experienced and capable radio officers.[26] He might have been a self-aggrandizing, 260-pound blowhard, but he was also regarded by his employers and immediate supervisors as both dependable and technically proficient.

Berndtson's reaction to Grogan's initial report of the mysterious Japanese radio transmissions was apparently not recorded either in the ship's log or in the later writings of anyone present at the time, but we can assume that the commodore of the Matson Line took seriously any information that might indicate a threat to his ship and those who sailed in her. His mission was to get *Lurline* safely to Hawaii, offload her passengers and cargo, and embark on the passage to San Francisco no later than December 5. It would be a fast turnaround; in the less than twenty-four hours she was scheduled to be in Honolulu *Lurline* would need to not only clear her inbound passengers and several tons of cargo, she'd also have to take on fuel, food, fresh water, and the mixed load of civilian and military travelers bound for California.

The latter task—boarding passengers in Honolulu for the return trip—turned out to be somewhat more challenging than usual. While all the ticketed San Francisco–bound travelers—including future baseball great Jackie Robinson[27] and Army second lieutenant Shigeru "Stu" Tsubota[28]—were aboard by *Lurline*'s scheduled noon sailing time, there was a hiccup in the normally smooth departure routine. As Leslie Grogan recalled,

> *Lurline* was all set for its . . . voyage home—the usual departure dock entertainment of music played by the Royal Hawaiian [Hotel] Band, and its accompanying singers . . . went through its usual Aloha [pier] farewell program. . . . Then, at exactly noon . . . instead of letting go its lines and backing away from the . . . pier [*Lurline*] . . . was being held at the dock for some unknown reason.[29]

The reason for the delay was revealed after several hours when a line of Navy trucks pulled onto the pier and began disgorging women and children. The new arrivals, all of whom were military dependents, were being evacuated to the mainland and their arrival ensured that the liner would be packed to the gunnels on the voyage to San Francisco. Indeed, adding the evacuees to the already boarded 502 first-class and 213 cabin-class passengers meant the ship would be short some seventy beds. The solution to the problem of where those additional passengers would sleep was simple if somewhat out of keeping with Matson's reputation for elegant service: Chief Officer Edward Collins ordered that the requisite number of wooden folding cots be brought up from the ship's holds and set out in the cabin-class lounge. Males and females were assigned cots on opposite sides of the room, and a cloth partition would be erected each night after dinner.[30]

With the evacuees finally aboard, *Lurline* let go her lines and, assisted by tugs, swung her bow toward the harbor entrance. From that point on the departure assumed its normal, festive course. Off Waikiki, as the ship passed Diamond Head, outrigger canoes filled with waving islanders raced alongside until the quickly accelerating liner left them behind. When the vessel pulled abreast of the Royal Hawaiian Hotel Berndtson ordered the traditional three whistle blasts, and civilian aircraft buzzed overhead, waggling their wings in a final aloha.[31]

As *Lurline* turned northeast to round Makapuu Point and pass through the Kaiwi Channel separating Oahu and Molokai, her captain, crew, and passengers might well have assumed the moderate seas and unusually fine December weather heralded a calm and relaxing passage. If so, they would soon learn how wrong they were.

———

As *LURLINE* STRUCK OUT ACROSS the open Pacific on her passage to San Francisco, the man for whom war was a foregone conclusion was some 1,400 miles to the northeast. On December 5, *I-26* was pounding her way through seas far more boisterous than those through which the Matson liner was traveling, and the "Climb Mt. Niitaka" message broadcast three days earlier ensured that Minoru Yokota's voyage was neither calm nor relaxing.

To the contrary, the sub captain would almost certainly have been walking the fine line between appropriate vigilance and outright anxiety. Though eager to play a role—albeit a relatively minor one—in what could well be the most significant combat action of his career, Yokota was no doubt acutely aware that his conduct over the coming hours could either contribute to victory or precipitate disaster. Because his ship was the farthest east of any Japanese vessel in the Pearl Harbor operation, discovery by American or Canadian naval forces could well result in *I-26*'s destruction and, more importantly, provide the U.S. Pacific Fleet with forewarning of the *Kido Butai*'s impending attack. Yokota thus had to race for his assigned barrier-patrol station with all possible speed, while at the same time doing all in his power to ensure that his vessel remained undiscovered.

Yokota was not the only member of *I-26*'s crew plagued by anxiety. Chief Torpedoman Takaji Komaba spent much of the passage south from the Aleutians worrying about whether the obsolescent "Sixth Year"–type torpedoes loaded in Yokosuka would be capable of hitting, let alone sinking, American warships or heavily laden cargo vessels. He shared his concerns with Chief Gunner Saburo Hayashi, who assured him that if the torpedoes couldn't dispatch an enemy vessel, the 5.5-inch deck gun's eighty-three-pound high-explosive shells would.[32] Whether *I-26*'s torpedoes would work as advertised remained an academic question for most of the submarine's passage south from Alaskan waters, however. Yokota's orders forbade him to engage any targets until after the assault on Pearl Harbor had begun and, more to the point, he'd sighted neither predators nor potential prey.

The later situation changed abruptly, however, late on the afternoon of December 6.[33] As Komaba later remembered,

> I was stationed on the bridge as the port lookout, when our watch officer, Lt. Satô, suddenly asked if anything was visible on that side. I could not see a thing. Satô, who had been standing on the periscope shears platform, descended and gave me a pair of 15 cm binoculars, suggesting that I should go up and replace him for a second. I climbed to that platform and . . . barely had I taken a look through the 10-power binoculars when I sighted a white light shining on our port beam. . . . The C.O. was informed of my sighting immediately.[34]

The unidentified vessel was at a range of about six miles, bearing almost due south and crossing the submarine's track from port to starboard. Yokota came up from the control room and, standing slightly below the lookout's perch, was soon able to make out the ship's white mast-head lights and red and green running lights with his naked eye.

Yokota noted his ship's position at that moment of first sighting as 145° west by 34° north. Then, not wanting the crew of the potential target to discover *I-26*'s presence, he cleared the bridge and took the sub down to periscope depth. Using the device's magnifying eyepiece to closely examine the mystery ship, he would have called out her identifying characteristics as they became discernable.

Though the vessel-identification handbooks carried aboard *I-26* would quickly have marked the anonymous craft as an American-built Laker, that determination would not have answered what must have been Yokota's most pressing question: whose flag did the mystery ship fly? In the years since World War I Lakers had joined virtually every major national merchant fleet on the planet, including Japan's,[35] and Yokota could not risk attacking a ship belonging to his own country, either of the Axis nations with which Japan shared common anti-Allied cause or a nonbelligerent nation such as Sweden. Because *Cynthia Olson*'s hull did not bear the large painted American-flag neutrality markings often seen on U.S.

vessels plying the North Atlantic, Yokota's only recourse was to get as close as possible and try to determine the ship's name and nationality.[36]

While we do not know how long it took the Japanese skipper to get *I-26* near enough to identify the mystery Laker as the American *Cynthia Olson*, we know beyond a shadow of a doubt that he did. We are also certain that, having identified the vessel and not wanting to give his presence away prematurely, the Japanese captain moved his ship into position several miles astern of the heavily loaded freighter and settled in to shadow her throughout the night.[37] As Yukio Oka later recalled, Yokota was so confident of the vessel's course, destination, and ignorance of the submarine's presence that he let *Cynthia Olson* get far enough ahead that "the lights of the freighter gradually faded until they were no longer visible."[38]

And, finally, we know that aboard that slowly disappearing vessel, Berthel Carlson and his crew had no inkling that fate was following in their wake.

CHAPTER 7

DESTRUCTION FROM
THE DEPTHS

That *Cynthia Olson* was the first American vessel to cross *I-26*'s path in the twenty-four hours before the *Kido Butai*'s scheduled attack on the U.S. Pacific Fleet at Pearl Harbor was, sadly, nothing more than simple bad luck for the men aboard the lumber freighter. For while on that early December morning the Pacific Ocean between the West Coast of North America and Honolulu might have seemed empty and endless—the Hawaiian Islands are, after all, among the most remote on the planet—the sea-lanes were far from deserted.[1]

Indeed, by dawn on December 7 no fewer than nineteen other U.S.-flagged military and commercial vessels were underway between Hawaii and West Coast ports—five eastbound and fourteen westbound.[2] In addition to *Lurline*, the former included three Matson cargo ships—*Manulani* and *Lahaina*, underway for San Francisco, and *Makiki*, headed for Seattle—and the San Diego–bound oceangoing Navy tug USS *Seminole*. Among the much heavier westbound traffic were the submarines USS *Pollack* and USS *Pompano*, en route to Pearl Harbor from California's Mare Island Naval Yard; the Navy-chartered cargo vessel SS *Jupiter*; SS *Montgomery City*, an Isthmian Lines cargo ship under Army charter; six Matson-owned freighters; and, perhaps the most valuable potential targets, four heavily laden Army troopships.[3]

The latter vessels—the USATs *Etolin*, *Tasker H. Bliss*, *President Johnson*, and *President Garfield*—were part of Operation Plum, a large War Department–directed effort to bolster Lieutenant General Douglas MacArthur's Philippines-based U.S. Army Forces Far East.[4] The intent was to ship some twenty thousand Army and Army Air Forces personnel and their equipment to Manila aboard eleven ships, which were scheduled to sail in several groups between November 21 and December 9. The first group of vessels had departed San Francisco in convoy on November 24, escorted by the cruiser USS *Pensacola*, and after calling at Pearl Harbor had pushed on for the Philippines.[5] *Etolin* (1,600 troops), *Bliss* (1,600), and *President Johnson* (2,500) had sailed out the Golden Gate on December 5 and were followed the next day by *President Garfield* (2,500). The final group of troopers, including the Army's *Will H. Point* and *Leonard Wood*, were scheduled to sortie on December 8 and 9.

With all of the vessels plying the Pacific between Hawaii and the West Coast, it is ironic that Yokota and *I-26* should have come upon arguably the least important of them. The humble *Cynthia Olson*—old, slow, and of virtually no military value in the greater scheme of things—was destined to die simply because she was in the wrong place at the very worst of times.

———

As THERE IS NO AUTHENTICATED record of *Cynthia Olson* breaking the radio silence Bert Carlsen had been ordered to observe, we can assume that the first six days of the Laker's passage to Hawaii were uneventful. That doesn't mean her crew was idle, of course, for the Laker was the product of a period in maritime history when ships were still highly labor-intensive, a time before automation in the engine room or the wheelhouse. Simply put, there was good reason why a vessel barely 250 feet long and weighing less than five thousand tons fully loaded had a crew more than twice as large as those found on many of today's massive oil tankers and container ships.

Perhaps the busiest and least comfortable members of *Cynthia Olson*'s crew during the voyage to Honolulu were those who labored away in the stifling engine room. A warren of pipes, valves, ladders, and landings where daytime temperatures routinely exceeded 120 degrees Fahrenheit, it was enveloped by a constant, head-splitting cacophony of sound and reeked of steam and hot oil. Located amidships, just aft of and several decks below the ship's single funnel, the cavernous space was dominated by the Laker's mechanical heart—the triple-expansion steam engine that kept her twelve-foot-diameter screw turning day and night. Built in Manitowoc Shipbuilding's own workshops, the immense power plant was some twenty feet tall, twenty-one feet long, and weighed more than one hundred thousand pounds. Its three cylinders had diameters of, respectively, twenty-one, thirty-five, and fifty-nine inches.

While Chief Engineer Harry Lofving kept a close eye on the engine and all of *Cynthia Olson*'s other machinery, it was up to the men on regular watches to provide the constant attention the engine demanded. For the assistant engineer in charge of each watch—whether Tom Muirhead, Charlie Taylor, or Tom Moore—there were myriad dials and gauges to monitor, logbook entries to make, and subsidiary duties (such as maintaining the ship's electrical equipment or ensuring the lifeboats and their davits were ready for immediate use) to perform. The fireman on watch— Sotero Cabigas, Isidro Montegrejo, or Benito Rodriguez—operated the oil-burning system that generated the steam for the ship's boilers. The unlicensed wiper, Maximo Terro, undertook whatever unskilled manual labor was required of him on any of the watches.

But it was arguably the three oilers—Anastacio Atad, Maximo Basbas, and Victoriano Pedro—who had the most dangerous job in *Cynthia Olson*'s engine room. Because the engine was lubricated entirely by gravity-feed, several times each hour the duty oiler made the rounds of the entire powerplant, hand-checking the surface temperature of such key components as bearings and adding oil wherever needed. While the engine's open design provided relatively direct access to its crankshaft, piston rods, and other important parts, it also meant that the oiler had to synchronize his temperature checks and use of the oil can to the rapid forty-two-inch strokes of the pistons. The slightest miscalculation around such potentially lethal machinery would be both catastrophic and immediate, with traumatic amputation of the oiler's hand or entire arm an ever-present danger.

While the members of *Cynthia Olson*'s Deck Department did not have to endure the noise and heat of the engine room, their tasks and the environment in which they performed them were arduous in their own ways. The work done on each watch and in any weather by the three ordinary seamen at the bottom of the department's pecking order—Sopromio Bajo, Conrado Jalocon, and Leo Kaay—could include anything from chipping paint and cleaning bilges to standing lookout on one of the bridge wings. The three were also at the beck and call of the ship's five able seamen— Jose Buta, Claro Maagma, August Santiago, Pedro Soliman, and Raymond Villa—who were one step up in the hierarchy. In addition to the jobs normally undertaken by able seamen on all merchant vessels—such things as operating deck machinery, standing wheel watches on the bridge, and repairing the ship's standing and running rigging—the able seamen aboard *Cynthia Olson* were also responsible for frequent inspections of the lumber tie-downs on the fore and aft well decks. This was an especially important task, for should the chains and heavy wire lines securing the Laker's deck cargo slacken, the resultant shifting of the stacks of logs and sawn lumber could cause the ship to list or even capsize.

Supervising the work of the ordinaries and able seamen was the job of bosun Joaquin Daguison, the senior unlicensed mariner on the ship and the man responsible for the maintenance and protection of all deck cargo and equipment. He was also the direct liaison between all of *Cynthia Olson*'s civilian ATS crewmen and Roland Dodd, who occupied the dual role of quartermaster and senior ATS representative aboard the freighter. As the former, Dodd supervised the men standing wheel watches, ensured that the ship's position was checked frequently, and oversaw the day-to-day operations in the wheelhouse. As the latter, he ensured that officers and crewmen alike understood and upheld the various requirements of *Cynthia Olson*'s ATS charter agreement.

Though technically subordinate to Dodd in matters pertaining to ATS regulations and procedures, Chief Steward Tony Bushka was essentially free to run the Mess Department as he saw fit. Providing full daily meals for thirty-five men working staggered watches—hardworking mariners for whom food provided both nourishment and distraction—was a task likely made more challenging by the crew's multiethnic composition. Given that twenty-two of the men aboard *Cynthia Olson* were Filipinos, it's probable that most of the meals served in the crew's mess on the voyage to Hawaii included steamed rice and such staples of Philippine cuisine as salted fish and pungent sauces. While the non-Filipino crewmembers may well have enjoyed such fare—many of the senior officers had voyaged throughout the Pacific and would have been familiar with foods that most

Americans of the time would have found overly exotic—it's a safe bet that most meals served in the officers' mess leaned more toward traditional "all-American" or, given the origin of Carlsen and several of his officers, even Scandinavian dishes.

Nor was menu planning the only challenge Bushka and his messmen faced. Compared to the restaurant-style kitchen the chief steward had worked in aboard his previous ship, USAT *Leonard Wood*, *Cynthia Olson*'s galley was tiny. Given that it incorporated two gas-fired ovens, a large range, a small refrigerator, several sinks, and all the normal paraphernalia associated with a commercial kitchen, food preparation would have necessarily required both extensive planning and economy of movement. Located on the bridge deck, just aft of the housing for the funnel, the galley was about thirty feet from the small pantry (just forward of the funnel housing) and slightly farther from the main saloon (just forward of the pantry). The engineers' mess was closer, just across a narrow passageway from the galley, but food intended for the rest of the crew had to be carried the length of the timber-packed aft section of the main deck, no matter what the weather or sea state, because the crews' mess was housed in the sterncastle at the base of the aft-most mast.

How Bushka planned, prepared, and served meals was probably not something Carlsen and his senior officers thought much about; their waking hours were consumed with other tasks. As the man ultimately responsible for the safety of ship, crew, and cargo, Carlsen would have spent most of his time in the wheelhouse during daylight. When not actually navigating the ship from the tall-legged, padded wooden captain's chair, he would have been in the small chartroom (in the left rear corner of the wheelhouse) or in his day cabin (in the right rear corner) updating the logbook or attending to the dozens of other managerial tasks to which all ship captains must resign themselves. Nor was he far removed from the bridge even at night, as his stateroom was one deck directly below and he would have been wakened immediately in the event of a nocturnal emergency.[6] Bill Buchtele, Carl Johnstad, and Jim Mills would also have spent most of each of their respective watches on the bridge, though when off-watch each had other duties—both operational and administrative—to perform.

While *Cynthia Olson*'s two military crewmembers didn't stand the same watches as their mariner colleagues, they were certainly no less busy as the Laker made its way westward.

We don't know how much medical care Dee Davenport actually had to provide during the voyage, but we can assume that he probably dealt with the sorts of relatively minor health issues common aboard any working merchant vessel. These would have included cuts caused by poorly spliced wire lines or carelessly handled tools, contusions and bruises resulting from falls during rough seas or tumbles from raised rigging or ladders, or even broken limbs or crushed digits. Davenport could draw from a fair range of medicines and other essential medical materials in the ship's compact four-berth sickbay—which was located on the port side of the bridge deck, just down a passageway from Bushka's galley—and the medic's training would have enabled him to handle most run-of-the mill illnesses and injuries.

When Davenport wasn't busy in the sickbay it's more than likely he would have been found in Sam Ziskind's domain, *Cynthia Olson*'s radio room. Also located on the port side of the bridge deck and separated from the sickbay by the two-bunk stateroom the two soldiers shared, the space was barely six by ten feet, and its forward bulkhead was dominated by the equipment that kept the Laker and her crew in touch with the outside world. Surviving records indicate the radio was most probably a Model 3U unit, which was installed soon after the Oliver Olson Company acquired the vessel and which had replaced an older and far less capable set. Manufactured by the Radio Marine Corporation of America, an RCA subsidiary, the 3U was widely used on small and medium-sized merchant ships of the period. It was a medium-frequency system, meaning it operated on frequencies below 650 kilocycles (Kcs)[7] and had a normal daytime range of 500 to 650 miles.[8]

The 3U was a modular unit made up of three frames, with a total width of about six feet and standing about five and a half feet tall. The operator sat at a desk-like work surface that spanned all three frames, with a Morse key and typewriter (for compiling his radio log and typing out weather reports and incoming messages to be passed to the captain) between him and the center console. Directly in front of him, at eye level, was a small wooden plaque bearing *Cynthia Olson*'s radio call sign, WUAP, in bold letters four inches tall.[9] The lower section of the wider center module housed the AR-8510 receiver, while the upper section was taken up by the much larger ET-8024A transmitter. The 3U's right-hand module held an ET-8025 low-power emergency transmitter, a battery charger (for the emergency unit's twelve-volt source), and the antenna transfer switch.[10] The left-hand module incorporated a Type C crystal radio, a Model 8601 auto-alarm receiver, and *Cynthia Olson*'s auto-alarm master switch.

These last two pieces of equipment were particularly important in terms of safety at sea. International maritime regulations first adopted after the 1912 sinking of RMS *Titanic*, and updated at the 1932 Madrid Radio Conference, established 500 Kcs as the primary frequency for maritime communication. Ships were to initiate contact on that frequency and then immediately switch to a "working" band so as not to block emergency communications. This was a vital point, for 500 Kcs was also the standard distress frequency. Maritime radio operators both afloat and ashore were required to suspend all transmissions on 500 Kcs for two three-minute "silence periods," beginning at fifteen and forty-five minutes after the hour, respectively, and monitor the airwaves for distress signals. While radio-room clocks (such as the one prominently displayed on the center module of *Cynthia Olson*'s 3U) all had the silence periods denoted by two bright-red triangles, the auto-alarm receiver was meant to ensure that no radio operator would miss an incoming SOS. Likewise, the auto-alarm master switch, when activated, would broadcast the series of four, twelve-second Morse dashes that would immediately precede the radio operator's outgoing keyed SOS.

The need to constantly monitor *Cynthia Olson*'s radios, record all pertinent traffic, and be within earshot of the auto-alarm receiver meant that Sam Ziskind would have spent virtually the whole voyage to Hawaii in, or very near, his radio room. Given that he and Davenport shared the stateroom next door, it's entirely likely that Ziskind would have asked the young medic to spell him at the radio console for quick smoke breaks, brief naps, or calls of nature. Since the two young men were friends who had more in common with each other than with their mariner shipmates, it's also probable they passed a fair amount of time listening to music picked up by Ziskind's receiver and doing what bored young soldiers have always done—smoking cigarettes and talking about women, sports, and home.

For all the men aboard *Cynthia Olson*, from Carlson to engine room wiper Terro, the days at sea would have been marked by the rhythm of work, sleep, and meals. And, when they had a chance, each man almost certainly would have gazed out at the passing ocean and thought about homes and loved ones left behind, of voyages past and future, and of the possibility of war. The thoughts of the younger men, and perhaps even the not so young, would also have inevitably turned to the contemplation of Honolulu's many diversions. While there would be work aplenty when the ship reached Hawaii—the cargo of lumber would have to be offloaded and then any U.S.-bound freight would have to be brought aboard and stowed—there would undoubtedly be time to unwind a bit. And for any sailor who has worked his way across the sea, whether above deck or below, landfall on a tropical isle promised unwindings of the most delightful sort.

Thus, when the sun rose on the morning of December 7, we can also assume that all aboard the freighter heaved sighs of relief that they'd made it safely through the night and were only three days' sail from Hawaii.

It was a haven they'd never reach.

———

WHILE THE PHRASE "NAUTICAL DAWN" is unfamiliar to most landsmen, for mariners it has two meanings. The first, and more specific, refers to that time in the morning when the sun is twelve degrees below the horizon and on the rise. The second, and more subjective, is when there is just enough sunlight for objects to be distinguishable. The latter determination can be influenced, of course, by such things as fog, bad weather, or by trying to view a particular object from a vantage point that is low in the water and whose stability is being affected by a heavy swell.

Unfortunately for the men aboard *Cynthia Olson*, nautical dawn on December 7 broke clear in that part of the northwestern Pacific through which they were passing, with calm seas, no rain, and virtually unlimited visibility. As Yukio Oka later remembered,

> The eastern sky was clearing up and several gigantic cumulonimbus clouds, characteristic of that area, piled up on the horizon. The rain had ceased and the weather was fine.[11]

As a result, the lookouts aboard *I-26* who had tracked the lumber carrier's running lights throughout the night had no trouble distinguishing her characteristic silhouette in the burgeoning light. Minoru Yokota, concerned that his vessel might itself be revealed by the quickly rising sun, ordered the bridge watch below and at 2:30 a.m., Japan Time, took *I-26* down to periscope depth and began maneuvering the sub into attack position.[12]

As he began his approach to the target, Yokota took a few moments to address the crew over the submarine's intercom. He first read the address that Yamamoto had composed regarding the necessity of war against America, and which the commander in chief of the Combined Fleet had ordered to be read aboard all Japanese vessels engaged in "Operation Hawaii." *I-26*'s captain then added his own words—which Oka later classified as a "pep talk" that "provided a tremendous boost to morale"[13]—as the Laker's screw noises became audible in the submarine's sound room. Then, according to Oka,

> Inside the conning tower the [commanding officer] and I exchanged glances. Except for the senior [petty officer], everybody could have a peek through the periscope at the freighter. . . . Both navigator and gunnery officer could observe the ship and they agreed it was unarmed.[14]

The determination that *Cynthia Olson* carried no armament prompted Yokota to make what Oka later recalled as a humanitarian gesture:

> "It would be unfair to sink them without warning," the C.O. suggested. "Let's surface at the prescribed attack time [3:30 a.m., JST], first give a warning [shot] and then sink that freighter after it has stopped."[15]

The Japanese commander carefully stalked the Laker until what he later said was exactly 3:30 a.m., Tokyo time, the hour appointed for the *Kido Butai*'s attack on Pearl Harbor. Then, as Oka recalled,

> "Stand by to battle surface for gunnery action," he ordered next.
> We had hoped for a chance to use our torpedoes, but our C.O., a man of small stature but possessing great authority, had decided against it. He first instructed the gunnery officer in a calm voice. From the control room, Gunner's Mate 1st Class Monma was also summoned to receive the instructions.
> After the navigator had reported 10 minutes were left until the surfacing, the C.O. repeated the instructions one more time: "We will fight

a gun action to starboard from 2,500 meters distance. Fire the first shot as an 'over.'"

The gunnery officer then instructed the gun crew himself. Its members lined up by the conning tower ladder, headed by the signals officer, a lookout carrying the portable rangefinder and the gunnery officer in person.

Finally the navigator announced: "The time is now 0330!"

"Do your best!" bellowed the skipper. "Blow the main tanks!"[16]

The massive, shark-like *I-26* quickly surfaced, and as soon as her semienclosed auxiliary bridge was clear of water Yokota ordered the main hatch opened and the gun crew rushed up the ladder. Squeezing past the twin 25-mm antiaircraft mount, the sailors—all wearing *hachimaki* headbands—vaulted over the low railing and onto the main deck.[17] As soon as the sailors had a round in the breech and the muzzle trained, Yokota had them fire a warning shot across the American vessel's bow. His intention, he later said, was to force *Cynthia Olson* to heave to and give those aboard a chance to take to their lifeboats before he sent their ship to the bottom.[18]

Then, as Oka later recalled, "Brown smoke wafted from the [sub's deck gun]. The first shell landed off the other side of the freighter, raising a column of water."[19]

We can be certain that the splash of a 5.5-inch shell just forward of their plodding Laker caught the Americans' immediate attention. We can also assume that they initially believed they were being fired on by mistake—probably by a German U-boat—because a large American flag was quickly run up *Cynthia Olson*'s main hoist. Bert Carlsen was obviously not taking any chances, however, for even as the Stars and Stripes were going aloft he ordered the ship brought to a halt. His World War I experiences had undoubtedly taught him that when unarmed merchantmen—neutral or not—disregard a warship's unmistakable order to stop, the consequences are usually catastrophic.

The submarine's appearance and the implied order to heave to would have galvanized *Cynthia Olson*'s crew. Even before they could determine *I-26*'s nationality or ultimate intentions, Carlsen or one of his officers would have rushed aft to Ziskind's radio room. The young soldier was obviously on the ball, for within minutes of the sub's warning shot he'd activated the auto-alarm master switch to send the series of four twelve-second dashes. Moments later he was keying a distress message, a signal immediately and clearly heard by Petty Officer Osawa, *I-26*'s radio operator (and one which will take on special significance later in this narrative).[20] When informed of the distress signal, Yokota ordered a second round fired ahead of the freighter, then told his signalman to use his flags to order the Americans off their vessel.

That second warning shot and the sub's flag signals would have erased any doubts in Carlsen's mind about what was happening. He would have immediately ordered the Laker's crew to abandon ship, and both lifeboats would quickly have been swung out on their davits. Once all of *Cynthia Olson*'s thirty-three men were loaded and accounted for, the boats would have lowered away. As soon as the hulls hit the water the men certainly rowed for all they were worth, undoubtedly wanting to get as far as possible from their obviously doomed ship. Carlsen, war veteran and former naval reservist that he was, would have already tossed into the sea the weighted bag containing the ship's copy of her Army charter agreement and Carlsen's ATC sailing orders. He knew that, if taken prisoner, he'd stand a better chance of convincing his captors that his ship was an innocent merchantman if there were no incriminating documents to prove otherwise.

The departure of the lifeboats was clearly seen by those aboard the attacking submarine. As Oka remembered,

> Our skipper ordered the gunnery officer to wait until both boats had cast off. . . . The distance was now down to 1,000 meters and the C.O. ordered [the gun crew] to fire another round at the freighter's stern. The projectile drew a shallow curve and disappeared into the hull of the ship. . . . A cloud of fire and steam emerged from the ship as it started to list to starboard.[21]

Shooting from a range of three thousand feet, *I-26*'s gunners landed about ten solid hits out of some twenty rounds fired.[22] Most of the shells were aimed at the Laker's waterline to flood her hull as quickly as possible, but several rounds hit the freighter's superstructure, blowing ragged holes in bulkheads, bringing down ladders and rigging, and sending shrapnel whizzing in all directions. The detonations also ignited fires within the stacked logs just forward of the amidships house, and a plume of thick smoke was soon spiraling into the air.

In a testament both to *Cynthia Olson*'s rugged construction and the added buoyancy provided by the lumber stowed in her holds—and undoubtedly to the amazement and frustration of those on the Japanese sub's bridge—the doughty Laker stubbornly remained afloat. After some thirty-five minutes of apparently ineffective fire, and fearing that the American vessel's SOS would bring antisubmarine aircraft zooming over the horizon, Yokota crash-dived *I-26* and moved off to await his prey's inevitable sinking.

Yet, when he surfaced sometime later, the Japanese sub skipper found *Cynthia Olson* not only still afloat but, her engines having not been shut down completely when her crew took to the boats, actually making a few knots of headway. As Oka recalled, "We fired several shells at the base of the foundation of the masts to hasten the sinking. It did not help."[23]

Wanting to dispatch the freighter as quickly as possible so she wouldn't become a beacon for American aircraft or warships, Yokota reversed his earlier decision and ordered her sunk with a torpedo. Though he was officially the diving officer, Oka

> mounted the portable target-bearing transmitter on the bridge overhead, near the periscope [casing]. One torpedo, in number 5 tube, was readied for firing. After the torpedo officer lined up his sights, it was launched from a distance of 450 meters.

Unfortunately, things didn't go exactly as the sub skipper anticipated, as Chief Gunner Saburo Hayashi later recalled, "We were dismayed because the old torpedo went wild, turned in mid-course, missed the target by a hair's breadth, then went dead in the water."[24]

Understandably annoyed that the obsolescent "Sixth Year"-type torpedo had failed, Komaba tried to convince Yokota that a second "tin fish" would certainly send the American vessel to the bottom. But, according to Oka, the sub's captain declined to fire a second torpedo, saying, "That ship is going to sink anyway. We shall cease the attack and dive immediately."[25]

Yokota took *I-26* back down and ordered that breakfast be served for the crew in honor of the sub's first kill. As Oka later recalled, the meal—steamed rice with azuki beans, grilled eels, and "plenty of fruit"—was served to a crew "elated" by being the first Japanese warship to sink an enemy vessel in this new conflict.[26] After about forty minutes, as Hayashi recalled, his commander took another look through the periscope, expecting to see the last throes of a sinking ship, but instead saw a vessel still stubbornly afloat:

> When we resurfaced [*Cynthia Olson*] was in heavy list. The gunners went back to the deck gun for more shooting. About one-third [of the way] through the 20 rounds fired, the [submarine's] electric ammunition elevator broke down, and the men had to hand-carry the heavy shells up through the hatch to the deck. After about 10 shells were carried, the electricians got the hoist working again.[27]

As the gunners were firing, Hayashi sought permission from First Officer Satô to leave his post in *I-26*'s conning tower and move to the open area aft of the periscope casing to photograph the listing, smoke-wreathed American vessel. With Satô's authorization, the chief gunner grabbed his favorite Reflex-Korelle camera and climbed to the top of the housing for the deck gun's rangefinder, at the extreme aft end of the conning tower. Aiming carefully, he then snapped the only photos known to exist of *Cynthia Olson*'s last minutes. The images depict the heavily damaged Laker with her starboard railing almost submerged and flames pouring from the base of her midships superstructure. Her lifeboat davits are empty and turned outward, indicating that both boats have been launched, but neither is visible.

Soon after Hayashi shot his photos—at what Yokota later estimated was approximately 3:00 p.m., Honolulu time—the sub commander decided that hours of effort and some forty rounds of 5.5-inch high explosive were more than enough. Besides, soon after *I-26* had begun been firing on the Laker the submarine's radio officer had picked up the *Kido Butai* attack force's "Tora, Tora, Tora" message indicating that it had accomplished its mission at Pearl Harbor and, with war now a reality, Yokota had other missions to carry out. He ordered the lookouts below and, with absolutely no regard for the welfare of the American mariners, submerged his vessel and sailed away.

———

MINORU YOKOTA'S CONCERNS THAT *CYNTHIA Olson*'s distress signal might have been heard by someone other than Petty Officer Osawa were

well-founded, for Sam Ziskind's auto alarm caught the immediate attention of a radio operator aboard the biggest ship at sea that day between
Hawaii and the U.S. West Coast. The radio operator was Leslie Grogan,
and the ship was *Lurline*.

Grogan later recalled that he had been on the 8:00 a.m. to noon radio
watch "but a little while" and was busy taking down weather reports
from other vessels for onward high-frequency transmittal to a commercial receiving station in San Francisco.[28] Then, at approximately 9:12 a.m.,
ship's time (the determination of which will be of special interest in the
following chapters), Grogan heard what he recorded as a "strong" transmission on 500 Kcs "making the 'SSS' signal, meaning in the International
Code that a submarine has been sighted or 'we are being attacked by a
submarine.'" He immediately asked for the freighter's position. Ziskind
replied in what Grogan called a "steady hand," reporting that his vessel
was being attacked by a surfaced sub and, a few minutes later, giving
Cynthia Olson's position as 33°42′ N by 145°29′ W, or about 1,120 miles
northeast of Honolulu's Diamond Head and some 320 miles due north of
Lurline. Immediately after giving the position data Ziskind abruptly went
off the air, prompting Grogan to record that the freighter's transmitter had
"sparked out like if a power failure took place."[29]

After waiting a few seconds to see if Ziskind would come back on the
air, Grogan acknowledged the position report and said he would immediately notify the Navy. He hoped to hear a response, but when none
was forthcoming, even from *Cynthia Olson*'s emergency transmitter, he
assumed the Laker had been torpedoed. Grogan and his supervisor, Chief
Radio Operator Rudy Asplund, then tried to contact the Navy radio stations at both Pearl Harbor and San Francisco. When they got no response—
which Grogan thought was "mighty strange"—they tried a different tack:

> We called NMC, the U.S. Coast Guard radio station at Point Bonita,
> Calif., . . . at the entrance to the Golden Gate. . . . We opened with the
> words "Distress Traffic," and NMC answered immediately on 500 Kcs.[30]

As soon as they'd established communication, the Coast Guard operator at Point Bonita instructed Grogan to move to *Lurline*'s "working" frequency, 468 Kcs. The radio operator did so and then began sending the
following in Morse:

AT 1838 GMT WUAP [the Laker's radio call sign] USAT *cynthia olson* SENT
FIRST AUTO ALARM SIGNAL FOLLOWED BY SOS SSS DE WUAP LAT 33 42
NORTH AND LONG 145 29 WEST SAYS NATURE OF SOS SUBMARINE ON SUR-
FACE WE ARE IN DIRECT COMMUNICATION WITH WUAP.[31]

When Grogan was halfway through relaying *Cynthia Olson*'s distress message, NMC informed him that *Lurline*'s medium-frequency signal was fading. The Coast Guard operator then instructed Grogan to switch to high frequency and pass the distress message to KTK, the Globe Wireless Company's commercial station at Mussel Rock, south of San Francisco.

The duty operator at KTK, Ray Ferrill, immediately answered and took down the details of *Cynthia Olson*'s message.[32] After telling Grogan he'd get back to him, Ferrill quickly got on the telephone and tried to reach the Navy radio station at Mare Island, just north of San Francisco. When he got no answer, he decided to go right to the top, calling the Office of Naval Communications in San Francisco's Federal Building. This time someone answered the phone immediately, and Ferrill passed on *Cynthia Olson*'s position and the gist of her message.

Unknown to Ferrill or the radio operators aboard *Lurline*, Ziskind's medium-frequency distress call caught the attention of three other parties. Two would be especially interested in the Laker's plight but would prove unable to help, while the third would ultimately play the most direct role in attempting to determine *Cynthia Olson*'s fate.

Ironically, the first two recipients of Ziskind's message were both Army transport ships involved in Operation Plum.[33] Two days out of San Francisco by the morning of December 7, USAT *Etolin* picked up the transmissions but was under orders not to deviate from her track or break radio silence unless she herself was under attack. The transport's master, a Captain Murray, thus had to sail on, knowing there was nothing he could do for his fellow mariners but no doubt believing that *Lurline* would direct help to the stricken Laker.

The other Army vessel, USAT *Will H. Point*, overheard the messages while still taking on cargo at Fort Mason. Though not required to monitor the 500 Kcs frequency while in port, one of the ship's radio operators was performing routine maintenance when his auto-alarm receiver activated. The radioman quickly copied down the details as Ziskind gave them to Grogan and then reported the exchange to *Will H. Point*'s captain. He, in

turn, sent the news to Colonel Mellon, the ATS superintendent, by mes-
senger. After scanning the message, Mellon rushed across the hall to the
office of SFPOE commander Colonel Frederick Gilbreath, who had only
been in the job two weeks and was in his office that Sunday morning to
stay ahead of his already prodigious workload.[34]

"The *Cynthia Olson* has been torpedoed by a Jap sub!" Mellon exclaimed
as he burst into Gilbreath's office. "We've just picked up her distress signal
on the wireless of the ship down at Fort Mason Dock 3."

A shocked Gilbreath picked up the telephone directly connecting him
with the Washington, DC, office of Major General Brehon B. Somervell,
the Army's assistant chief of staff for logistics.[35] As the two men were discussing the ramifications of the attack on *Cynthia Olson*, Mellon burst back
in to inform Gilbreath of the Japanese attack on Pearl Harbor.

And at that precise moment the plight of a small, civilian-crewed lumber freighter ceased to be of immediate concern to the SFPOE commander
and, indeed, the Army at large. The outbreak of war brought an instan-
taneous and irrevocable shift in priorities, the most important of which,
from Gilbreath's point of view, was the safety of the ships involved in
Operation Plum. He ordered that all Army-owned or -controlled vessels
still in San Francisco be held at their piers and directed the immediate
recall of *Etolin*, *Tasker H. Bliss*, *President Johnson*, and *President Garfield*.
Troopships and cargo vessels already en route from Hawaii to the Philippines were to be diverted to Australia or other Allied ports.[36]

The news that forced *Cynthia Olson* off Gilbreath's priority list also
diverted the attention of those aboard *Lurline* away from the Laker. Almost
immediately after receiving Ziskind's distress signal, and as Grogan was
contacting KTK in San Francisco, Asplund had passed news of *Cynthia
Olson*'s plight to the liner's chief officer, Edward Collins. As he later recalled,

> I took [a copy of the message] to the chartroom, where First Officer
> John Van Orden was working at the chart table on the morning's navi-
> gation. I gave him the message and then notified Commodore Berndt-
> son. Van Orden plotted the *Cynthia Olson*'s position: about 300 miles
> bearing 005 degrees true from the *Lurline*.[37]

Collins's announcement put an end to the church service Berndtson
had been conducting in the ship's lounge, as the commodore called an

immediate gathering of his top staff. But even before the liner's officers could begin discussing how they might be able to assist the stricken lumber freighter, another, more shocking message arrived. When Collins returned to the radio shack, he was handed the transcript of a Navy signal—the famous "This is no drill" message—announcing the attack on Pearl Harbor. When he relayed this latest bit of bad news to Berndtson, *Lurline*'s master immediately vetoed any further action regarding *Cynthia Olson* and ordered the liner blacked out. Determined to ensure the survival of his vessel, his crew, and his passengers, he then rang up "Full Speed Ahead" on the ship's engine-order telegraph and raced for the safety of San Francisco Bay.[38]

The third entity to hear of Sam Ziskind's distress call, and the only one to actually attempt to respond, was the Royal Canadian Navy. A radio operator sitting in a windowless room in Esquimalt, BC, intercepted a retransmission of *Cynthia Olson*'s SSS that had been broadcast in the clear by NPC, the U.S. 13th Naval District's radio station at Bremerton, near Seattle. The Canadian sailor logged the intercept at 7:02 p.m., Greenwich Mean Time (GMT), (which was 11:02 a.m., British Columbia time), typed a transcript of the Morse code, and passed the information up the chain to the Commanding Officer Pacific Coast (COPC), Commodore W.J.R. Beech.[39]

Himself a former submariner, Beech was still digesting the significance of an obviously hostile sub operating halfway between North America and Hawaii when a second, more urgent message explained everything. At 8:18 GMT the same radio operator who passed on *Cynthia Olson*'s distress call received, and immediately forwarded to all COPC subordinate organizations and ships,[40] the fateful news: "Air raid on Pearl Harbour [*sic*]. U.S. hostilities with Japan have commenced."[41] With the reason for *Cynthia Olson*'s distress message now clear and any doubts of its authenticity erased, Beech ordered that the lumber schooner's report of the attack and her last-known position be sent to the RCN vessel closest to that position. And that vessel was none other than HMCS *Prince Robert*.

Over the previous forty-eight hours the converted liner had made good time, though an incident on the night of December 5–6 had left her captain and crew more than a little shaken. As the ship was racing through the dark a flare suddenly shot into the sky from a point just off *Prince Robert*'s port beam. Hart immediately ordered searchlights trained on the flare's point of origin, and gun crews scrambled to man their weapons. As it turned out, the flare had been fired by an American submarine, apparently bound for Honolulu and concerned that the hard-charging Canadian vessel might inadvertently run her down.[42] That *Prince Robert*'s lookouts and admittedly primitive surface-search radar (still referred to as RDF, meaning "radio direction finding" equipment) had failed to detect the surfaced sub must have caused Hart more than a little anxiety, but once the American vessel had been identified he had no choice but to continue his headlong rush toward Esquimalt.

The first message destined to interrupt that voyage on *Cynthia Olson*'s behalf was sent to *Prince Robert*—in the clear—at 8:31 GMT, or 12:31 p.m., on December 7, some ninety minutes after the first intercept and just thirteen minutes after Hart had received the Pearl Harbor message:

> FROM: COPC
>
> HMCS *PRINCE ROBERT*, IMMEDIATE
>
> USAT *CYNTHIA OLSEN* [sic] SENT DISTRESS REPORT ENEMY SUBMARINE LAT 33.42 NORTH LONG. 145.29 WEST 07 1902[43]

While this first message did not direct *Prince Robert* to undertake any specific action, a second one, sent at 9:42 p.m. GMT, did. This latter message was transmitted in naval code—a terse notation on the cover form cites "34 Groups of Cyphers"—and directed Hart to go to the Laker's aid.[44] As *Prince Robert*'s captain later noted in his "Report of Proceedings,"

> On Sunday, 7th December, information that hostilities had broken out with Japan and also that the U.S. Army Transport *Cynthia Olsen* [sic] had been sunk C.O.P.C.'s 2142Z/7. As H.M.C.S. "*Prince Robert*" was only 150 miles from the position mentioned [for *Cynthia Olson*], course was at once altered and speed increased to 21 knots.[45]

Prince Robert's deck log shows that the course alteration and speed increase were made at 11:47 a.m. ship's time. At twenty-one knots the converted liner would have covered the 150 miles to *Cynthia Olson*'s last reported position in just over six hours, putting the Canadian vessel on station by approximately 5:45 p.m. ship's time. Though darkness had fallen,[46] search conditions were ideal—the sea was calm, the night was clear, and there was what Hart called a "brilliant moon."[47] The Canadian commander ordered a methodical search, and over the following three hours *Prince Robert* covered several hundred square miles of ocean. Her lookouts, augmented by other members of the ship's company and by the vessel's primitive surface-search radar, scanned the sea is all directions and found nothing. No burning hulk, no floating wreckage, and no drifting lifeboats.

Cynthia Olson had vanished without a trace.

CHAPTER 8

BAD NEWS TRAVELS . . .

WHILE NEWS OF THE *KIDO Butai*'s attack on Pearl Harbor quickly diverted official attention from *Cynthia Olson*'s distress message, the Laker's plight did not go publicly unannounced. Indeed, the first radio news flash to mention *I-26*'s attack on the freighter hit the airwaves in the United States even as the Japanese submarine was struggling to send the stubborn Laker to the bottom.

Though surviving records do not clearly indicate how Sam Ziskind's hurriedly dispatched distress call had been relayed to Washington, DC, we know that it had by the time the second wave of Japanese attackers appeared over Oahu at 2:22 p.m., Eastern Standard Time, which was 8:52 a.m. in Hawaii. At that moment White House Press Secretary Stephen Early was releasing a statement to the nation's three main wire services—Associated Press, International News Service, and United Press. Speaking from his home in northeast Washington via the White House operator, he said,

> The Japanese have attacked Pearl Harbor from the air and all naval and military activities on the island of Oahu, the principal American base in the Hawaii Islands.[1]

Early then directed the operator to distribute the statement to all of the country's major radio networks and newspapers and, after making a second brief telephone statement regarding the attacks on the Philippines, he hurried to his White House office. He was immediately mobbed by radio, print, and wire-service reporters, and at 3:20 made the U.S. government's first official reference to the attack on *Cynthia Olson*:

> The president has just received a dispatch from the War Department reporting the torpedoing of an Army transport, 1,300 miles west of San Francisco. Fortunately, the transport was carrying a cargo of lumber rather than personnel of the Army.[2]

While Early's implication that there were no Army personnel aboard the ship was inaccurate and his seeming disregard for the safety of the civilian crew more than a little insensitive, his brief statement was passed up the journalistic food chain with breathtaking speed. At 3:24 p.m. EST, near the end of a regularly scheduled news program that had consisted almost exclusively of bulletins about the initial Pearl Harbor air raid, NBC radio commentator H. V. Kaltenborn broke the news of what he called a "torpedo attack" on an unnamed, lumber-carrying Army transport. When CBS Radio's John Daly interrupted the network's broadcast of the New York Philharmonic Society (playing Dmitri Shostakovich's Symphony No. 1 in F Minor) at approximately 3:35, he too spoke of a torpedo attack on what he termed "an Army lumber transport" and repeated the location information provided by Early.[3] Within an hour of Kaltenborn's initial mention of the event, the news that an Army vessel had been attacked by what was widely assumed to be a Japanese submarine was getting airplay on radio stations across the nation.

Despite the fact that it was readily apparent even from the first hurried reports that the Japanese had inflicted massive damage at Pearl Harbor, it is not surprising that the fate of a single "unnamed Army lumber transport" should have gotten the attention it did from major news organizations. While the attacks on Oahu were obviously heavy blows militarily and would finally bring the United States into the war on the Allied side, the Japanese onslaught was in some ways too big a story—too many dead, too much destruction, too many potentially historic ramifications. Many editors trying to fill air minutes or column inches sought to personalize the coming of war by concentrating on a journalistically ideal human-interest story—the tale of a single, unarmed ship treacherously attacked on the high seas. That details of the reported assault remained sketchy detracted not a whit from the story's news value.

Indeed, it is entirely possible that the lack of hard information actually increased public interest in the saga of the anonymous lumber transport. Many Americans perceived Hawaii to be a colonial outpost far out in the vast Pacific and did not feel immediately threatened by the momentous events at Pearl Harbor. However, news that enemy submarines were active within three or four days' steaming of the West Coast did seem to touch a collective national nerve and almost certainly helped precipitate the increasing number of "sightings" of Japanese activity reported from Seattle to San Diego as December 7 wore on.[4]

Despite the day's increasing volume of detailed news reports coming from Hawaii—a second wave of attackers had begun unleashing further destruction on Oahu beginning at 2:24 p.m. EST—the story of the anonymous Army lumber freighter remained oddly compelling for many Americans, even those in the White House. First Lady Eleanor Roosevelt was the first of the executive mansion's occupants to mention the incident during her regular Sunday evening radio broadcast, "Current Events":[5]

> Good evening, ladies and gentlemen, I am speaking to you tonight at a very serious moment in our history. The Cabinet is convening and the leaders in Congress are meeting with the president. The State Department and Army and Navy officials have been with the president all afternoon. In fact, the Japanese ambassador was talking to the president at the very time that Japan's airships [sic] were bombing our citizens in Hawaii and the Philippines and sinking one of our transports loaded with lumber on its way to Hawaii.[6]

While the First Lady's assertion that the lumber transport had been sunk was premature given what was actually known at the time she spoke, the mere fact that she mentioned the attack is an indication that the White House realized the American people's interest in the Laker's fate. It may also have been a subtle and shrewd attempt to shape American public opinion: by connecting the attack on a humble, unarmed lumber schooner with the assaults on the military bastion in Hawaii and initial air raids in the Philippines, the First Lady (and, by extension, her husband's administration) might well have been attempting to instill in Americans' minds the idea that the rapacious Japanese would strike any target, whether or not it had true military significance.[7]

The other resident of the White House made his own, somewhat more oblique reference to the attack the following day. During his famous "Day of Infamy" speech, given at 12:30 p.m. EST to a joint session of Congress, President Franklin D. Roosevelt said:

> The attack yesterday on the Hawaiian Islands has caused severe damage to American naval and military forces. Very many American lives have been lost. In addition, American ships have been reported torpedoed on the high seas between San Francisco and Honolulu.[8]

While FDR's implication that *Cynthia Olson* had sailed for Hawaii directly from San Francisco was incorrect (and which is an error still widely repeated today), his mention of the incident ensured that the story of the anonymous lumber transport remained in the news in the days immediately following the speech and Congress' subsequent declaration of war.

Mrs. Roosevelt's December 7 mention of the attack on a Hawaii-bound lumber transport and her husband's veiled reference the following day were the first chilling indications the families and friends of those aboard *Cynthia Olson* had that something had happened. Typical was the experience of Sam Ziskind's wife, Bernice, and her family, as recalled by her sister, Inez:

> We were all together on Dec. 7, and [Bernice] knew [Sam's] ship was on the way to Pearl Harbor, and we all sort of thought something happened to him, right then and there.[9]

Confirmation of those first dreadful inklings that *Cynthia Olson* was the anonymous "Army lumber transport" so much in the news was not immediately forthcoming, however. For though Mellon, the ATS superintendent at Fort Mason, and San Francisco Port of Embarkation commander Gilbreath had both learned of the Laker's distress call within minutes of its transmission (thanks to the radioman aboard *Will H. Point*), they understandably chose to wait for additional details before notifying either the Oliver J. Olson Company or the families of the ship's crewmembers.

And those details had to wait for the arrival in San Francisco of Matson's *Lurline*.

After being notified of the attack on Pearl Harbor, Commodore Berndtson had ordered his ship blacked out, put her on a zigzag course meant to spoil the aim of any lurking enemy submarine commanders, and rang up "Full Ahead" on the engine-order telegraph. The liner pounded eastward, her master determined that she and those aboard her would reach San Francisco unscathed. That they did at 3:00 a.m. on December 10, and within minutes of *Lurline*'s arrival at Pier 32 her voyage radio log—which contained the only complete record of what would soon become known as the *Cynthia Olson* incident—was being confiscated by the U.S. government. As Leslie Grogan recalled,

> Lieut. Comdr. Preston Allen of the Navy, whom I knew personally in WWI, entered the Radio Room and requested that the voyage radio log be turned over to him. Rudy Asplund, our Chief Operator, and myself realized this Log contained a full picture of events that took place, and we told Lieut. Comdr. Allen that we were still under the Orders of the Merchant Marine, and accordingly, the Master of the *Lurline* is our immediate superior, and we will turn the Log over to the Master, getting a receipt for the same—and he can do whatever he wishes with it.[10]

Allen, a member of the 12th Naval District's intelligence staff, accompanied Asplund and Grogan to the liner's bridge. After signing a quickly prepared receipt for the radiomen, Berndtson officially handed the log over to Allen, who then left the ship with almost unseemly dispatch.

We do not know what ultimately became of the radio log (a mystery into which we will delve later in this volume), but we can be certain that the information it contained was of great interest to the Office of Naval Intelligence (ONI). The attack on *Cynthia Olson* was by all indications the first on an American vessel by a Japanese fleet submarine, and the agency was understandably eager to glean from the document any nuggets of information that might shed light on Japanese undersea capabilities, methods, or intentions.[11] Allen's sudden appearance in *Lurline*'s radio room, and his insistence on leaving with the only copy of the radio log, are both indications that the Navy believed the document had at least some intelligence value.

Allen was not slow to share the information contained in the log. Within hours of seizing the document he dispatched via secure teletype a classified summary of the information it contained regarding the attack on *Cynthia Olson* to the ONI's Coastal Intelligence Section in Washington, DC. That organization, known within the Navy as Op-16-B-8, promptly passed the details on to several other key Navy bureaus in a "Confidential" message signed by Lieutenant Commander C. P. Baldwin and carrying the subject heading "Submarine Attack on United States Steamer CYNTHIA OLSEN [*sic*]":

> A teletype received from the 12th Naval District at 1415 on December 10, 1941, states that information obtained from Class "A" source to the effect that the United States steamer LURLINE at 8:00 a.m. local time, December 7, heard the United States steamer CYNTHIA OLSEN [*sic*] give an S.O.S. call stating that she had been attacked by a submarine and the CYNTHIA OLSEN [*sic*] gave her position as Latitude 33° 42 minutes North, Lo. 145° 29 minutes West. She stated that submarine was on the surface, and then she went off the air and was not heard again. The LURLINE was 320 miles due South from position given by CYNTHIA OLSEN [*sic*]. The LURLINE then headed on course South and proceeded to San Francisco by around about [*sic*] route.[12]

While news of the attack on *Cynthia Olson* was passed with some speed through the military services and other branches of government, it was left to Whitney and George Olson to confirm to the crewmembers' anxious family members the identity of the "Army lumber transport." The brothers were apparently briefed on the contents of *Lurline*'s radio log soon after the document's seizure by the Navy, for by December 11 they had spoken by telephone with most of the wives or other family members of the crewmembers who resided in the United States. As Berthel Carlsen's wife, Thyra, disclosed in a December 12 interview with the San Pedro *News-Pilot*, the Olsons had few details to share:

> "Transport" Reported Sunk Commanded by San Pedran

> The "Army transport" reported sunk while en route to Hawaii when Japanese planes last Sunday attacked Pearl Harbor was commanded by a San Pedro man, Carl Berthel Carlsen, 64.

This was disclosed by the captain's wife, of 1415 Le Grande Terrace. Her report was based on information from former owners of the vessel. She has received no confirmation of it.

Mrs. Carlson was told, she said, that an SOS from the transport, a former coastwise ship long familiar here, was picked up by several other vessels. It indicated the transport was being attacked by a submarine. The ship was en route to Honolulu from a northwest port with lumber cargo.

Captain Carlsen has been a master mariner for 27 years. He and Mrs. Carlsen are widely known among shipping people. Today, Mrs. Carlsen expressed all confidence that her husband and his crew had been picked up by other ships.[13]

———————

As DECEMBER WORE ON AND America's military fortunes in the Pacific continued to deteriorate, the story of the disappearance of the still publicly unnamed lumber transport and her crew gradually faded from the news. It did not, however, fade from the minds of those whose loved ones had been aboard the ship. While most appreciated the Olson Company's initial December 11 notification of the attack, they were puzzled and more than a little angry that it took the Army Transport Service office at Fort Mason until the third week of December to officially notify them that the ship was overdue. And as C. M. Dodd, brother of ATS quartermaster Roland Dodd, later recalled, even that official notification—delivered by telegram—contained precious few details: "just the name [of the ship], date and approximate location [of the attack]."[14]

Two family members—Katherine Buchtele and Thyra Carlsen—were especially persistent in their efforts to get more facts about the ship's fate out of the Olson Company and the Army. In a December 20 letter to Whitney Olson, the former asked "for any scrap of additional information" the company might be able to provide. Olson's December 22 reply offered sympathy, but little in the way of news:

Dear Mrs. Buchtele;

We are today in receipt of your air mail letter, and we are still at a loss to know what to say to you as we have been unable as yet to get an official announcement out of either the Army Department or Navy Headquarters as to the fate of the SS "CYNTHIA OLSON" and its crew.

. . . We have been hoping each day that some encouraging word would arrive advising us of the safety of the crew and the vessel, but no such word has been received.

We appreciate how worried and anxious you must be and it is not our desire to withhold any information to which you are rightfully entitled. We can assure you that the moment we hear anything definite we will advise you and we are all hoping that we will receive encouraging news assuring us of the safety of your husband, as well as the balance of the crew.

. . . We have been able to contact Capt. Sax, of the Army Department, and he is getting a wire off to Washington tonight to get a definite line on all communications regarding the "CYNTHIA OLSON" and as soon as we receive this from him we will immediately relay it to you.[15]

The "Capt. Sax" to whom Olson referred was Captain Samuel E. Sax, Mellon's assistant at the Fort Mason ATS office. Katherine Buchtele decided not to wait for the young officer to contact her; on the same day she received Whitney Olson's letter, she wrote to Sax, asking if there was any new information. He replied on December 24:

My dear Mrs. Buchtele:

We have your letter of December 22, requesting information on the SS "CYNTHIA OLSON." We sincerely regret that present communications with the islands are so restricted that no reports have been received, either good or bad, concerning the fate of this vessel or its crew.

We can do no more than assure you that this vessel was provided with adequate life-saving equipment and life-boats. If the vessel had been torpedoed it is most likely that the crew had ample time to take to the life-boats and may have been picked up by other vessels in the vicinity.

We regret that we have no more detailed information, but wish to assure you that you will be advised when this matter is cleared.[16]

While Bill Buchtele's wife sought information from the ATS at Fort Mason, Thyra Carlsen chose to go right to the top. On December 21 she wrote directly to Major General Edmund B. Gregory, the chief of the Army's Quartermaster Corps and the man who technically "owned" all Army vessel operations at that time.[17] In a reply dated December 26, Colonel C. H. Kells, chief of the Water Transport Branch in the Office of the Quartermaster General, was able to provide only a few new tidbits of information:

Dear Mrs. Carlsen:

It is regretted that no definite information can be given you of the fate of the crew of the CYNTHIA OLSON. The Army, however, has not given up the whole crew of this vessel as lost without trace.

It is true that early on the morning of December 7 the CYNTHIA OLSON sent an SOS stating she was being attacked by an enemy submarine. Nothing further was ever heard from this vessel or the crew. The Japanese press announced the vessel had been torpedoed and sunk. Our Army and Navy used all means possible to locate some trace of this vessel or its crew. The location in the ocean last given by the CYNTHIA OLSON in her SOS was searched by the United States Navy and nothing was found. While the vessel is long over-due, it is still hoped that some of the crew may have escaped in life boats to either the mainland of the United States or Canada, or to some small island in the Pacific. It might further develop that if it is true CYNTHIA OLSON was torpedoed by a Japanese submarine, that this submarine took aboard it the members of the crew and, as is customary in cases of this kind, will keep such information a secret until the submarine returns to its home base or to a port where the crew can be put ashore.

The Army Transport Service is deeply grieved over the loss of this vessel, and cannot believe that the vessel and its crew would entirely disappear. That is the one reason this office has hesitated to announce the CYNTHIA OLSON as lost. Until some definite information can be given, it is best to hope that sooner or later this gallant crew will return safely to our country.

Everyone joins in extending their deepest sympathy to you in these long and anxious hours. We hope to be able to give you more definite information within a short time.[18]

The sympathy expressed to family members of *Cynthia Olson*'s crewmen by Sax, Kells, and other Army officials was certainly genuine, and their repeated statements that they had no additional information to impart was entirely accurate. Indeed, the Army's failure to provide any substantive information about the fate of *Cynthia Olson* and her crew in the weeks immediately following the ship's disappearance stemmed not from any official desire to safeguard classified information or somehow stonewall the next of kin. It was, instead, simply because the service had no further details to offer. The Royal Canadian Navy had passed on to ONI and other U.S. military agencies the negative results of HMCS *Prince Robert's* search soon after the auxiliary cruiser had returned to Esquimalt, and not one of the increasing number of U.S. naval or merchant vessels voyaging between Hawaii and the West Coast had reported any sign of *Cynthia Olson*, her missing crew, or her lumber cargo.

The continuing lack of information led to a variety of official suppositions about the Laker's ultimate fate, perhaps the most interesting of which was raised in a January 22, 1942, message from the commander of the Seattle-based 13th Naval District to the Navy Department in Washington:[19]

In view of having received no reports of any trace of the vessel, [her] appurtenances, cargo, or personnel, and in consideration of the amount of traffic passing in the vicinity of the last reported position of the OLSON, and the nature and type of the cargo carried by the OLSON, it is very possible that the vessel has been taken as a prize by the enemy.[20]

While the theory that the Laker had been captured intact and hustled off to a Japanese-controlled port apparently did not gain many adherents in Army or Navy circles, the other points made in the January 22 message helped convince the War Department that—despite Kells's intimation to Thyra Carlsen that the Army would not give *Cynthia Olson* up as lost until something definite was learned—the time had come to make an official determination regarding the presumed fate of both ship and crew. The process of making that determination was well under way by February 5, 1942, on which date the Army's Office of the Adjutant General sent to the Office of the Quartermaster General two memos, each bearing the subject heading "Report of Death." One of the documents concerned Dee Davenport, and the other Sam Ziskind. After listing such basic facts as each soldier's date and place of birth, rank, arm of service, and next of kin, the memos carried the words "Missing at sea since Dec. 7, 1941" in the space titled "Date and place of death."[21]

Though the memos seem to indicate that the Army had already determined that Davenport and Ziskind were dead, the official notification telegrams sent to the soldiers' families by the Office of the Adjutant General on February 5 did not reflect that conclusion. The one sent to Davenport's mother, Mrs. Pauline Clifton, for example, read as follows:

THE SEC. OF WAR DESIRES ME TO EXPRESS WITH DEEP REGRET THAT YOUR SON ERNEST J. DAVENPORT HAS BEEN REPORTED MISSING AT SEA SINCE ABOUT DECEMBER SEVENTH. THE VESSEL ON WHICH HE SAILED FROM SEATTLE HAS BEEN LONG OVERDUE SINCE DEC. TENTH. LETTER FOLLOWS.

Nor was that following letter—also dated February 5 and signed by Major General Emory S. Adams, the adjutant general—any more illuminating:

Dear Mrs. Clifton:
    It is with profound regret that I confirm the recent War Department telegram informing you that your son . . . has been missing at sea since about December 7, 1941.
    . . . The report received did not furnish any definite information as to the circumstances connected therewith. When further information as to his status is received at this office you will be informed immediately.[22]

After notifying all *Cynthia Olson* family members having U.S. mailing addresses, the War Department issued its official statement about the Laker on the evening of February 6. The following day, the *New York Times* reported the gist of the announcement in an article headlined "Army Freighter Lost with 35 Men Aboard":

The Army freight transport Cynthia Olson, with thirty-five persons aboard, was given up as lost by the War Department tonight as a result of enemy action in the Pacific.
    The steamship was under charter to the United States Army. She has been unreported since Dec. 7, 1941. On that date she wirelessed that she was being attacked by a Japanese submarine.
    At the time of the attack the vessel gave her position as about 1,200 miles west of Seattle. She was en route to Honolulu with a cargo of lumber when attacked and was due in Honolulu on Dec. 10.

The vessel was . . . owned by the Oliver J. Olson Company. At the
time of the attack there were thirty-three civilian members of the crew
and two American soldiers on board. All of them are presumed to have
been lost.[23]

While the War Department's official announcement of the name and
presumed fate of the previously anonymous "Army lumber transport"
and the issuance of regret letters by the adjutant general went some way
toward filling the information void that had existed since the attack on
Cynthia Olson, two significant issues remained. The first concerned the
families of the Filipino crewmembers, and the second grew out of the
fact that a determination of "missing at sea" was not sufficient to trigger
the death benefits and other governmental support that would ease the
increasingly dire financial straits in which most of the family members
were beginning to find themselves.

Though the War Department sent notification telegrams and follow-up
letters to the U.S.-resident families of *Cynthia Olson*'s Filipino crewmembers, efforts to notify families still living in the Philippines were, of course,
severely hampered by the military situation in those islands. Japanese
naval infantry units of Lieutenant General Masaharu Homma's 14th
Army had begun initial landings on the beaches of northern Luzon on
December 8, Japan time, followed four days later by a larger assault on the
island's southern end. On December 22 the main Japanese invasion force
began hitting the beaches along the Lingayan Gulf, and by Christmas Eve
General Douglas MacArthur was beginning the withdrawal of American
and Filipino forces to Bataan. Under such conditions it was impossible to
notify the Philippines-resident families of *Cynthia Olson*'s Filipino crewmen that their loved ones were presumed lost, and in the vast majority of
cases that official notification was not made until after the end of the war.

For family members in the United States the issue was not notification,
it was finances. The November 18, 1941, charter agreement between the
Army Transport Service and the Oliver J. Olson Company had stipulated
that the U.S. government would "at its own expense, man, operate . . .
and pay all . . . costs and expenses incident to the use and operation of
the vessel." That meant that the crews' normal salaries were to be paid
by the Army Transport Service rather than by the Olson Company, and
before the ship left San Francisco for Puget Sound at the end of November

all members of the ship's complement were supposed to have filled out allotment forms that would allow the Army to send the majority of their salaries to whomever the men designated. While Bill Buchtele and several other crewmembers told their wives that the allotment forms had been signed and submitted, the forms somehow went astray. As Mellon, the Fort Mason ATS superintendent, told Katherine Buchtele in a January 22 letter,

> With reference to your not having received allotment which you state your husband said would be paid to you, there is no record in this office nor in the Shipping Commissioner's office at this port of any allotments made by the crew of this vessel.[24]

Given the hasty nature of *Cynthia Olson*'s departure from San Francisco, it is entirely possible that the signed allotment forms were never taken ashore. Perhaps ATS quartermaster Roland Dodd—the man responsible for managing all paperwork pertaining to the ship's charter and subsequent administrative operations—intended to submit the forms to the ATS office in Seattle and did not have the chance to do so. Or, perhaps the forms were never signed and Buchtele and others were confusing them with other documents they'd had to fill out during the hurried preparations to sail.

Whatever the reason, the lack of allotment forms was a serious problem for the family members of all those aboard the Laker. The ATS-Olson Company charter agreement had effectively negated any personal or union-provided life insurance the mariners might have carried, while at the same time making the payment of crew wages and benefits a government responsibility. But no wages had been paid by the time the ship left Seattle on December 1, nor had any payments been made by the time *Cynthia Olson* and those who'd sailed aboard her were declared "presumed lost" on February 5, 1942. Since there were no allotment forms that would have permitted the Army to provide some amount of each man's monthly salary to a designated beneficiary, the February 5 determination of the ship's status meant that no funds could be passed to the family members. Nor could the families apply for government death benefits, for though "missing and presumed lost" the men aboard *Cynthia Olson* had not been officially declared dead.

It was a classic catch-22 situation, and one that put the family members in increasingly difficult circumstances. Katherine Buchtele's case, as explained in an April 24, 1942, letter to the War Department, was a common one:

> My husband was, as I understand, on a straight salary basis of $240.00 per month, to be paid by the Quartermaster, U.S. Army. . . . I have been completely without funds after having spent the last money received by my husband in November, 1941, prior to his shipping out on the *Cynthia Olson*. . . . The American Red Cross has been assisting me in the meantime. . . .
>
> I am endeavoring to secure work to support myself and my daughter [Eleanor Beck], but at the present time what work I am able to find is insufficient to care for us. Prior to Mr. Buchtele's last trip he gave me an average of $150.00 per month for household expenses and miscellaneous bills.
>
> In view of the above circumstances, I am writing this letter to request your assistance in helping determine whether I am eligible for benefits or a portion of my husband's pay as of the date he was reported missing at sea.[25]

Katherine Buchtele joined Thyra Carlsen and Chief Engineer Harry Lofving's wife, Hulda, in a concerted effort to get the War Department to provide some sort of financial assistance to the families of *Cynthia Olson*'s crewmen. The three women asked for, and received, Whitney Olson's assistance in their quest, and on May 22, 1942, he wrote to Colonel Kells regarding the situation. In his May 26 reply to Olson, Kells—by this time executive officer of the Water Division in the Transportation Service—was able to pass on some positive news:

> Arrangements are now being made by the War Department to extend to the wives and dependents of sea-going personnel who are reported missing benefits either under the Compensation Act or through some other medium.

The "Compensation Act" to which Kells referred was the December 2, 1942, amendment of the 1916 legislation that created the United States

Employees' Compensation Commission (USECC). Originally intended to provide workmen's compensation benefits for federal employees injured in the course of their official duties, through the 1942 amendment it was extended to cover, among others, eligible employees "who suffer injury or death as a result of a war risk hazard" and authorized payments to "dependents of employees missing from the place of employment due to the belligerent action of an enemy."[26] Because the terms of the Army Transport Service's charter agreement with the Oliver J. Olson Company effectively made all the civilian members of *Cynthia Olson*'s crew federal employees (not just those who were already on the ATS payroll), and because they were most certainly missing because of enemy action, on June 9, 1942, the USECC determined that the crewmen were covered by the amended legislation despite the fact that no finding of death had yet been issued.[27]

The determination cleared the way for family members of *Cynthia Olson*'s crewmembers—and, indeed, the dependents of civilian mariners listed as missing, injured, or killed throughout World War II—to apply for compensation, and all who could be reached were so informed during the last two weeks of June. Virtually all of the *Cynthia Olson* dependents resident in the United States subsequently submitted compensation applications, though the process was something of a bureaucratic nightmare. Wives, for example, had to provide the USECC with certified copies of their marriage licenses. In those cases where a wife had been previously married, she had to also provide a certified copy of the decree terminating the earlier marriage. Moreover, applicants were also required to provide certified copies of birth certificates for any dependent children on behalf of whom additional compensation was being requested.

The family members must ultimately have wondered if the amount of compensation was ultimately worth all the paperwork. Katherine Buchtele's case is typical: after some two months of back-and-forth interaction with the USECC, she was awarded a monthly compensation payment of $61.25, plus an additional $17.50 per month for her daughter, Eleanor. There were, of course, the usual caveats attached to the payments: Katherine's checks would only continue so long as she remained unmarried, and Eleanor's,

> until she dies, marries or reaches the age of eighteen, or if over eighteen and incapable of self-support on account of some physical or mental disability, until she is able to support herself.[28]

The letter informing Katherine of the award also tersely noted that "No greater amounts can be awarded under the law."[29]

While the compensation amounts awarded by the USECC to the family members of *Cynthia Olson*'s civilian crewmembers were relatively modest, they were considerably more than the Army initially provided to the families of Dee Davenport and Sam Ziskind—which was nothing. Despite the Army's February 5, 1942, memos listing both soldiers as "Missing at sea since Dec. 7, 1941," neither of the young men had been officially declared dead, meaning that their families could not collect on either their $1,000 G.I. life insurance policies or their back pay and allowances. While this state of affairs did not pose much a problem for Davenport's mother, it was a real hardship for Ziskind's wife, Bernice.

Soon after hearing from Colonel Mellon that Sam's ship was indeed the "Army lumber transport" attacked on December 7, the young woman had given up the small Marina District apartment she and Sam had shared and moved in with a female friend, Eleanor Lee. While the roommates lived frugally, Bernice could not find a suitable teaching position and found it increasingly difficult to make ends meet. At the end of January 1942 she therefore moved back to Los Angeles to live with her mother, stepfather, and younger sister. She stayed in the family home even after landing a job in the Los Angeles County public school system, and several times made train trips to San Francisco to personally seek additional information about Sam's status from Mellon at Fort Mason.[30] While sympathetic to the young woman's plight, the ATS superintendent could do nothing but repeat the Army's pledge to immediately inform her of any new developments.

As it happened, the news that Bernice Ziskind and the other *Cynthia Olson* family members would ultimately get of their loved ones would not be what they wanted to hear. On March 7, 1942, the 77th Congress passed Public Law 490, the "Missing Persons Act." The legislation's Section 5, in essence, gave the military services permission to assume for legal and administrative purposes that a service member or government civilian employee was dead if the person had been listed as "missing in action" for a year and a day and no new evidence had been uncovered that indicated the possibility of the individual's survival. This "presumptive finding of death" would allow family members or other designated beneficiaries to receive life insurance payouts and checks for their loved ones' back pay and allowances, and soon after the legislation's passage the chief of the Casualty Branch in the Army's Adjutant General Office (AGO) began issuing such findings in a wide range of cases.

By February 1943 AGO staffers had sorted through what little was known about *Cynthia Olson*'s loss, and on February 25 changed the status of the thirty-five men aboard the Laker from "missing in action on Dec. 7, 1941" to "presumed to be dead as of Dec. 7, 1942." Each crewmember's listed next of kin was notified of the change of status, though thirteen whose addresses were in the Philippines could not be contacted.

In addition to allowing family members to receive payouts on certain life insurance policies and at least partial payments of their loved one's back pay and allowances, the "presumptive finding of death" allowed the dependents of *Cynthia Olson*'s crewmembers to apply to the War Shipping Administration for reimbursement for the mariners' personal items lost in the Laker's sinking. The WSA made such payments out of a revolving war-risk insurance fund created pursuant to the 77th Congress's 1942 passage of Public Law 523. In the case of senior officers Carlsen, Buchtele, Johnstad, and Mills, the requested reimbursements were not inconsiderable sums, given that each man had taken aboard his own navigation books and instruments, dress uniforms, and other costly items.[31]

While the "presumptive finding of death" resulted in some financial assistance for the dependents of *Cynthia Olson* crewmembers, it was not the final word on the mariners' status in that the government did not issue official death certificates. In late 1946, as part of an ongoing postwar effort to finally resolve a vast backlog of wartime "missing in action" cases, the Casualty Section of the Adjutant General Office's Personnel Actions Branch initiated a comprehensive review of the *Cynthia Olson* case. Myrta Ethel Cawood, a veteran investigator in the Casualty Section's Status Review and Determination Sub-Section, undertook an exhaustive search for all pertinent records. Not only did she comb Army, Navy, and War Shipping Administration files in Washington, DC, she obtained documents from the Olson Company, Matson, the San Francisco Port of Embarkation, and the 12th, 13th, and 14th Naval Districts.

On March 11, 1947, Cawood submitted her "Reports of Death of Personnel of USAT 'Cynthia Olson'" to Lieutenant Colonel Earle M. Ewing, chief of the Casualty Branch. After reviewing the details of the charter agreement between the ATS and the Olson Company, and listing all known facts pertaining to the attack on the Laker and the subsequent disappearance of her crew, Cawood stated that

> An extended search has been made of Casualty records but no report after 7 December 1941 was ever received either on the USAT *Cynthia Olson* or any person known to have been on board. All available records—Casualty, Decimal Files, Confidential Files, Transportation Corps, Japanese Prisoner of War records, and the 201 files of the 35 individuals—fail to disclose the faintest trace of additional information as to the fate of the *Cynthia Olson* or its crew.[32]

Cawood recommended that her findings be accepted as the basis for

> an official report of death, and that casualty reports be issued stating that the two enlisted men and the 33 civilian employees of the Army Transport Service, Quartermaster Corps, USAT *Cynthia Olson* . . . were killed in action on 7 December 1941 in the Central Pacific Area as result of enemy submarine attack.[33]

Ewing's laconic response, "Approved: Action will be taken," was typed neatly on the report's final page just above his signature. His acceptance of Cawood's findings resulted over the following weeks in the issuance of official death certificates for all of the thirty-five men aboard *Cynthia Olson*, which in turn allowed the next of kin to apply for payments of any monies whose release had not been effected by the earlier "presumptive finding of death." And for many of the family members, the final death decree came not a moment too soon. As Cawood had pointed out in her report, as of the date she sent it forward to Ewing, the estates of only eleven of the men on board the Laker had been paid the amounts owed them under the provisions of Public Law 490, only two of the estates had received both life-insurance and personal-effects payments, and just six estates had gotten personal-effects payments only.

Ewing's signature on Cawood's report was thus intended to finally address all outstanding financial claims by all eligible family members of those who had by now been officially deemed to have died aboard *Cynthia Olson*. It did so, but the effort took far longer than the Casualty Branch had planned. Owing to a mix-up in addresses and the names of next of kin for crewman Sotero V. Cabigas, his Philippine-resident family members did not receive a final estate payment until June 1954, and then only after a six-month effort that required the intervention of the Army's Adjutant General's Office and the U.S. Army Finance Center in St. Louis, Missouri.

———

THE FAMILY MEMBERS OF *CYNTHIA OLSON*'s crewmen were not the only ones seeking financial compensation following the ship's disappearance. Almost immediately after being briefed on the contents of *Lurline*'s radio log during the second week of December 1941, Whitney and George Olson approached San Francisco ATS superintendent Mellon with questions about how the Army would reimburse the Olson Company for the loss of the vessel. Mellon, by this point inundated with the massive amounts of paperwork necessary to convert his ATS office to a wartime footing, asked the brothers to submit a formal invoice that could be passed up the chain of command.

The Olsons lost no time in producing the requested invoice, submitting it to Mellon during the second week of January 1942. The document likely took the ATS superintendent's breath away, for the Olsons asked for a total reimbursement of $346,600 for the twenty-three-year-old vessel. In support of their request, the brothers cited their original purchase price as $113,000 and noted that they'd spent an additional $69,000 on repairs and improvements. In addition, they pointed out that in May 1941 *Cynthia Olson*'s hull and machinery had been insured for $160,000, which was increased to $200,000 on November 19, 1941, as part of the ATS charter agreement. As required by that agreement, the Olson Company had prepaid the premiums for the entire six-month charter period, a total of $7,397.26, though the premiums did not figure in the Olsons' initial claim.[34]

Mellon passed the reimbursement request up the chain of command, noting in his transmittal letter that he considered the $346,600 figure "entirely too high for a vessel of [*Cynthia Olson*'s] age and condition." His superiors obviously agreed, for no reimbursement was immediately forthcoming. Indeed, as of June 1943 the Olsons' invoice was still "under review" by the Legal Office of the Transportation Corps' Water Division. On June 8 the Legal Office attorney dealing with the Olsons' claim issued a report upon which the ATS would base its counterproposal. It read, in part,

> It is also noted that the San Francisco Port of Embarkation, together with the Maritime Commission, have approved a valuation of $100.00 per dead weight ton for war risk insurance for this vessel.
>
> . . . It is the opinion of this Branch that a valuation of $100.00 per dead weight ton for the vessel in question is entirely too high, and in collaboration with the Maintenance and Repair Branch in the Water Division, it has been developed that the value carried in the charter party; namely, $200,000 for insurance purposes; is adequate and should be an equitable adjustment of the loss for all concerned.[35]

When notified of the government's counteroffer the Oliver J. Olson Company found it neither adequate nor equitable and refused to accept it. While the Olsons had their corporate hands full operating a number of ships on charter to both the Army and Navy, they nonetheless found time over the following two years to file repeated requests for reimbursement of the $346,600 they'd originally requested. By the spring of 1945, it had become all too clear that the U.S. government had no intention of meeting that figure, and in April the Oliver J. Olson Company filed suit in federal court in San Francisco against the Army Transport Service, claiming violation of the terms of the November 18, 1941, *Cynthia Olson* charter agreement.

Because the operation and insurance of all noncombatant civilian vessels chartered by the Army and Navy had become the responsibility of the War Shipping Administration following that agency's February 1942 creation, the Olsons' suit ultimately made its way to the WSA's Office of General Counsel. On June 2, 1945, Arthur M. Becker, the staff attorney tapped to oversee the agency's response to the suit, sent a telegram to the WSA's Los Angeles office:

> IN CONNECTION WITH THE DEFENSE OF SUIT ON SS CYNTHIA OLSON PLEASE SECURE AT EARLIEST CONVENIENCE COMPLETE ABSTRACT OF TITLE ON THIS VESSEL (EX COQUINA) FROM BUREAU OF CUSTOMS (HOME PORT SAN FRANCISCO) AND SEND IT TO UNITED STATES ATTORNEY SAN FRANCISCO FOR ATTENTION OF JUSTICE DEPARTMENTS ATTORNEY MR. COLBY AND SEND COPY THEREOF TO WSA IN WASHINGTON.[36]

The "Mr. Colby" to whom Becker referred was Leavenworth Colby, the Washington, DC–based chief of the Justice Department's Admiralty and Shipping Section. It would fall to him to actually litigate the case on the government's behalf, aided by Assistant Attorney General John F. Sonnett.

Given the pressing backlog of similar wartime cases waiting to be heard, the Olsons' suit did not come before the U.S. Court of Federal Claims in Washington until the spring of 1947. Once in court, the Olsons—represented by Alan B. Aldwell of the prestigious San Francisco law firm Brobeck, Phleger & Harrison[37]—not only maintained their initial claim for $364,600, they added to it the $7,397.26 in insurance premiums. In addition to reviewing the ship's operational and maintenance history from the time of her launching through the date of her disappearance, Aldwell—for reasons about which we can now only speculate—stated for the record that the Oliver J. Olson Company had originally purchased *Coquina* in 1930, a misstatement that was not challenged by the government. He then detailed the terms of the charter agreement and offered the testimony of an expert witness to support the Olsons' claim that the Laker's value at the time of her loss was not less than $325,000. Perhaps not coincidentally, the expert witness was none other than Captain A. F. Pillsbury, of the shipbrokers Pillsbury & Curtis, who in 1925 had purchased then-*Coquina* from the Emergency Fleet Corporation and in years thereafter orchestrated her repeated sales.

Colby, in his remarks, conceded the government's liability for *Cynthia Olson*'s loss. He also accepted without dispute Aldwell's recitation of the Laker's history and the plaintiff's interpretation of the government's responsibilities as laid out in the charter agreement. Indeed, Colby said, the sole issue to be decided was the value of *Cynthia Olson* on the day she was sunk. To that end, the government introduced its own expert witness—a "highly experienced ship surveyor" named Captain Jeans—who set the ship's value on December 7, 1941, at no more than $200,000. Colby also pointed out that because there were no sales of American-flag vessels of *Cynthia Olson*'s size and type in all of 1941, there was no clear evidence that would establish the Laker's fair-market value at the time of her destruction.

Having considered all the evidence, on May 5, 1947, the five-judge Court of Federal Claims rendered its written opinion:

Considering all the evidence and circumstances—including the intrinsic worth of the vessel, the demand for vessels of this type, the

onditions, the restricted market . . . and other pertinent
~e find that the fair and reasonable value of the *Cynthia*
December 7, 1941, was $222,000. . . . We think the plaintiff
ntitled to recover the amount expended by it for insurance,
as provided for the six-month period of the contract . . . in the sum of
$7,397.26, [for] a total of $229,397.26.[38]

While the final award was far less than the $371,997.26 for which the
Olson Company had brought suit, it was apparently an amount the shipping firm could accept. On May 9, Aldwell signed the necessary papers
agreeing to the judgment and accepted a check on the Olsons' behalf.

THE COURT OF FEDERAL CLAIMS judgment closed the book on *Cynthia
Olson* as far as her erstwhile owners were concerned, and the succession
of government decisions about the status of the men who'd sailed in her
helped their next of kin eventually achieve varying measures of financial
security and emotional acceptance. Yet no one—not owner, family member, attorney, or government official—had been able to solve the two basic,
underlying riddles of the *Cynthia Olson* incident: what really happened
to the ship on December 7, 1941, and, more importantly, what became of
her crew?

In 1966 a Hawaii-based newspaper editor named Riley H. Allen—an
eyewitness to the *Kido Butai*'s attack on Pearl Harbor and a man who pas-
sionately believed that the *Cynthia Olson* story might be able to shed new
light on the events of that dark day—decided it was time to start looking
for the answers to both questions.

Laid down in the summer of 1918, *Coquina* was one of 331 oceangoing freighters built for the U.S. Shipping Board for World War I service and one of 33 Design 1044 variants constructed by Wisconsin's Manitowoc Shipbuilding Company. The 1044's standard features—"three-island" silhouette, single stack, and masts fore and aft—are clearly visible in this January 1919 photo of the nearly completed *Coquina*. (*Wisconsin Maritime Museum*)

Coquina moves from the builder's yards toward Lake Michigan soon after completion in April 1919. Finished too late to see transport service in World War I, the vessel was laid up within sight of where she was built until chartered to the Philadelphia-based Earn Line Steamship Company. *Coquina* went on to haul miscellaneous cargo—including whiskey—between the U.S. East Coast, the West Indies, Panama, and the east coast of South America. Laid up in New York between 1921 and 1925, the Laker was ultimately sold to the San Francisco ship brokerage firm Pillsbury & Curtis. (*Wisconsin Maritime Museum*)

Coquina was purchased by San Francisco's Olson Steamship Company in April 1940 and renamed *Cynthia Olson*, and is seen here alongside a Pacific Northwest pier awaiting a cargo of lumber. The Laker subsequently made several coastwise voyages, usually under Captain P.C. Johnson, hauling some 2 million board feet of lumber on each passage. (*U.S. Army Heritage and Education Center*)

Arriving from Southern California to load a cargo of timber, *Cynthia Olson* maneuvers in the harbor at Coos Bay, Oregon. It was one of several West Coast ports the vessel frequented in the months leading up to its chartering by the Army. Note the Olson Line's large white "O" on her funnel. (*Coos Historical and Maritime Museum*)

Captain Berthel Carlsen's license clearly indicates the 64-year-old, Norwegian-born mariner's mastery of his trade. A veteran of both World War I and the postwar humanitarian-relief effort, Carlsen had sailed the Atlantic, Pacific, and Mediterranean. Though qualified to command any ship of any size on any ocean, he preferred smaller vessels such as the Olson Line's lumber carriers. (*National Archives*)

Born Wilhelm Buchtele Petersen in Vordingborg, Denmark, Berthel Carlsen's *Cynthia Olson* first mate had changed his name to William Petersen Buchtele upon his 1929 naturalization. He had known and sailed with Carlsen before embarking on *Cynthia Olson*'s final voyage. Both men were last-minute replacements for the vessel's usual master and mate. (*Courtesy Eleanor Beck Robinson*)

Only two years younger than his captain, Swedish-born chief engineer Konrad "Harry" Lofving was equally well qualified for his job. Despite his taciturn mien, he was a jovial and well-liked man who knew his ship inside and out. (*National Archives*)

While all of *Cynthia Olson*'s senior officers were native-born or naturalized Americans of European heritage, most of her crewmen were Filipinos. Many of them—including oiler Anastacio M. Atad—had previously served on the Army troopships that carried soldiers to and from peacetime garrison duty in Hawaii and the Philippines. (*National Archives*)

When *Cynthia Olson* sailed from Seattle on her final voyage she carried two soldiers—Privates Ernest J. Davenport and Samuel J. Ziskind—as part of her crew. "Dee" Davenport, a 24-year-old from North Carolina, had enlisted in the Army in 1939 and was trained as a medic. Before being assigned to the San Francisco Port of Embarkation—and, ultimately, as *Cynthia Olson's* sole medical practitioner—he'd spent time with the Hawaii-based 11th Medical Regiment. He's seen here during a quiet moment in the unit's sick-call office at Oahu's Schofield Barracks. (*Courtesy Loretta Phelps*)

The epitome of the worldly and street-savvy urbanite, Brooklyn-born Sam Ziskind enlisted in the Army in September 1940 to gain the training he'd need to snag a post-service job in the civilian radio broadcasting industry. Posted to San Francisco's Fort Mason in March 1941, he married Bernice Lerner the following June. The couple is seen here during an outing in Golden Gate Park just days after the wedding. (*Courtesy Inez Lerner Grover*)

In what may well be the last photograph taken of *Cynthia Olson* before her sinking, the ship steams slowly away from a Seattle pier, bound for the open sea and Hawaii. Though it's impossible to know for sure, the two figures on the starboard bridge wing may well be Captain Carlsen and First Mate Buchtele. (*Courtesy Eleanor Beck Robinson*)

Admiral Isoroku Yamamoto, commander in chief of the Imperial Japanese Navy's Combined Fleet and architect of the surprise assault on Pearl Harbor, tasked 27 submarines to undertake key roles in "Operation Hawaii." *I-26*'s role was initially to be a supporting one, reconnaissance of American installations in the Aleutian Islands, followed by the detection and interdiction of American vessels attempting to reach Hawaii after the Japanese attack. (*U.S. Naval History and Heritage Command*)

A B1-type fleet boat, *I-26* was designed to be a globe-circling reconnaissance platform and was one of the world's most advanced submarines when launched in November 1941. In addition to her torpedo and deck-gun armament, the vessel was capable of embarking a small floatplane, though none was aboard when she sailed on what became her first wartime voyage. (*U.S. Naval History and Heritage Command*)

Born in land-locked Okayama Prefecture in western Honshu, Minoru Yokota was admitted to the Imperial Japanese Naval Academy at age 17. Following his graduation in 1923 the young officer attended submarine school, and after progressing steadily through the ranks gained his first command in 1936. Three years later he was assigned the plum position of equipping officer for the as-yet-uncompleted *I-26* and was ultimately named the advanced submarine's first commanding officer. (*U.S. Naval History and Heritage Command*)

Yokota and several of his officers pose for an informal (and sadly unfocused) group photo. Widely known as a fair and relatively humane officer, *I-26*'s commander was nonetheless highly professional and extremely competitive. (*U.S. Naval History and Heritage Command*)

I-26's chief torpedoman, Takaji Komaba, was concerned that the 10 older torpedoes loaded aboard the submarine before it left Yokosuka wouldn't be capable of sinking heavily laden American cargo ships and their nimble escorts. (*U.S. Naval History and Heritage Command*)

Chief Gunner Saburo Hayashi's confidence in the lethality of I-26's 140mm deck gun was ultimately proved well-placed, though it took some 40 rounds to sink the buoyant lumber-carrier. (*U.S. Naval History and Heritage Command*)

As I-26's gunners were firing, Saburo Hayashi climbed to the highest point on the vessel's conning tower and took a picture of the now-burning *Cynthia Olson*. By this point the Laker's crew had taken to their two lifeboats (the empty davits are just visible) and moved well away from the stricken ship. (*U.S. Naval History and Heritage Command*)

Built in 1930 as a coastal passenger liner for Canadian National Steamships, *Prince Robert* was requisitioned for military service in 1939. Extensive modifications turned the vessel into one of the most powerful warships in the Royal Canadian Navy at the time of her July 1940 commissioning. In late 1941 *Prince Robert* helped move the Canadian "C" Force to Hong Kong, and it was while returning from that mission that the warship was tasked to search for *Cynthia Olson*. (*U.S. Naval History and Heritage Command*)

Matson Navigation's 18,163-ton *Lurline* had been a fixture on the California-to-Hawaii passenger route since soon after her 1933 maiden voyage. The liner's departure from Honolulu was delayed by the need to take aboard military dependents being evacuated from Hawaii; therefore, she was less than 350 miles south of *Cynthia Olson* when radio operator Leslie Grogan picked up Sam Ziskind's distress SOS/SSS message. (*U.S. Naval History and Heritage Command*)

Master mariner and commodore of the Matson Line, Charles A. Berndtson had been extensively briefed about the possibility of hostile Japanese actions in the Pacific before he took his vessel to sea from Honolulu. Any inclination he might have had to divert *Lurline* toward the Army lumber transport vanished immediately upon being notified of the attack on Pearl Harbor. In accordance with standing orders, he blacked out his ship and raced for safety in San Francisco. (*U.S. Naval History and Heritage Command*)

White House press secretary Stephen Early made the U.S. government's first official reference to the attack on *Cynthia Olson*, when at 3:20 EST on December 7 he told print and radio reporters gathered in his office that President Franklin Roosevelt had just received a dispatch reporting the "torpedoing of an Army transport, 1,300 miles west of San Francisco." Within minutes of Early's statement the news of the lumber transport's plight was being broadcast on both NBC and CBS radio. (*Courtesy of the Franklin D. Roosevelt Library and Museum, Hyde Park, New York*)

First Lady Eleanor Roosevelt was the first of the White House's occupants to publicly mention the attack on *Cynthia Olson*. On the December 7 broadcast of her regular Sunday evening radio program "Current Events" she spoke of the "...sinking of one of our transports loaded with lumber on its way to Hawaii." (*Courtesy of the Franklin D. Roosevelt Library and Museum, Hyde Park, New York*)

At 12:30 p.m. EST on December 8 President Franklin D. Roosevelt delivered his now-famous "Day of Infamy" speech to a joint session of the U.S. Congress. His brief mention of the torpedoing of American ships "...on the high seas between San Francisco and Honolulu..." ensured that the story of the thus-far anonymous lumber transport remained in the news in the days following the speech and Congress' subsequent declaration of war. (*Courtesy of the Franklin D. Roosevelt Library and Museum, Hyde Park, New York*)

Cynthia Olson was not the only victim to fall prey to Minoru Yokota and *I-26*. In June 1942 the Japanese skipper and his crew sank the American freighter *Coast Trader* off Washington state's Cape Flattery, and the following August inflicted minor damage on the aircraft carrier USS *Saratoga* in the Solomon Islands. In November 1942 *I-26* sank the light cruiser USS *Juneau* during the First Naval Battle of Guadalcanal. The already damaged American warship sank within 20 seconds, and only 10 members of her 700-man crew were ultimately rescued. (*U.S. Naval History and Heritage Command*)

Editor of the Honolulu *Star-Bulletin* since 1912, Riley H. Allen was arguably Hawaii's best-known and best-connected newspaperman. Long interested in the *Cynthia Olson* story, his 1947 speech to the Hawaii Social Science Association included most of the information then known about the vessel's demise. His 1966 suggestion that reporter Alf Pratte "follow up on that story" led to the latter's multipart *Star-Bulletin* article. (*Hawaii State Library*)

As a 35-year-old Naval Reserve officer working in Tokyo immediately after the war, historian Gordon W. Prange located and secured historically valuable Japanese military records. As the civilian head of General Douglas MacArthur's historical section, Prange interviewed hundreds of former Japanese military and naval officers—including Minoru Yokota. The historian was the first to hear the former sub captain's account of *Cynthia Olson*'s demise. (*Courtesy of the Gordon W. Prange Collection, University of Maryland Libraries*)

After the war, and following the death of his first wife, Minoru Yakota converted to Christianity. He ultimately married a widow named Hasegawa, took her last name, and raised her three daughters as his own. Here he is seen (bottom row, far right) in a late 1950s family photo with his wife, mother in law, the daughters and their husbands. (*Courtesy Philip Z. Hirai, via Isamu Murahashi*)

Oregon-based photographer and local historian Bert Webber corresponded with and met Minoru Yokota/Hasegawa and several of *I-26*'s wartime crewmembers, and included the *Cynthia Olson* story in several editions of his book dealing with Japan's World War II attacks on the U.S. West Coast. (*Hoover Institution Library and Archives*)

PART TWO

PART TWO

CHAPTER 9

REBIRTH OF A MYSTERY

ON THE EVENING OF MONDAY, November 3, 1947, Riley Harris Allen rose from his chair in the crowded meeting room of a hotel just off Honolulu's Waikiki Beach. He walked briskly to a lectern set atop a low stage at the front of the room, absentmindedly shuffled the sheaf of typewritten pages in his left hand, and prepared to give the keynote talk at the monthly meeting of the Hawaii Social Science Association.

It was a familiar venue for Allen, the sixty-three-year-old editor of the *Star-Bulletin*, one of Honolulu's two highly competitive daily newspapers.[1] Widely known for both his public-speaking skills and his encyclopedic knowledge of Hawaii's history, culture, and politics, he was a longtime association member and a frequent—and popular—speaker at its gatherings. He was also arguably Hawaii's best-known and best-connected newspaperman; he'd been editor of the *Star-Bulletin* since 1912 and personally knew nearly every leading political, social, commercial, and military leader in the territory.

The audience that night knew only that he would speak about some aspect of World War II, and many assumed it would have to do with the activities of both the editor and his newspaper on December 7, 1941. Allen had been at his desk since 6:00 that Sunday morning, as was his custom every day of the week, and was the only member of the *Star-Bulletin*'s editorial staff in the building. When the first bombs began to fall on Pearl

137

Harbor Allen quickly began calling in every available staffer, and over the course of the day the paper put out three special editions.[2] Following the U.S. declaration of war Allen ensured that the *Star-Bulletin* spoke often and loudly in support of the rights of Hawaii's citizens of Japanese descent, and when the tide in the Pacific began to turn in America's favor after the June 1942 Battle of Midway his was among the loudest voices speaking in favor of a speedy end to military rule in the territory.[3]

As it turned out, however, the gathered members of the Social Science Association were to hear Allen's thoughts on a new and, to most of those present that November evening, completely unknown topic. He had titled his speech "A Footnote to the History of World War II: First Shot of the War in the Pacific,"[4] and in his introductory remarks Allen acknowledged that his topic might at first seem of little importance:

> In such a colossal phenomenon as war, inevitably there are thousands, millions of unrecorded deeds, witnessed by only a few minor actors on the global stage, unrecognized by the narrators of broadly outlined history for the generations to come. . . . In modern warfare . . . many an event . . . disappears into the already clogged records, perhaps never to be resurrected. . . . Days and weeks and months and years go by. . . . And unless by some odd chance brought to public attention, it remains in the vast bourne which like some lonely, musty library, buries in accumulating dust the written records and the memories of events that once meant life and death of human beings.[5]

Pausing briefly for effect, he then dropped something of a bombshell:

> It is of such an event that I speak tonight—the story of a tragedy, an attack at sea—which, given only brief reference at the time because of military secrecy may yet, if fully described and documented, change the opening chapter of World War II in the Pacific.[6]

Having skillfully grabbed his audience's attention, Allen went on to say that the incident of which he was about to speak

> does not appear in any popular history. It is not, so far as I know, in the voluminous report of the Roberts Commission,[7] or the far more

extensive report of the joint Pearl Harbor Investigating Committee of Congress—a report comprising 40 volumes, and measuring, on our *Star-Bulletin* library shelves, three and one-half linear feet.[8]

Allen was talking, of course, of the attack on *Cynthia Olson*, and he went on to give his listeners the essential facts of her story. Initially referring to the ship as "a small schooner," he briefly outlined her history, said she was crewed by "31 officers and men," and traced her intended route from Tacoma to Honolulu.[9] He then spoke of *Lurline*'s interception of *Cynthia Olson*'s distress signal and of how that message was passed by Globe Wireless to the proper Navy authorities in San Francisco.

Allen then did something highly unusual for a professional newsman— he confessed a certain level of ignorance. He admitted that during the war years he'd never heard of *Cynthia Olson*'s disappearance, despite the fact that the story of the missing "Army lumber transport" had been widely mentioned on radio and in print in the first days after the Pearl Harbor attack and the ship's name had been released to the public as early as February 1942. He said, in fact, that he'd only learned of the freighter's story in December 1946, when a few brief sentences in a fairly routine corporate news release caught his eye:

On Saturday, December 7, 1946, fifth anniversary of the [Pearl Harbor] attack, Globe Wireless issued a statement at San Francisco announcing the reopening of its Mussel Rock station—which had been taken over by and operated for the Navy during the war. In this statement it is said that "Operators on duty at KTK [Mussel Rock's call letters] that ill-fated Sunday morning (Dec. 7, 1941) heard what was probably the first overt act of the war, inasmuch as it occurred prior to the onslaught of the planes at Pearl Harbor. . . . A few minutes later the Globe Wireless marine station at Honolulu reported that Pearl Harbor was under attack."[10]

Having personally witnessed the *Kido Butai*'s devastation of Pearl Harbor, Allen was fascinated by the idea that Japan's first shot of the Pacific war might actually have been aimed at *Cynthia Olson*.[11] So fascinated, he told his audience, that immediately upon reading the Globe Wireless release he'd jumped wholeheartedly into researching what was thus far known about the lumber freighter's loss. In his quest for information he contacted both Rudy Asplund and Commodore Berndtson, as well as Globe Wireless, the Army's Adjutant General's office, and Captain John B. Heffernan, director of Naval Records and Library.

While Allen said in his presentation that "The available records of Globe Wireless bear out this belief that the attack on the *Cynthia Olsen* [sic] preceded that of the carrier planes on Oahu," he added that Heffernan had informed him, in a "very courteous letter," that Navy records thus far available "do not bear out the theory that the attack . . . was the first gunfire from the Japanese in the history of World War II in the Pacific." The Navy's position, Heffernan said, was that "the Japanese submarine had attacked and sunk the *Cynthia Olsen* [sic] at 8:08 Honolulu time, 13 minutes *after* the first bombs fell on Pearl Harbor."[12]

Dogged reporter that he was, Allen did not accept Heffernan's statement at face value or as the last word on the timing of the attack on *Cynthia Olson*. He continued to dig and presented the few facts then known in several short *Star-Bulletin* articles in 1946. But, as he told the gathered members of the Social Science Association,

> the record is not complete—that is, the record as publicly known.
> . . . Neither the log of the *Lurline* that Sunday morning nor the log of the Globe Wireless station is available. Each was taken into official custodianship and each was classed as top drawer secret during the years of World War II. . . . Fixing the exact time of the attack . . . must therefore await the opening of official records still sealed to the public.[13]

And why, Allen rhetorically asked his listeners, was it so important to determine the Laker's fate? He said, in essence, that there were three reasons.

First, if the Japanese submarine (whose identity was not yet known outside the Office of Naval Intelligence) fired on the freighter before the beginning of the Pearl Harbor raid it would be Japan's first shot of World War II in the Pacific, and *Cynthia Olson* would hold the historical distinction of being the first American vessel attacked by Japan in that conflict. Second, and perhaps more important, if the attack on the lumber transport actually occurred almost an hour *before* the Pearl Harbor raid, might not the news "have stirred the armed forces to complete alertness and shocked the nation to immediate action,"[14] thus possibly changing the course of the war?

And as he began winding up his speech, Allen pointed out that newspapermen and historians weren't the only ones interested in learning the truth about *Cynthia Olson*'s demise:

> On April 1 of this year I had a letter from the widow of the *Cynthia Olsen*'s [sic] skipper.
>
> Mrs. Thyra Carlsen wrote me from Oakland, California, having seen in our newspaper a brief story about the incident. She, too, had been informed that the call sent from her husband's vessel preceded the attack on Pearl Harbor, but no official records to verify it.
>
> She is today awaiting, with sad anticipation, the full telling of the story—the story which, for her, really ended when the little transport went to the bottom carrying with it, presumably, all the officers and men.[15]

By the time Allen stepped down from the podium on that night in 1947 he'd raised, but not answered, three important questions. When did the attack on *Cynthia Olson* actually occur? Could news of the attack have prevented the carnage at Pearl Harbor? And, finally, what happened to the Laker's crew? The questions were important both because the answers could well change the history of World War II in the Pacific, and—on a far more personal and emotional level—because thirty-five men remained unaccounted for.

As it happened, no one—not journalists, historians, or next of kin— would find quick or easy answers to the questions raised by *Cynthia Olson*'s disappearance. Indeed, Allen's talk on that balmy Hawaiian night would be the last public discourse on the ship's fate for almost twenty years. And, fittingly perhaps, when the discussion finally began again, it would be Riley Allen who revived it.

———

THAT NEARLY TWO DECADES ELAPSED before Allen and the *Star-Bulletin* again took up the *Cynthia Olson* story did not imply any diminution of the legendary editor's interest in answering the three questions he'd raised before the Social Science Association. Rather, it was simply a reflection of how busy—and turbulent—Allen's personal and professional lives were in the years following the November 1947 speech.

Soon after that event the editor's beloved wife of thirty-seven years, Suzanne, a former opera singer, was diagnosed with an illness that led to her death in July 1950.[16] And as if that personal tragedy weren't enough, the 1954 passing of *Star-Bulletin* general manager Joseph R. Farrington— son of the paper's founder and since 1943 an influential member of the U.S. House of Representatives—sparked a bitter battle for ownership and control of the newspaper between Farrington's sister and his wife, Betty. Allen tried to remain neutral in the long and drawn-out legal squabble, instead focusing his editorial attention on such things as supporting Hawaii's statehood and arguing against the establishment of legalized gambling in the islands. Betty Farrington's eventual success in gaining control of the newspaper had the unintended effect of ending her close friend Allen's forty-eight-year tenure as editor, for her appointment of him as a trustee of the Farrington estate ultimately required him to relinquish all participation in the paper's editorial activities, and he retired from the *Star-Bulletin* in 1960.[17]

Yet despite the upheavals in his life, or perhaps as a counter to them, Allen had continued his own personal research into the *Cynthia Olson* story. Over the years he corresponded with a variety of people—including crewmembers and passengers who'd been aboard *Lurline* on that fateful December 1941 voyage, historians in both the United States and Japan, and family members of some of the men who'd perished aboard the Laker. On occasional trips to the mainland he searched for useful information in Matson's historical files, Army and Navy records, and in the morgues of such newspapers as the Seattle *Post-Intelligencer* and the San Francisco *Chronicle*.[18] Indeed, after his 1960 retirement what had initially been a diverting hobby became something of an obsession, and Allen eventually found a way to get his search for answers to his three *Cynthia Olson* questions back into the public eye.

While his status as a trustee of the Farrington estate ostensibly kept Allen out of the *Star-Bulletin*'s newsroom, it in no way reduced his considerable influence in the paper's boardroom. His close friendship with Betty Farrington and the fact that his handpicked successor, William Ewing, now filled the editor's chair ensured that his editorial and political views continued to shape much of the paper's tone and content. Among the stories Allen frequently put forth for Ewing's consideration was that of *Cynthia Olson*, but it took a chance meeting between Allen and a young *Star-Bulletin* reporter to finally get the subject slotted into the paper's editorial calendar.

In early 1966 Canadian-born Alf Pratte was pursuing a master's degree in journalism from the University of Hawaii while working full-time as a general-assignment reporter at the *Star-Bulletin*. He decided to do his thesis on the history of the newspaper and interviewed Allen—by now suffering from a terminal illness—as part of his background research.

"Before I left I said, 'Mr. Allen, is there anything else you'd like to tell me before I go?'" Pratte recalled in an interview with the author.[19] Allen's eyes lit up as he mentioned his interest in the *Cynthia Olson* story and his 1947 talk before the Social Science Association.

"He said, 'Alfie, why don't you follow up on that story? There's a lot more that could be done with it, and I'd like you to do it,'" Pratte remembered. "When I got back to the *Star-Bulletin* I talked with my editor, Bud Smiser, about the idea of doing the story. Bud had been in Hawaii a long time, and he said he'd heard about the ship, but that as far as he knew, nobody had done an in-depth story about it."

Pratte's editors decided that he should indeed do a multipart series on *Cynthia Olson*'s disappearance. The articles would attempt to answer the three questions Allen posed in 1947, and the series was slated to run beginning on December 3, 1966, just before the twenty-fifth anniversary of the Pearl Harbor attack. Pratte was told to do regular reporting every day until noon, after which he was to devote the rest of each workday to the ship's story. The young reporter jumped into the task with gusto.

Using Allen's research as a starting point, Pratte began by contacting the history branches of both the Army and the Navy, requesting copies of any and all official documents relating to *Cynthia Olson*. He was especially interested in obtaining a copy of *Lurline*'s voyage radio log—the one confiscated in San Francisco by Navy Lieutenant Commander Preston Allen on December 10, 1941—knowing that it could very possibly answer the question of exactly when the attack on the Laker occurred. Unfortunately, Pratte's hopes regarding the quick rediscovery of the radio log were soon dashed. In a June 12 letter to the reporter that accompanied photocopies of the few pertinent documents held by the Navy, Dr. Dean C. Allard, a staffer[20] in the Naval History Division in Washington, DC, said he had contacted the Federal Communications Commission

> regarding the radio logs you mention. The Commission tells us that logs dating from 1941 have been removed from their records and destroyed. There is a possibility, however, that the parent company has copies.[21]

The "parent company" to which Allard referred was, of course, Matson Navigation. Pratte had contacted the firm earlier requesting a range of information, including a copy of the radio log, only to hear the same news regarding the latter document: Matson did not have a copy, and the FCC had destroyed the original. Disappointed but undeterred, Pratte had reached out to one of the key people involved in compiling the log— Rudy Asplund—hoping he might be able to provide a new lead. Though *Lurline*'s former chief radio operator had said he could no longer remember when the first distress message was received from *Cynthia Olson* and did not have a copy of the log, he told Pratte that his erstwhile assistant, Leslie Grogan, believed the original log had not been destroyed and even claimed to know its whereabouts. Understandably excited by this bit of news, Pratte had asked his editors to contact the *Star-Bulletin*'s San Francisco bureau chief to ask his help. The resultant teletype message, sent June 7, read, in part,

> ASPLUND ADVISES THAT HE BELIEVES LESLIE E GROGAN OF 13 BELFORD DRIVE, DALY CITY[22] WHO WAS IN RADIO SHACK OF LURL THAT MORNING, HAS LOCATED THE LURL LOG X WLD U PLS . . . CALL OR WRITE GROGAN TO SEE IF HE HAS LOCATED LOG X STAR-BULLETIN PARTICULARLY ANXIOUS TO GET TIME MESSAGE FROM CYNTHIA OLSON RECEIVED BY LURL X IF GROGAN NO HELP PLS ASK HIM IF ANYONE BESIDES HE AND ASPLUND WERE IN RADIO ROOM WHEN MESSAGE RECEIVED X.[23]

It seems highly unlikely that Grogan actually had a lead on the original log; he had most probably been spinning a self-aggrandizing yarn for Asplund's benefit. In any event, when contacted by the *Star-Bulletin*'s San Francisco bureau chief, the former Matson radio operator was unable to provide either the radio log or any useful information about its fate.

Disappointed yet again, Pratte tried one more tack. After locating and corresponding with Ray Ferrill, the KTK radio operator who'd picked up *Lurline*'s initial notification of *Cynthia Olson*'s distress call, he attempted to locate the station's incoming message logs for December 7, 1941. Sadly, the reporter's hopes were again dashed—the logbooks had apparently been destroyed in the late 1950s following Globe Wireless's absorption by the World Communications Company, a New York–based subsidiary of the sprawling International Telephone & Telegraph Corp.

Though repeatedly stymied in his search for radio logs that would help him determine the time of the attack, Pratte had far better luck when he went looking for people either directly involved in the event or who were relatives of *Cynthia Olson*'s crewmen. "I got a lot of the names from Riley Allen's research, and one person led to another," Pratte recalled.[24] In addition to *Lurline*'s Berndtson, Asplund, and Grogan and Globe Wireless's Ferrill, the reporter corresponded with Thyra Carlsen; C. M. Dodd, brother of ATS quartermaster Roland Dodd; and Arra J. Woods, aunt of Third Officer James Mills. Ms. Woods, a spry eighty-year-old by the time she spoke with Pratte, told the reporter that she had never been officially notified of her nephew's status, despite the fact that she was his official next of kin. And, in an oddly touching aside, she told Pratte that the thirty-six-year-old Mills had taken a canoe aboard the Laker for later use in Hawaii.

As difficult and time-consuming as his research into the *Cynthia Olson* story was, Alf Pratte was fortunate in that many details not available to Riley Allen in 1947 had since come to light. And in October 1966 Pratte uncovered two pieces of information that proved just how lucky he was. While poring over a belated answer to an inquiry he'd made to the historian of the 13th Naval District, the reporter came across two startling nuggets—the identity of the submarine that sank *Cynthia Olson* and the name of the Japanese vessel's captain.

———

WHILE ATTACKING *CYNTHIA OLSON* HAD been entirely in line with the orders Minoru Yokota received before taking *I-26* to sea, the sub captain and his crew were anxious to find prey more important to the Allied war effort than a lowly lumber freighter. Believing he'd have a better chance of locating more lucrative targets closer to the U.S. West Coast, Yokota set an eastward course almost immediately after turning *I-26* away from the burning, listing, and obviously doomed Laker.[25] For three days he gradually zigzagged his way in the general direction of San Francisco, hoping to stumble across a major warship or heavily laden tanker. But he found no targets and was on the verge of shifting his search farther south when, on December 10, he received an electrifying message from Vice Admiral Shimizu.

The 6th Fleet commander was broadcasting from aboard his flagship, *Katori*, which by this time was anchored in the vast lagoon at Kwajalein in the Marshall Islands. He reported that at 8:40 a.m., local time, on December 9, Lieutenant Commander Michimune Inaba of the Submarine Squadron 1 boat *I-6*, patrolling the Kauai Channel southwest of Oahu, had sighted a U.S. Navy *Lexington*-class aircraft carrier and two cruisers heading northeast from the Hawaiian Islands, apparently bound for a West Coast port. Shimizu's message directed *I-26* and all other Submarine Squadron 2 boats to immediately locate and attack the carrier and her escorts. Yokota plotted the American ships' most likely track between Hawaii and both San Diego and San Francisco, then spent the next four days fruitlessly attempting to intercept the enemy vessels.[26]

On December 14 *I-26* was one of nine submarines ordered to take up station just off the U.S. West Coast and attack any shipping they might encounter. Yokota's assigned patrol area was the waters off Washington's Cape Flattery and the entrance to the Strait of Juan de Fuca, but even as he shaped a course for the Pacific Northwest the Japanese skipper received a message from IJN headquarters that instructed him and the commanders of the other subs to undertake a coordinated surface attack on the night of December 25. Each sub was to fire thirty deck-gun rounds at targets such as harbor facilities, coastal defenses, bridges, and oil refineries, then attack any ships that came looking for them. *I-26* arrived off Cape Flattery on December 20, but two days later Admiral Yamamoto postponed the attack until December 27. However, by the night of December 26, most of the subs assigned to the attack were running perilously short of fuel, so 6th Fleet commander Shimizu canceled the operation and ordered all nine boats to make for the anchorage at Kwajalein.

I-26 reached the Marshall Islands on January 11, 1942, with her fuel tanks almost empty. Over the following weeks Yokota and his crew labored to get their boat back into fighting trim, a process that was rudely interrupted on February 11 when aircraft from USS *Enterprise* raided Kwajalein, damaging *Katori* and several other vessels. *I-26* escaped harm by submerging at her anchorage until the American attackers departed. Over the following months Yokota and *I-26* took part in a variety of operations, including supporting the unsuccessful March 5 Japanese flying boat attack on Pearl Harbor.[27] The submarine then returned to Yokosuka for a much-needed overhaul and was still in dry-dock on April 18 when a U.S. Army Air Forces B-25B Mitchell light bomber flown by Lieutenant Edgar E. McElroy attacked the naval base as part of the famed "Doolittle Raid" launched from the carrier USS *Hornet*. *I-26* was not damaged in the attack, and on May 11 she departed Yokosuka for a familiar destination: the entrance to the Strait of Juan de Fuca.

As on her first voyage, *I-26* headed north after leaving Japan. Reassigned to Submarine Squadron 1 and operating in company with Commander Meiji Tagami's *I-25*, Yokota reconnoitered Kodiak and several nearby Alaskan islands in preparation for the Japanese invasion of Attu and Kiska, though by the time the landings took place on June 6 and 7 *I-26* was already patrolling some thirty-five miles southwest of Cape Flattery. It was there, on Sunday, June 7, that Yokota and his men found and sank their second victim.[28] Peering through his periscope, the Japanese sub captain must have had a sense of déjà vu—though not a Laker, the 3,286-ton freighter SS *Coast Trader* had the same "three-island" silhouette as *Cynthia Olson*. And there were other parallels, though Yokota couldn't have been aware of them at the time. Built in 1920 and owned by the Coastwise Line, the 324-foot-long vessel had been under Army charter since just after Pearl Harbor, and when spotted by *I-26* she was carrying timber products—some 1,250 tons of newsprint—from Port Angeles, Washington, to San Francisco.

Given his proximity to the U.S. mainland, Yokota elected to attack with torpedoes rather than his deck gun and made no attempt to stop the vessel first to allow Captain Lyle Havens and his fifty-five-man crew to take to the lifeboats. Just after 2:00 p.m., local time, the Japanese skipper ordered Lieutenant Satô to fire a single "Sixth Year" torpedo, which almost to the surprise of the Japanese submariners ran straight and true, hitting the freighter in her starboard side, aft of the midships house. The explosion caused massive damage, killed the ship's engine, and created an immediate list that prevented the vessel's Army gun crew from engaging the enemy sub. Havens, realizing his ship was doomed, ordered everyone into the boats and all—save one man who died from exposure—were rescued over the next two days by the fishing boat *Virginia I* and the Royal Canadian Navy corvette HMCS *Edmunston*.

Buoyed by their success, the men of *I-26* spent the next thirteen days attempting to recreate it. They were unable to locate a suitable target, however, and Yokota ultimately decided that there were other ways to inflict damage on the enemy. Just after 10:00 p.m., local time, on the night of June 20 he surfaced the boat some three thousand yards off the Estevan Point lighthouse on the west coast of Vancouver Island, and over the next thirty minutes his gunners fired nearly a score of 5.5-inch rounds at the structure. It was not the Japanese sailors' best example of marksmanship, however, for though the concussion of the exploding shells broke the lighthouse's windows, the gunners failed to actually hit the one-hundred-foot-tall tower or any of its associated structures. The attack—the first enemy shelling of Canadian soil since 1812—was not a complete failure, though; the Canadian government's subsequent decision to extinguish the light caused significant disruptions to shipping in the approaches to the Strait of Juan de Fuca.

I-26 did not fire her weapons again for just over a month, but when she did her target was vastly more important and her aim far better. By the last day of August the submarine was operating far from British Columbia, off Espíritu Santo in the New Hebrides, as part of the Japanese task force battling U.S. Navy units in the aftermath of the August 7 American invasion of Guadalcanal. Just after midnight on September 1 Yokota surfaced the boat to recharge her batteries, and almost as soon as his lookouts reached their perches atop the conning tower they sighted the lights of what quickly proved to be several American ships. Yokota ordered a crash dive, then spent several hours playing a potentially lethal game of cat and mouse with American escort ships. When *I-26* surfaced at about 6:30 a.m. the U.S. vessels were nowhere to be seen, though scarcely an hour later the lookout manning the sub's night binoculars sighted a very large ship at a range of about a mile and a half. A quick look convinced Yokota that he was looking at a *Lexington*-class carrier, and as he ordered the decks cleared for diving, he was already formulating his attack plan.

Once at periscope depth Yokota quickly determined the target's course and speed, and to his deep disappointment realized that he would not be able to set up a firing solution on the carrier before it moved out of range. Just as he was about to admit defeat the target and her escorts changed course back toward him, and Yokota ordered the forward tubes readied. When the carrier, which by this point the Japanese sub skipper had identified as *Saratoga*, was within one thousand yards, Yokota ordered Satô to fire a six-torpedo spread, only to be told there had been some sort of malfunction. By the time the issue was resolved *Saratoga* had changed course again, and Yokota had no choice but to try to maneuver back into firing position. He did so by 7:46 a.m., at which point he fired the six torpedoes and immediately took his ship down to her maximum depth of 330 feet. Barely two minutes later, as *I-26* was making off at flank speed, Yokota and his crewmen felt the satisfying concussion of a torpedo hit. Though the Japanese were certain they'd crippled or even doomed the carrier, *Saratoga* suffered no casualties and was only slightly damaged by the torpedo. She was back in action after repairs at Pearl Harbor.

I-26's next victim did not get off so lightly. Just before noon on November 13, 1942, the submarine sighted the American cruisers *San Francisco*, *Helena*, and *Juneau*. All three had been damaged before dawn that morning in the wild melee that historians would later call the First Naval Battle of Guadalcanal and were limping toward Espíritu Santo for initial repairs.[29] Seeing a once-in-a-lifetime opportunity, Yokota quickly fired a spread of three torpedoes.[30] *San Francisco* and *Helena* both escaped unscathed, but one of the weapons slammed into *Juneau*, detonating on her port side, midships, in the exact spot where she'd been hit in the earlier surface battle. The torpedo ignited a massive explosion in the damaged cruiser's main magazine, and the effect was both immediate and catastrophic: *Juneau* was blown in half and sank within minutes. Fearing further Japanese attacks— and in keeping with standing orders—the captains of *San Francisco* and *Helena* did not stop their vessels to rescue survivors, of whom there were about one hundred out of the now-vanished ship's seven-hundred-man complement. Rescue forces did not return for more than a week, and by the time they did sharks and exposure had killed all but ten of those who had survived the sinking.[31]

After helping to evacuate Japanese troops from Guadalcanal *I-26* went on to participate in the March 1943 Battle of the Bismarck Sea, and the following month found her patrolling off the east coast of Australia. It was a good hunting ground for Yokota and his men; during an April 11 attack on a convoy southeast of Cape Howe, Victoria, they sank the 4,732-ton Yugo-slav freighter *Recina*, and on April 13, they destroyed the 2,125-ton steamer *Kowarra* (another dead ringer for *Cynthia Olson*) of Australia's Howard Smith Line off Queensland's Sandy Cape. After surviving a particularly determined depth-charge attack by a Royal New Zealand Air Force Hud-son patrol bomber off Suva, Fiji, in June, *I-26* returned to Yokosuka near the end of August for a much-needed yard period.

Soon after seeing his boat safely into dry-dock, Minoru Yokota received orders to pass command of *I-26* to Lieutenant Commander Toshio Kusaka and take up a position on the staff of Submarine Squadron 1.[32] That job was only temporary, however, for the IJN had bigger things in mind for the man credited with sinking *Juneau*. Barely six weeks after leaving *I-26* Yokota was named equipping officer of *I-44*, a Type B-2 boat laid down in June 1942 and nearing completion at Yokosuka's Naval Arsenal.[33] Though outwardly identical to *I-26* and the other *I-15*-class vessels, *I-44* and the five other *I-40*-class B-2s built as part of the IJN's Maru Kyū Pro-gram[34] were constructed of higher-quality steel and had diesel engines of a simpler and more economical design.[35] Yokota shepherded the new sub through her fitting-out and was officially named her commander on the day of her commissioning, January 31, 1944.

Though Yokota hoped to use the new submarine to wreak havoc on Allied shipping, his eight months in command of *I-44* were a decided let-down.[36] Not only did two war patrols fail to produce a single victory, on the second voyage *I-44* herself very nearly became a casualty. On May 27, 1944, while running on the surface near New Ireland in the Bismarck Archipelago, the Japanese submarine was jumped by an Allied aircraft. The attacker, who had not been detected by *I-44*'s Type 13 air-search radar, managed to score several near misses with bombs before Yokota crash-dived the sub. *I-44* was then set upon by patrol boats vectored in by the aircraft, and over the next harrowing hours Yokota and his crew endured a merciless depth-charging that left their vessel heavily damaged and tak-ing on water. After determining that the attackers had moved on, Yokota surfaced his stricken ship only to find that he could not dive again. The nine-day voyage back to Kure was thus made entirely on the surface, and several radar sightings of Allied aircraft along the way ensured that nei-ther captain nor crew got much sleep.

Upon *I-44*'s return to Japan Yokota oversaw her extensive repairs, and on September 16 he relinquished command of the submarine to

Lieutenant Commander Genbei Kawaguchi. After more temporary staff work Yokota was "kicked upstairs," becoming the commanding officer of Submarine Division 52 on July 20, 1945, and in the process gaining promotion to captain. It was a short-lived billet, of course, for World War II in the Pacific was rapidly coming to an end. The atomic bombings of Hiroshima and Nagasaki on August 6 and 9, respectively, led Emperor Hirohito to accept the inevitability of defeat. In a recorded August 15 radio address he announced to his people that Japan had accepted the Allies' demand for unconditional surrender, adding that a cease-fire would go into effect immediately.[37]

Yokota, like the vast majority of his countrymen, was shocked by the capitulation. Though happy and somewhat surprised that he'd survived the conflict—both *I-26* and *I-44* had ultimately been lost with all hands[38]—he was dismayed by the rapid change in his own circumstances; from respected and highly decorated naval officer he was reduced within a matter of weeks to being both penniless and jobless. He later recalled of that period,

> I was confused and in despair. I had lost my home to firebombing; I did not have any vocational skills; I didn't have the courage to take my own life; I was a fish out of water who was not able to do anything, so I just moved in with my elder brother in the house of my birth. I was thinking that I could borrow a room and work as a farmer, but even this plan didn't work out.[39]

To add to his difficulties, Yokota was among hundreds of former Japanese naval officers interrogated by Allied war-crimes investigators in the months following the surrender. The IJN had participated in many of the worst atrocities committed against Allied combatants and civilians during the war—a topic we shall later examine in greater detail—and as both a former sub captain and senior IJN staff officer Yokota was closely questioned about his own wartime actions and those of others. The U.S. Navy had not at that point completed the process of collating the names of Allied vessels sunk by Japanese submarines with the identities of either the subs or their commanders, so it is unclear whether either *Cynthia Olson* or *Juneau* came up during the questioning.

While the records of Yokota's interrogation have not survived, we can assume he must not have been under suspicion at that point, for on

January 3, 1946, "the fish out of water" was offered the chance to go back to sea. Much to his surprise, Yokota was recalled to service and told he was to captain a warship.

Japan's capitulation had left hundreds of thousands of the nation's service members stranded throughout Southeast Asia and the Pacific. In the months immediately following the surrender, Tokyo—under the supervision of the Allied occupation authorities—put together an ambitious plan to repatriate Japanese military personnel as quickly as possible. The remnants of the former Imperial Japanese Navy were tapped to play the primary role in the repatriation effort, and dozens of surviving warships were hastily converted into crude passenger vessels. One of the ships so converted was the light cruiser *Kashima*, one of two sisters to *Katori*, the erstwhile flagship of the IJN's submarine fleet. After having the barrels of all her main guns cut off and with the addition of a deckhouse constructed around her main mast, the ship departed on October 10, 1945, on what was to be the first of twelve repatriation voyages.

On January 17, 1946, *Kashima* returned to Kure from New Guinea at the end of her third trip, carrying nearly one thousand repatriated troops. Almost as soon as the cruiser was securely tied to her pier, Minoru Yokota walked up her gangplank and officially relieved Captain Shojiro Iura. One week later Yokota got the ship underway on the first of eight repatriation trips the ship would make under his command. Over the next ten months *Kashima* called at ports in Thailand, French Indochina, the Marshall and Solomon Islands, Formosa, and Indonesia as well as at Hong Kong and Singapore. She returned to Japan each time packed to the gunnels with men, and by the time she was withdrawn from service in November 1946 she had repatriated some six thousand troops.

The end of *Kashima*'s postwar repatriation duty also marked the end of Minoru Yokota's life at sea. At loose ends again, the former sub skipper moved back in with his brother. "After returning home I tried my hand at many different jobs while helping with the family farm," he later recalled, "but everything ended in failure."[40] Giving up on the idea of a rural life, Yokota left his family home and moved back to Yokosuka where, ironically, he found a job doing menial work for the U.S. Navy. The job paid poorly and the hours were long, but it was not until the 1950 repeal of the U.S.-instituted law banning former military officers from public jobs that Yokota was able to find a position that made better use of his skills. The job—as a teacher of science and mathematics at a high school in Fujisawa, on the shore of Sagami Bay in Kanagawa Prefecture—paid well enough to support both Yokota and, following his marriage in 1951, his wife, Utako.[41]

Things finally seemed to be looking up for Minoru Yokota, but in May 1957 the better times all too quickly ended:

> Just when I felt that we would be able to lead a stable life, my wife sud-
> denly succumbed to the hardships she had endured [during the war],
> and since we didn't have any children, I found myself all alone. I had
> lost all my goals and felt that I had nothing to live for.[42]

It is at this lowest of low points that Yokota's life took a completely unexpected—one is tempted to say miraculous—turn. A few months after his wife's death he met a Yokosuka-based Christian missionary with whom he developed a friendship. The two met occasionally to discuss life, death, and other weighty subjects, and in the course of their talks the missionary often told Yokota that he should confess his sins and live a religious, meaning Christian, life. By doing so, the missionary said, Yokota would discover "a glorious road" that would be even better than the navy life he'd previously led. Though initially skeptical, Yokota agreed to accompany the missionary to a three-day evangelical meeting to be held at a large church in Tokyo's commercial Marunouchi district. It was a jour-ney that would change the former sub captain's life forever.

The event began on May 12, 1957, and while Yokota felt "a certain attraction" to the ideas being discussed, his skepticism remained. As he later recalled,

> I knew there was no way that I could meet the moral levels that were
> expected. . . . Because I had spent 55 years living in sin and lived at
> sea for much of that time, so that my morals were disfigured much as
> a pine tree [is disfigured] by the sea, I didn't think I would last three
> days [as a Christian] even if I confessed my sins and was forgiven
> by God. Although I had regrets, I didn't have the courage to reform
> myself and started to head home [after the final session].[43]

While Yokota never publicly revealed the nature of the "sins" that so burdened him, it is logical to assume that his wartime actions may have contributed to what he saw as his moral disfigurement. After all, in the process of becoming one of the more successful submarine captains in the Imperial Japanese Navy he had knowingly sent enemy sailors and merchant mariners to their deaths by torpedoing their ships and leaving survivors to die of starvation, exposure, and, in the case of *Juneau*, shark attack. But were there other wartime sins for which he felt remorse?

Whatever the cause of his "regrets," they were apparently significant enough that even the possibility of divine understanding and forgiveness could not prevent him from leaving, unconverted, from that final meeting. But before he could make it out the door he was taken aside by one of the foremost, and apparently one of the most convincing, Japanese Christian leaders of the twentieth century. The man, Reverend David Tsugio Tsutada, was the scion of a prominent family and had been schooled in England. But he was no stranger to hardship and struggle: like many Japanese Christians he'd been jailed for most of the war on trumped-up charges of sedition against Emperor Hirohito. Released following Japan's surrender, he'd established a large church in Tokyo—the Immanuel General Mission—and by the time he met Minoru Yokota that May evening in 1957 he was widely referred to as the "John Wesley of Japan" and was the leader of one of the country's largest Christian organizations.[44]

Tsutada stopped Yokota as he was leaving, and, as the latter recalled,

He told me that if I were to believe and ask Jesus for forgiveness, that all my past sins would be forgiven and that I would be reborn. . . . That's when I made my decision. I decided to be courageous, leave the sinful life I had been leading and jump into Jesus's arms. . . . I believed that the Lord had accepted me and went home happily.[45]

Yokota's conversion from Buddhism to Christianity was sealed ten days later by his baptism. And there was more change to come. Soon after his initiation into the church the former sub captain met Matsuko Hasegawa, a Christian widow with three young daughters. At the time of their marriage in October 1957 Yokota adopted his new wife's last name, a fairly common practice in Japan when a man marries a widow with female children. And whether Yokota considered it or not, the change also relieved him of a name that would within a few years be irrevocably connected with the IJN, the war, and the deaths of several hundred Allied seamen.

In the years following his second marriage Minoru Hasegawa, as he was now known, continued teaching mathematics at the high school in Fujisawa, where his wife taught home economics. He also played a major role in helping to raise Matsuko's three daughters and, in what spare time he had, he did volunteer work in the Department of World Missions of Tsutada's church and the related Immanuel Bible Training College. It was by all accounts a busy and fulfilling life, and one that allowed memories of the war to slowly fade from Hasegawa's mind.

Until, that is, one fall day in 1966 when a note left on the front door of his modest Yokosuka home brought them all rushing back.

CHAPTER 10

A STORY LONG DELAYED

THOUGH ALF PRATTE'S SEARCH FOR Americans connected to *Cynthia Olson* had been highly successful, his efforts to find Japanese participants in the story had been anything but. Many IJN veterans were understandably reticent to talk about the war, and a vast number of Japan's wartime records had been destroyed either in the Allied bombing or in the immediate postwar period by individuals and agencies seeking to hamper war-crimes investigations.[1] Moreover, while the identity of the submarine that had attacked the Laker became known to U.S. Navy intelligence officers fairly quickly after Japan's capitulation, that information—and the names of the submarine's captain and crewmembers—did not become publicly available in the United States until the early 1960s.

Indeed, until he received the letter from the 13th Naval District historian, Alf Pratte had been unable to determine the identity of the submarine that sank *Cynthia Olson* and the name of the Japanese commander. Understandably elated by these new and important nuggets of information, the young reporter quickly set about trying to track down Minoru Yokota. The latter's 1957 name change hampered the search somewhat, but Pratte was ultimately able to determine that Yokota and the Fujisawa high school teacher named Hasegawa were one and the same. Having made that determination, Pratte and his supervising editor, Ed Edwards, then had to decide how best to set up and conduct what would obviously be one of the planned article series' most important interviews.

The answer to that particular logistical question turned out to be fairly straightforward. Another young *Star-Bulletin* reporter, Tomi Kaizawa Knaefler, was already scheduled to travel to Japan. Hawaii-born and of Japanese ancestry, Knaefler was in the process of doing her own multipart series for the paper, focusing on how World War II separated Japanese Americans from loved ones in Hawaii and on the mainland.[2] Edwards asked her to schedule some time during her stay in Tokyo to meet with Hasegawa and ask him a series of fifty questions prepared by Pratte regarding the sinking of *Cynthia Olson*. Knaefler readily agreed, adding that she would have the considerable assistance of her brother, former U.S. Army translator Stanley Kaizawa, who'd worked as an interpreter for the Allied occupation forces and stayed on in Japan after the occupation ended in 1951 to work for the U.S. government.[3] With Knaefler on board, Edwards and Pratte considered calling Hasegawa to set up the interview in advance, but then decided that by doing so they risked spooking the former submarine captain. Given the importance of the information they believed he would be able to provide, Edwards and Pratte ultimately determined that Knaefler and her brother should simply show up unannounced at Hasegawa's home.

With the tactics of the interview agreed upon, Knaefler journeyed to Tokyo in early November 1966. She met up with her brother, and together they determined Hasegawa's address and went to his home. When their knocking on the door went unanswered they left a note explaining who they were and what they wanted, and then anxiously waited for a reply. To their great relief, Hasegawa called them at their hotel a few days later and—despite his obvious surprise at their interest in his wartime activities—agreed to meet them. That encounter took place the next day in a location that was obviously both familiar and comfortable for the former sub captain: Tsutada's Immanuel General Mission in Tokyo.

Hasegawa and his wife arrived promptly at the appointed time. "They were both very quiet and humble, and obviously very devoted to each other and to the church," Knaefler later recalled. "And they obviously lived a very quiet life."[4] After some introductory small talk—Knaefler learned that Hasegawa's three adopted daughters had all married Japanese Christian missionaries—the group settled into chairs in the church basement to begin the interview.

With her brother acting as interpreter, Knaefler launched into the questions Pratte had prepared. She began by asking Hasegawa about the timing of the attack on *Cynthia Olson*, and he calmly insisted that he had not opened fire until 3:35 a.m. on December 8, Tokyo time, some ten minutes after the first bombs had begun falling on Pearl Harbor. Over the next several hours, Hasegawa "didn't hesitate to answer any of the questions," Knaefler said. "In fact, I got the impression he was relieved to finally talk about it all." The young reporter found the former captain of *I-26* to be "very calm and straightforward, and so humble that it was hard to believe he'd ever commanded a submarine in combat."[5] Indeed, as Knaefler remembered it, the only time Hasegawa lost his composure was when she mentioned that there had been no survivors from *Cynthia Olson*. He was adamant that the American crewmen had been alive and well in the lifeboats at the time of *I-26*'s departure from the scene, and he had always believed, he told her, that the mariners had ultimately been rescued.[6]

When the interview ended Knaefler and her brother treated the Hasegawas to dinner, then the four parted company. Back in her hotel room the young reporter looked over her notes, added a few comments of her own, then carefully put her notebook away in her suitcase. As interesting as the conversation with Hasegawa had been, she had her own project to think about.

————————

TOMI KNAEFLER STAYED IN JAPAN for about ten days, and by the time she returned to Honolulu Alf Pratte was fairly chomping at the bit to see what she'd been able to find out from Minoru Hasegawa.

Pratte's anxiety was understandable, given that he and others had very high hopes for his *Cynthia Olson* series. "Everybody in the newsroom was enthusiastic about the project; it was a team effort," he recalled, and though he was the sole writer, Knaefler and others had helped immeasurably. Supervising editor Edwards's input was especially valuable, Pratte said. "He really helped me, because I was writing the series of articles as though they were a master's thesis. Ed helped calm me down, and of course he trimmed thousands of words from it."[7]

All the effort Pratte and others put into the *Cynthia Olson* story came to fruition when the *Star-Bulletin* opened the "Prelude to Pearl Harbor" series on Saturday, December 3, 1966. To understand Pratte's conclusions, a quick review of each article is indicated.[8]

PART 1: "THE STORY OF THE CYNTHIA OLSON," DECEMBER 3

The initial article covered the basic outlines of the ship's early life as both *Coquina* and *Cynthia Olson*, her charter by the Army, and a few details about her crew. Pratte then gave a broad overview of the "time question," adding that

> Information furnished 25 years ago by two men who were aboard the *Lurline* [referring to Asplund and Grogan] indicates that the *Olson* was sunk from a half hour to an hour before the attack on Pearl Harbor began. This evidence is bolstered by information furnished by a radio operator [referring to Ray Ferrill] who was monitoring the air waves on the West Coast on the day of the attack.

PART 2: "CYNTHIA OLSON'S BLIND DATE WITH DEATH," DECEMBER 5

The second installment—the shortest of Pratte's articles—introduced both Yokota and *I-26*.[9] Though Pratte succinctly and correctly outlined the submarine's mission as part of the Advance Force, he wrongly stated that on her first voyage *I-26* had called at Kwajalein before going north to scout the Aleutians (she first visited the Marshall Islands after sinking *Cynthia Olson*).

PART 3: "THE CYNTHIA OLSON'S RENDEZVOUS WITH FATE," DECEMBER 6

Pratte's third article opened with details of *Lurline*'s delayed departure from Honolulu, then diverged from the narrative to introduce some of the uncertainties surrounding the timing of the Matson liner's reception of *Cynthia Olson*'s distress signal. As Pratte put it,

> One of the first things to note in regard to time was that it was customary to move clocks ahead one-half hour each midnight as *Lurline* traveled from Hawaii to the West Coast. Thus, if the captain of the Matson

liner began to advance his clocks shortly after the *Lurline* left Honolulu December 6, there would have been a difference of one hour between the ship and Honolulu on the morning of December 7, 1941.

The young reporter then added a second important point for his readers to bear in mind:

Today, Hawaii observes the time in the 10th standard time zone which is 10 hours earlier than Greenwich, England, and two hours earlier than the West Coast. But in 1941, Hawaii was using a standard time of 10 1/2 hours earlier than Greenwich Mean Time (GMT) and 2 1/2 hours earlier than the Pacific Coast.[10]

Pratte then wrote of *I-26*'s discovery and stalking of *Cynthia Olson* and pointed out that Yokota was very specific about the Laker's location when first detected: 34° north, 145° west.

PART 4: "CYNTHIA OLSON'S FATE SEALED—BUT WHEN?" DECEMBER 7

After speculating about what *Cynthia Olson*'s crewmen were doing when *I-26*'s warning shot suddenly streaked across the Laker's bow, Pratte's penultimate article revisited the "time issue." He cited Ray Ferrill's 1946 assertion to Riley Allen that KTK, Globe Wireless's Mussel Rock station, received *Lurline*'s rebroadcast of *Cynthia Olson*'s distress message at 9:30 a.m., San Francisco time, which would have been 7:00 a.m., Honolulu time. Pratte then added,

In addition to Ferrill's testimony, *Lurline* Commodore C.A. Berndston [*sic*] and radio operator Asplund both recollected in 1946 that the luxury liner picked up the first distress call at about 8 a.m., ship time, or 7 a.m., Honolulu time.

Pratte went on to mention the disappearance of *Lurline*'s radio log, then wrapped up the fourth article with Yokota's memories of the attack. Pratte pointedly included the former sub skipper's emphatic assertion that "No shots were ever fired at the men in the lifeboats at any time."

PART 5: "CYNTHIA OLSON MIGHT HAVE BEEN FORGOTTEN," DECEMBER 8

In the final article of the "Prelude to Pearl Harbor" series, Pratte cited Riley Allen's initial interest in the *Cynthia Olson* story, then went on to attempt to definitively answer Allen's three questions—when did the attack occur, could news of it have changed what happened at Pearl Harbor, and what happened to the crew?

In addressing the first question, Pratte first reviewed the opinions of individuals Allen had mentioned in his 1947 paper. The young reporter then added information from several new sources, arguably the most authoritative of whom was Toshikazu Ohmae, a former captain in the IJN and, by the time Pratte contacted him, chief of Military Operational Analysis in the Foreign Histories Division of the Office of Military History at Headquarters, U.S. Army, Japan.[11] In the article, Pratte said,

> Ohmae wrote this reporter to state that evidence he had uncovered showed the *I-26* had fired on the *Olson* before the air attacks on Pearl Harbor. "Although the precise time [of the firing on the *Olson*] is not available," Ohmae wrote, "it is reasonably believed to be at 7h 41m–45m. In consideration of the fact that the first air attack by dive bombers [at Pearl Harbor] was commenced at 7h55m, the bombardment of *I-26* was preceding the air attacks although the time interval was only small minutes."

Ohmae's belief that *I-26* had fired on *Cynthia Olson* before the air attack at Pearl Harbor was echoed by Whitney Phillips, the Olson Company's Honolulu-based district representative:

> Phillips has told this reporter a number of times that he and most of the members of the Olson family have long been aware that the *Cynthia Olson* was the first casualty of World War II for the United States, and was fired on before the Oahu attack. "But the Army told us to keep quiet about it," Phillips said in an interview June 7. "And the family doesn't like to talk about it."

In attempting to determine whether earlier notification of the attack on *Cynthia Olson* might have changed the course of events at Pearl Harbor, Pratte offered the differing opinions of two highly credible sources.

The first, Dr. W. J. Holmes, was a former Navy intelligence officer and past dean of the University of Hawaii. He stated unequivocally that an earlier warning "wouldn't have made any difference" and added that by prompting the ships of the Pacific Fleet to hurriedly put to sea such a warning might even have caused greater losses. Instead of being sunk in shallow water from which they were raised and put back into service, U.S. warships might have been sent to the bottom in deep water, from which they could not have been recovered.

But Pratte's second and equally credible source, official World War II Navy historian (and rear admiral) Samuel Eliot Morison, strongly disagreed with Holmes:

> Morison said that if there had been an alert, more anti-aircraft guns would have been in a better position to fire, and more American planes could have been in the air rather than parked on landing strips as sitting ducks. "There is no doubt that even a one-half hour warning would have made some difference. And an hour would have made a lot of difference," Morison said.

Having addressed the questions of the attack's timing and whether forewarning could have changed what happened at Pearl Harbor, Pratte closed out the final article in his series by addressing the fate of her crew. And that is where the young reporter's editors failed him, for they allowed him to make two fundamental journalistic errors: reliance on information provided by a single—and possibly self-serving—source and failure to explore possible alternatives to the story provided by that source.

The single source upon whom Pratte relied when pondering the fate of *Cynthia Olson*'s crew was, of course, Minoru Hasegawa. Having allowed the former sub captain to assert in part 4 of the series that "No shots were ever fired at the men in the lifeboats at any time," Pratte and his editors apparently accepted that statement at face value. Indeed, after writing that the Americans were "last seen by the crew members of the Japanese

submarine as the two lifeboats moved away from the *Olson* toward Honolulu," Pratte added only

> Did [the Americans] have enough rations to last them for part of their
> 1,000-mile journey? Or did their boats capsize in the winter ocean
> within days after they hurriedly left the *Olson*? How far did they row
> from the spot where the Japanese submarine was firing on the *Olson*?

Swayed, perhaps, by Hasegawa's Christianity and his "honest and
cooperative" eyes (as Tomi Knaefler described them), Pratte never once
mentioned the possibility that the former sub captain—a man with an
obvious vested interest in having the world believe that Carlsen, Buchtele,
and the rest did not perish in a hail of automatic weapons fire—might not
be telling the truth. Nor did Pratte ask the obvious question: could the
men aboard *Cynthia Olson* have been among the hundreds of Allied merchant mariners proven to have survived the sinkings of their ships only to
be killed by the crews of Japanese submarines?

Pratte's focus in the concluding paragraphs of the last article in his
five-part series was not on the fate of *Cynthia Olson*'s crewmen, but rather
on how the man who sank the Laker managed to survive a war that killed
the majority of Japanese submariners. The former captain, the young
reporter wrote,

> said he entered the war with the attack on the *Olson* with the feeling
> that he "would not come out of it alive. But I guess I was good at escap-
> ing," he added.

Having spent seven months researching and writing the "Prelude to
War" series, Alf Pratte and those who'd supported his efforts put the work
before the public with great, not to say impossible, hopes.

"We really thought the series might be nominated for a Pulitzer, but
in hindsight that was ridiculous," Pratte told the author. "Even though
it was done in five parts, it really lacked the depth needed for Pulitzer
consideration."

When asked what kind of public reaction the articles elicited, Pratte
sighed and said, "It was basically ho-hum, which was the saddest thing
that had happened in my life to that point. We'd all been talking about a

Pulitzer, and then nobody seemed excited about the series. In fact, most of the comments I heard were things like 'It's too damn long.'"

Long it may have been, and a labor of love on Alf Pratte's part it obviously was. But definitive "Prelude to War" most definitely was not. Despite Pratte's best intentions, the mystery of *Cynthia Olson* remained robustly alive. And though new information about the events surrounding the Laker's sinking would come to light in the following decades, several writers would find it just as difficult to answer Riley H. Allen's three lingering questions.

WHILE ALF PRATTE'S "PRELUDE TO War" series did not prove to be as successful as the young reporter had hoped, it definitely impressed—though somewhat belatedly—an Oregon-based photographer and prolific writer of local histories named Ebbert True Webber.

An Army Signal Corps photographer during World War II and postwar owner of a commercial photography business in Washington state, Bert Webber went on to earn an undergraduate degree in journalism and a master's in library science. In 1967 he'd published the first of several dozen books on various topics of Pacific Northwest history, and by 1974 was at work on a volume examining Japan's World War II naval activities along the U.S. West Coast. In the course of his research he came across Pratte's *Star-Bulletin* series and, knowing a good story when he saw one, decided to delve further into *Cynthia Olson*'s fatal encounter with *I-26*.

Webber first wrote about the Laker's demise in a December 7, 1972, article in the *Oregon Journal*, an afternoon daily in Portland.[12] His piece was obviously based entirely on Pratte's earlier work, and while there were slight differences—Pratte's Sam "Zisking" became "Sisking" in Webber's article, for example—the latter closely followed both the chronology and conclusions of the *Star-Bulletin* series.

Then, determined to include a more comprehensive version of the *Cynthia Olson* story in his forthcoming book, *Retaliation: Japanese Attacks and Allied Countermeasures on the Pacific Coast in World War II*, in the spring of 1973 Webber obtained Minoru Hasegawa's address and wrote him a letter containing a number of fairly specific questions about *I-26*'s attack on the Laker.[13]

Somewhat to the American author's surprise Hasegawa not only replied, he answered the questions at some length. He repeated several of the points he'd made to Tomi Knaefler in 1966—including that he'd waited to engage the lumber freighter until after the scheduled hour of the *Kido Butai*'s strike on Pearl Harbor; that the American mariners had all gotten into their lifeboats and moved away from their ship before *I-26* opened fire; that the submarine's radio operator had picked up the Laker's distress signal; and that it had taken several hours to inflict what Hasegawa ultimately determined to be fatal damage on the ship. Interestingly, the former sub captain specifically said that he never fired a torpedo at the American vessel, relying solely on *I-26*'s deck gun.

As helpful as Hasegawa's written answers were, Webber soon had the chance to follow up with the former IJN officer—in person. In July 1975 the American author and his wife, Margie, traveled to Japan to attend a reunion of the crews of *I-25* and *I-26*. Over the course of several days Webber was able to speak at length with Hasegawa as well as with Saburo Hayashi, *I-26*'s former chief gunner, and several other one-time crewmembers.[14] The visit was apparently extremely cordial, though it revealed some important differences in the way the Japanese veterans remembered the events of December 7, 1941.

Hayashi, for example, agreed with his former commander that all the Americans had left their doomed ship in lifeboats, but he was adamant that when gunfire seemed incapable of sinking *Cynthia Olson*, *I-26* had fired one torpedo that missed (it is this description of the torpedo attack that appears in chapter 7 of this volume). Hayashi's version of events was corroborated by former torpedoman Takaji Komaba and former diving officer Yukio Oka. None of the men added any further information about the ultimate fate of the Laker's crew.

Webber incorporated the accounts of both Hasegawa and Hayashi, as well as the latter's photo of the burning *Cynthia Olson*, into the original 1975 edition of *Retaliation* and the 1976 second imprint. He then included two new and important bits of information in an expanded version of the work published in 1983 as *Silent Siege: Japanese Attacks Against North America in World War II*. After saying that *Cynthia Olson*'s crewmen had entered lifeboats but were "never rescued from the sea," Webber added,

Mr. Hasegawa wrote to me in September 1983 that before the survivors disappeared, submarine *I-19* saw them drifting helplessly and pulled alongside. *I-19*'s medical officer observed the sailors closely then directed the submarine's skipper to make food available to the men in the boats. This done, *I-19* departed.[15]

This marks the first time that a second Japanese submarine is mentioned as a player in the *Cynthia Olson* drama, and it is interesting and not a little puzzling that Hasegawa had not mentioned *I-19*'s purported humanitarian gesture to Tomi Knaefler in 1966 or to Webber during the 1975 reunion. A second and decidedly more astonishing statement from *I-26*'s former captain also appears in *Silent Siege*. As Webber wrote,

> When *I-26* attacked *Cynthia Olson*, Commander Yokota (Hasegawa) determined his submarine's position for his first hostile action to be 29°N–140°W. This would be about midway and about on a line between Honolulu and San Jose, California.[16]

This statement immediately prompts several questions, the first of which is why Webber chose to abandon the position Yokota gave to Alf Pratte in 1966—34° north by 145° west—and which Webber himself included in his 1975 article in the *Oregon Journal*. That original position was entirely consistent with *Cynthia Olson*'s final location as transmitted by Sam Ziskind. Which leads us to wonder whether Webber ever saw the actual contents of *Cynthia Olson*'s distress message—which he did not use in any of his accounts of the Laker's sinking—because if he had, he should have realized that the altered position Hasegawa gave for the attack and the position Ziskind sent are more than 450 miles apart. Moreover, given that *Cynthia Olson* had departed from Puget Sound rather than San Francisco Bay, for the Laker to have been sunk anywhere near 29° N by 140° W would have meant that Bert Carlsen had deliberately taken his ship far to the south of the normal track between the Pacific Northwest and Honolulu. There would have been no logical reason to do so since war had not yet broken out, and such a diversion would therefore have been a waste of both time and fuel.

Webber retained both the mention of *I-19*'s encounter with *Cynthia Olson*'s lifeboats and Hasegawa's puzzling position report in the 1988 and 1992 updates of *Silent Siege* (II and III). Both later versions also included an intriguing addition; inserted directly after Hayashi's account of the sinking was the statement, "Mr. Hayashi said Imperial authorities never quizzed him about the sinking and apparently did not know he had taken pictures."[17] It may be that this statement was added in response to some criticism Hayashi might have received in Japan after the original publication of his photo of the burning *Cynthia Olson*, though no explanation was provided.

While Webber's friendship and correspondence with Minoru Hasegawa and other *I-26* veterans obviously gave the American author a unique perspective on the *Cynthia Olson* story, he was ultimately unable or unwilling to apply any sort of rigorous journalistic evaluation to what he heard from the former submariners. Nowhere in any of his published writings on the events of December 7 did Webber seriously dispute the details provided by the Japanese veterans. Like Alf Pratte, he seemed willing to accept without question the version of events provided by Hasegawa, especially with regard to the ultimate fate of the Laker's crew.

Nor were Pratte and Webber the only writers to take a surprisingly nonjudgmental view of Minoru Hasegawa's statements regarding *I-26*'s attack on *Cynthia Olson*. A far more eminent author—quite possibly the world's foremost expert on Japan's assault on Pearl Harbor and the events surrounding it—would prove just as forbearing when it came to relating the former sub captain's version of the death of *Cynthia Olson*.

———

IN 1945 A THIRTY-FIVE-YEAR-OLD U.S. Naval Reserve officer named Gordon W. Prange arrived in Tokyo to join the Allied occupation effort headed by General Douglas MacArthur. No ordinary staff officer, from 1937 to 1942 Prange had been a professor of history at the University of Maryland, and upon his arrival in Tokyo he was assigned to the office tasked with locating and securing Japanese military records that might prove to be of historical value. Upon his October 1946 release from active duty he chose to stay on as a civilian employee in the same office and was subsequently named chief of the one-hundred-member historical section in the office of MacArthur's deputy chief of staff for intelligence. Over the following five years Prange had unprecedented access to wartime Japanese records and, more importantly, was able to personally interview hundreds of former Japanese military officers.

On February 23, 1951, as he was wrapping up his time in Japan and preparing to return to his teaching position in Maryland, Prange interviewed Minoru Yokota (as he was still called at that time). Over the course of several hours the former sub captain, by then teaching at the high school in Fujisawa, told Prange of *I-26*'s departure from Japan in November 1941 and her subsequent reconnaissance of the Aleutians. While it was the submarine's activities as part of the Advance Force that most interested Prange, he also asked Yokota about the attack on *Cynthia Olson*. The former IJN officer told essentially the same version of the story that he would later recount to Pratte, Webber, and others, emphasizing that he did not open fire on the freighter until after the scheduled time of the *Kido Butai*'s assault on Pearl Harbor. Interestingly, Yokota specifically told the American historian that *I-26* launched two torpedoes at the listing and burning Laker, but that both missed. And while Yokota wrapped up his account of the action against *Cynthia Olson* by saying that the American mariners were all safe in their lifeboats when *I-26* left the area, he made no mention of *I-19* or any other Japanese sub chancing upon the lifeboats or providing their occupants with food or water.

For nearly three decades following his return to the University of Maryland Prange labored diligently—indeed, some might say obsessively—on what would become arguably the best-known and most authoritative account of the Pearl Harbor attack. Built upon key U.S. and Japanese documents—many of which Prange himself had collected during his years in Tokyo—and including information the historian had distilled from his hundreds of postwar interviews, the manuscript had grown to some 3,500 pages by the time Prange died of cancer on May 15, 1980. In accordance with his wishes, the final editing and organization of what became *At Dawn We Slept: The Untold Story of Pearl Harbor* was undertaken by Dr. Donald M. Goldstein and Katherine V. Dillon. The book was published to almost universal acclaim in 1981 and spent forty-seven weeks on the New York Times Best Seller list.[18]

While Prange and his editors included Minoru Yokota's account of *I-26*'s Aleutian reconnaissance, *At Dawn We Slept* makes no mention of the attack on *Cynthia Olson*. This is an odd omission, given the book's truly exhaustive examination of virtually every other event in any way connected with Japanese naval operations on December 7, 1941. The oversight was corrected in a follow-on Prange volume also edited by Goldstein and Dillon, 1988's *Dec. 7, 1941: The Day the Japanese Attacked Pearl Harbor*. Strangely, the book referred to the Laker as a "small wooden craft" and a "little wooden ship" and misspelled her name as *Cynthia Olsen*. Yokota was described as waiting "chivalrously" for the American mariners to get into the lifeboats and away from the ship before opening fire, and the account states unequivocally that *I-26* fired two torpedoes during the engagement.[19] Footnotes indicate that the paragraphs pertaining to Yokota and his sub were based on Prange's 1951 interview and, interestingly, also contained information drawn from Alf Pratte's 1966 series in the *Star-Bulletin*.

The approach Prange and his editors took to the information drawn from Yokota/Hasegawa's interview and Pratte's articles seems to be the same—unquestioning acceptance. There is no indication that the version of events presented by the former commander of *I-26* in either the interview or the *Star-Bulletin* series was subjected to any process of corroboration. And while the second of the two Prange volumes dispenses with the question of the timing of Yokota's attack on the Laker by simply observing (in a footnote) that he "was positive that he did not jump the gun," there is no mention or speculation at all of the fate of Berthel Carlsen and his crew.[20]

The same unquestioning approach has been taken by virtually every one of the handful of writers since Prange who has touched on the *Cynthia Olson* story—a not unexpected result, given that Prange and Pratte remain to this day the most-often cited sources. And while two authors, Stanley Weintraub and David H. Grover,[21] produced magazine articles in 2001 suggesting that Minoru Hasegawa had been less than truthful about both the timing of *I-26*'s attack and the fate of the Laker's crew, no one has yet been able to definitively answer the three questions Riley H. Allen posed in 1947: When did the attack on *Cynthia Olson* actually occur? Could news of the attack have prevented the carnage at Pearl Harbor? And, finally, what happened to the Laker's crew?

CHAPTER 11

MYSTERIES RESOLVED

BEFORE WE ATTEMPT TO ANSWER the three questions Riley Allen posed in 1947 we must, of course, first ask, What's the point? The attack on *Cynthia Olson* occurred seventy-five years ago, at the very beginning of a world-wide conflict that ultimately killed some sixty million people through combat, disease, starvation, and extermination.[1] What importance is there, then, in trying to finally determine what happened to thirty-five Americans whose disappearance so quickly became no more than an historical footnote?

The answer to that question is twofold.

First, history is never static. As new information comes to light we con-tinuously edit, modify, broaden, and restate our accounts of past events in an effort to more clearly and accurately describe and understand the actions and motivations of our predecessors. This drive to refine the past is especially important when we are writing about war, for anything that helps us better comprehend the causes and conduct of mankind's most enduring form of mass insanity must—if we are truly able to see beyond our national, cultural, and religious prejudices—help us find ways to either avoid military conflicts or conduct them in less destructive ways. And, of course, if *Cynthia Olson* truly was the first American vessel to be sunk by the Japanese in World War II, it would rewrite—albeit it in a mod-est way—the first chapter of the Pacific war's history.

The second reason to seek answers to Riley Allen's three questions is less about setting straight the historical record than it is about honoring the men who sailed aboard *Cynthia Olson* and those who waited, in vain, for some final word of the mariners' fate. Like the rest of the more than seventy-three thousand American service members and merchant seamen still listed as missing from World War II, the men lost aboard the Laker deserve our best efforts to determine their ultimate fate as accurately as we can.[2] *Cynthia Olson*'s crewmembers—American and Filipino, young and old, seamen and soldiers—died in service to the United States. The nation therefore owes them and their families debts of both honor and gratitude, an obligation that can be at least partially discharged by attempting to discover, once and for all, the way in which they died.

———

THE EXACT TIMING OF *I-26*'s attack on *Cynthia Olson*—and whether it took place before or after the commencement of the *Kido Butai*'s assault on Pearl Harbor—has been the subject of heated debate virtually from the minute Sam Ziskind pounded out that first, hurried SOS. Throughout his life—and in sharp contrast to contradictions that arose in his recounting of other aspects of the attack on *Cynthia Olson*—Minoru Hasegawa steadfastly maintained that he did not fire that first warning shot across the Laker's bow until *after* the scheduled start time of the initial air raid on Oahu. It was a point he first made to Gordon Prange in 1951 and which he repeated to Tomi Knaefler, Bert Webber, and others over the years.

Hasegawa's reasons for insisting that he waited until 3:30 a.m., Japan Standard Time, before acting are not difficult to fathom.

First, and probably most important to someone who'd spent two decades of his life as an officer in one of the world's most rigid military hierarchies, he would not have wanted to jeopardize the success of the *Kido Butai*'s surprise attack by violating his very explicit orders to avoid engaging enemy forces until after the first bombs had fallen on Hawaii. He would almost certainly have assumed that *Cynthia Olson* was equipped with a radio capable of instantly broadcasting word of his attack, and he knew that any precipitate action on his part could well have alerted the American military forces on Oahu and given them time to prepare a strong defense. The possibility of later being branded as the man who single-handedly ensured the failure of Japan's most important military operation in a generation would have been anathema to him.

Second, in the years immediately following his nation's defeat and occupation Hasegawa would certainly not have wanted to become known as the officer who was so eager to spill American blood that he actually struck before the rest of the Imperial Japanese Navy. Like most of his countrymen, he was only too aware of the disgust virtually all Americans felt with regard to Japan's "sneak attack" at Pearl Harbor. In the lean and extremely difficult first years of the occupation—a time when the occupiers could withhold food, shelter, medicine, and work—to be labeled "sneakier" than even those who attempted to bomb the U.S. Pacific Fleet into oblivion would have been a literal death sentence.

Hasegawa's unwavering contention that he waited until 3:30 a.m., JST, has, of course, been challenged. Globe Wireless's 1947 press release, for example, stated that operators on duty at the company's Mussel Rock station near San Francisco

> heard what was probably the first overt act of the war [referring to the reception of Leslie Grogan's message regarding his receipt of *Cynthia Olson*'s distress call], inasmuch as it occurred prior to the onslaught of the planes at Pearl Harbor.[3]

And in his *Star-Bulletin* series Alf Pratte cited the opinions of such knowledgeable parties as Globe Wireless's Ray Ferrill, Japanese military historian Toshikazu Ohmae, and the Oliver J. Olson Company's Whitney Phillips, all of whom agreed that *I-26*'s attack had preceded the air assault on Pearl Harbor.

Writers on both sides of the question—those who insist that *I-26* struck prematurely and those who accept her captain's protestations to the contrary—have traditionally resorted to detailed and occasionally arcane ruminations on the ways in which time was being measured aboard *Lurline* on December 7, 1941. Such measurement is important, of course, because in his "Record for Posterity" Leslie Grogan stated that he received *Cynthia Olson*'s first automated alarm signal at 9:12 a.m., ship's time, and virtually all attempts to pin down the time of *I-26*'s initial attack on the Laker have been extrapolated from that figure. As noted maritime historian (and former merchant mariner) David H. Grover has observed, "The question of the time of the attack on *Cynthia Olson* hinges on which local time the *Lurline* was keeping on the morning in question."[4]

Because the Matson liner's voyage radio log was confiscated upon her December 10 arrival in San Francisco, Grover pointed out that determining which time was being observed aboard the ship "must be done inferentially."[5] He was referring, as Alf Pratte had done in part 3 of his *Star-Bulletin* series, to the fact that aboard Matson vessels traveling eastward from Hawaii it was customary to move clocks ahead thirty minutes each midnight the ship spent at sea. If *Lurline*'s clocks were advanced in accordance with that schedule beginning on the night of her December 5 departure from Honolulu, by the morning of December 7—two midnights later—"local time" aboard the liner would have been one hour later than Honolulu time.

While this seems to be a fairly straightforward calculation, there has always been a perplexing and potentially significant wrinkle. As stated earlier in this volume, in December 1941 Hawaii observed Greenwich Mean Time plus ten and a half hours, rather than the plus ten hours that would have been appropriate to its longitude.[6] This becomes an issue if one assumes that as *Lurline* moved east from Hawaii, out of the fairly small spatial confines of the territory's self-adopted time zone, Commodore Berndtson chose to adjust the ship's clocks in keeping with the plus-ten zone. If he did so, then, as Grover pointed out, *Lurline*'s "local time" would have been

> one half hour later than that of Hawaii, meaning in comparative terms that 8:00 a.m. at the ship would coincide with 7:30 a.m. in Honolulu.[7]

There are indications that *Lurline* might, in fact, have been operating on plus-ten time: Several of the liner's officers—including Chief Officer Edward Collins—later voiced the opinion that *Cynthia Olson*'s distress message was received at 8:00 a.m., ship's time, rather than the 9:12 figure mentioned by Grogan. If the 8:00 a.m. reception time was correct, of course, it would have meant that Grogan picked up Sam Ziskind's signal thirty minutes before the Japanese attacked Pearl Harbor.

There is, however, a simpler, more logical, and arguably more convincing way to look at the entire "time issue." And it does not require either acceptance of one person's testimony or an attempt to discern a liner captain's feelings about time measurement some seventy-five years after the fact. More importantly, it is based on the reality that all of the non-Japanese radio operators who participated in any way in the events surrounding *Cynthia Olson*'s loss—no matter their location, the sophistication of their equipment, or the hour in their local time zones—had one thing in common. Each one had been trained, and was required by national law, military regulation, or company policy, to log incoming and outgoing messages in Greenwich Mean Time, not local time. Each radio room—whether ashore or afloat—had at least two clocks to which the operator could refer, one set to local time and the other to GMT. We can therefore compare the GMT transmission or reception times recorded by various operators to "fix" the time of *Cynthia Olson*'s initial distress signal.

Leslie Grogan's first transmission regarding *Cynthia Olson* was logged by station KPH in Bolinas, California, at 6:47 p.m., GMT, on 500 Kcs.[8] As we saw earlier, that first message said that Grogan had received the Laker's initial auto-alarm signal at 6:38 p.m., GMT, some nine minutes earlier, and gave the lumber transport's position as 33°42' north by 145°29' west. Grogan's message was actually directed to NERK, the radio call letters standing for "All Navy Vessels," in an attempt to pass Ziskind's distress call to any naval ships and shore installations within range for relay to Pearl Harbor. At 6:48 p.m., GMT, the Navy station at Point Reyes, California, NMC, queried KTK, Globe Wireless's Mussel Rock station, about the message, which NMC had been unable to understand. At 6:51 p.m., GMT, Ray Ferrill at KTK asked Grogan for clarification, and six minutes later Ferrill passed the relayed distress call to NPG, the Navy station at Mare Island, just north of San Francisco. At 7:00 p.m., GMT, Ferrill forwarded the message to NMC, asking the Navy operator to "rush" the information to all other Navy stations on the West Coast. At 7:02 p.m., GMT, the Royal Canadian Navy station at Esquimalt, British Columbia, logged receipt of the U.S. 13th Naval District's rebroadcast of Grogan's transmission, just fifteen minutes after *Lurline*'s first message was picked up by KPH in Bolinas.

Grogan's statement that he received *Cynthia Olson*'s first auto alarm at 6:38 p.m., GMT, essentially solves the "time question." As a career radioman he would not have gotten wrong so fundamental a piece of information as the receipt time of an incoming distress message, and KPH's logging of his call just nine minutes after the stated time of the first auto-alarm transmission reinforces the belief that Grogan and Asplund—whatever their individual personalities or character flaws—were professionals who knew their business. And despite their later disagreements about the local time being kept aboard *Lurline* at the time *Cynthia Olson*'s first signal was received, both Grogan and Asplund—and, for that matter, Chief Officer Collins—all stated independently and repeatedly over the years that *Lurline* began trying to notify the world at large of the Laker's distress within minutes of receiving the first auto-alarm message.[9]

While some official U.S. government documents[10] list the starting time of the *Kido Butai*'s air attack on Oahu as early as 7:43 a.m., Honolulu time, or 6:13 p.m., GMT, the commonly accepted time (and the one cited in the various military services' official accounts of the event[11]) is 7:55 a.m., local time, or 6:25 p.m., GMT. Minoru Hasegawa's oft-repeated statement that he waited until 3:30 a.m., JST, or 6:30 p.m., GMT, to launch his attack on *Cynthia Olson* therefore seems, ironically enough, to be true. The timing was certainly close—just eight minutes separated the beginning of the initial air attacks on Oahu from *I-26*'s warning shot across the lumber transport's bow—but the evidence clearly indicates that *Cynthia Olson* was not the victim of Japan's first Pacific war attack on an American target.

———

HAVING ANSWERED THE FIRST OF Riley Allen's three questions about the sinking of *Cynthia Olson*, we can make fairly short work of the second: could news of the attack have prevented the carnage at Pearl Harbor?

The obvious answer is no, given that the *Kido Butai*'s assault on Oahu had already begun by the time *I-26* fired across the Laker's bow. Japan and the United States were effectively at war even as Sam Ziskind sent the first auto-alarm signal, and by the time *Lurline* received that message, soldiers, sailors, and marines were already dead or dying at Kaneohe Naval Air Station and Wheeler and Ewa Fields.

Moreover, speculating about whether news of the Laker's plight might have prevented the carnage at Pearl Harbor—had *I-26* attacked the Laker before 3:30 a.m., JST—is ultimately pointless because we know for a fact that an event that actually *did* occur failed to do so. At 6:53 a.m., Honolulu time—almost a full hour before the first bombs fell—the destroyer USS *Ward* radioed that it had attacked an unidentified submarine operating just off the entrance to Pearl Harbor.[12] Simply put, if the report of an actual attack on a presumed Japanese sub right outside the U.S. Navy's most important Pacific anchorage couldn't trigger the type of vigorous and proactive defense that might have changed the course of history, then a message from a small civilian freighter some one thousand miles at sea certainly wouldn't have either.

Which brings us to the final and most important question about *I-26*'s fateful encounter with *Cynthia Olson*: what happened to the Laker's crew?

IN SEEKING AN ANSWER TO that question we are faced with several obvious difficulties. One, of course, is the simple fact that none of the American mariners survived to provide details of the events of that long-ago encounter. Added to that is the reality that the only eyewitnesses to the Laker's demise—the Japanese aboard *I-26*—simply cannot be considered as unbiased sources, for reasons we'll examine below. And, finally, the destruction during the final days of World War II of virtually all official IJN records dealing with the service's wartime submarine operations means that we have precious little documentary evidence to work with.

How, then, do we go about attempting to unravel this final mystery? We first sift through what evidence does exist, looking for facts upon which we can build. Then we make a few educated and hopefully sound suppositions based on information that has come to light in the nearly eight decades that have passed since *Cynthia Olson* vanished.

Let's first review the few facts available to us: We know that *Cynthia Olson* reported at 6:38 p.m., GMT, on December 7, 1941, that she had been stopped by a surfaced enemy submarine at position 33°42' north by 145°29' west. We also know that official U.S. government documents credit the submarine *I-26* with the Laker's destruction and that several of the Japanese sub's crewmen (including her captain) have repeatedly acknowledged that *I-26* was indeed the vessel that fired on *Cynthia Olson* that Sunday morning. We know, further, that at 9:42 p.m., GMT, on the same day HMCS *Prince Robert* was ordered to proceed to the position given in Sam Ziskind's distress message, that the warship undertook a thorough search of the area, and that she found absolutely no trace of the

Laker or her crew. And, finally, we know that *Cynthia Olson* and the men aboard her have not been seen since.

Then there are the facets of the story provided by Minoru Hasegawa and others who were aboard *I-26* when she encountered *Cynthia Olson*. These nuggets can help flesh out the narrative of the Laker's demise, but we must be wary of accepting them at face value.

Why such caution? First, most of the accounts were given years or even decades after the fact and, memory being the most inaccurate and capricious of human faculties, differ extensively or even fully contradict each other. Second, the absence of official Imperial Japanese Navy records—*I-26*'s logbook the most important among them—makes it extremely difficult to verify any of the details provided by the sub's crewmembers. And third, while journalists and historians must always be cautious when dealing with personal reminiscences of significant events (vanity, ego, and the impulse toward self-aggrandizement have, after all, always been part of human nature) the Japanese participants in the attack on *Cynthia Olson* had a particularly strong motive for recounting the event—and their individual roles in it—in the best possible light. Simply put, the post–World War II revelations of Japanese brutality at sea obviously would have prevented *I-26*'s former crewmembers from revealing information about the attack on *Cynthia Olson* that might in any way have been construed as an admission of complicity in a war crime.

Bearing these caveats in mind, the accounts by Hasegawa, Yukio Oka, Takaji Komaba, and Saburo Hayashi are remarkably consistent regarding the general details of the attack on *Cynthia Olson* and the initial disposition of her crew. The accounts agree that the Laker was unarmed; that *I-26*'s attack was initiated as a surface action; that a warning shot (or possibly two) across her bow brought the lumber transport to a halt; that Sam Ziskind's distress message preceded the final abandonment of the American vessel; that between thirty and fifty rounds of deck-gun ammunition were fired at the Laker; and that *I-26* submerged and resurfaced at least once during the course of the encounter.

The Japanese accounts also agree that both of *Cynthia Olson*'s lifeboats were in the water before *I-26* opened fire on the Laker. While we can't verify the stories of *I-26*'s sailors, we do know a fair amount about the lifeboats; both were examined and found fully functional—as were the ship's thirty life preservers and twelve life rings—by inspectors from the Commerce

Department's Bureau of Marine Inspection and Navigation the day before the ship left San Francisco at the beginning of her first passage to Hawaii.[13] Each of the two nonmotorized, open-top, thirty-five-foot-long steel craft was capable of carrying up to thirty-six people, and each was equipped with oars, freshwater casks, and watertight containers of emergency rations.

It is also important to understand how Bert Carlsen and his men would have launched the lifeboats. The craft were located on either side of the boat deck, abaft the third mast, with boat no. 1 to starboard and no. 2 to port. The keel of each rested in two wooden chocks that raised the small vessel about eighteen inches off the deck, and each boat was suspended by bow and stern lines from old-fashioned radial davits. The base of each crook-shaped davit was fitted into a socket that allowed the lifeboat to be carried inboard so it did not project over the ship's side. In an emergency the boat would be swung outboard on its davits, the canvas cover would be removed, and the crewmen would board, and the lifeboat would then be lowered into the water using blocks and tackle. Once the craft was riding normally in the water the men would cast off the bow and stern lines and move the lifeboat away from the ship.

Though apparently straightforward, the process of launching a lifeboat carried on simple radial davits has always been inherently risky. A snagged line or jammed davit on either end can prevent the lifeboat from being swung outboard. Once fully suspended the loaded boat must be carefully lowered on an even keel to prevent its occupants from being spilled into the sea and keep it from swamping should either bow or stern plunge into the water prematurely. And, perhaps most importantly, if the ship has taken on any significant degree of list the boats on the high side cannot be launched because the davits are unable to project them outward far enough to clear the ship's hull.

Saburo Hayashi's photo of the burning *Cynthia Olson* clearly shows that the heavily listing ship's davits had been swung outboard and are empty. Neither lifeboat is visible in the picture, though it's entirely possible that no. 2 is hidden from view by *Cynthia Olson's* elevated port side. The photo cannot, of course, tell us at what point in the attack the boats were cast off or whether all the Americans made it into the small craft before they were rowed away from the ship.

While we can assume that a veteran master mariner like Carlsen would have ensured that all his men were safely in one or the other of the boats before abandoning *Cynthia Olson* and, further, that no one would choose to remain aboard a vessel that was so obviously about to be either captured or sunk, we can't be certain. That none of the Japanese accounts mention American crewmen being aboard the Laker when the first shells hit is only to be expected, for any such revelation would have opened its author to exactly the sort of moral and possibly legal ramifications most former Japanese military personnel were seeking to avoid in the immediate postwar period.

In the final analysis, then, there are really only four possible answers to the final, lingering question about the fate of *Cynthia Olson*'s crew. First, some or all of the men were killed aboard their ship by gunfire (and possibly torpedoes) from *I-26*, and the rest died when the ship sank. Second, the American mariners did, in fact, make it off their doomed vessel but were then killed in the water by gunfire, ramming, or some other hostile act on the part of *I-26*'s crew. Third, the Americans were safe when *I-26* departed, but were killed by the second sub that Hasegawa told Bert Webber had chanced upon the lifeboats days after the initial attack. Or, fourth, the Americans made it into the two lifeboats and, unmolested by any Japanese attackers, drifted off into the vast Pacific to die a slow and agonizing death from starvation, thirst, and exposure.

While none of these is an appealing scenario, each deserves examination.

————

THE FIRST POSSIBILITY—THAT *I-26* OPENED fire on *Cynthia Olson* without allowing the American vessel's crew time to escape—is the least likely. We know that the submarine held its fire long enough after surfacing that Sam Ziskind had time to send both the first auto alarm and the follow-up SSS message and position report. Why would Yokota have allowed the American vessel time to transmit such important information if his intent all along was to kill the Laker's crew? And while the SSS code Ziskind sent could mean either "a submarine has been sighted" or "we are being attacked by a submarine," the young radio operator did not indicate that his ship was actually under fire and communicated (in Morse) twice with Leslie Grogan in what the latter termed "a steady hand." Though the abrupt termination of that exchange prompted *Lurline*'s assistant radio officer to comment that the Laker's transmitter had "sparked out like if a power failure took place," it is also conceivable that Ziskind's sudden silence was due to the fact that, having sent the distress message, he had shut down his apparatus and dashed from the radio room to take his place in one of the lifeboats.[14] And, finally, Hayashi's photo shows that both of *Cynthia Olson*'s lifeboats had been launched, an act that would have been virtually impossible if Japanese fire had been raking the Laker's superstructure.

The second scenario—that the Americans made it off the ship but were then killed by Yokota and his men—is both illogical and highly improbable. Why would the Japanese skipper have allowed the merchant mariners time to send a fairly specific distress and position report that, for all he knew, could well have included the submarine's identity (the number "26" was clearly painted on both sides of her conning tower) only to expend further time and ammunition trying to kill thirty-five men who would certainly have done everything they could to avoid being hit? Yokota—who was having a hard enough time trying to send *Cynthia Olson* herself to the bottom—was expecting the imminent arrival of American ships and aircraft. It would have been military stupidity of the most extraordinary kind—and completely out of character for the consummate naval professional that Yokota's record shows him to be—to attempt a maritime massacre that in all probability would have been both incomplete and interrupted by the arrival of enemy forces. Though it is certainly a fact that later in the war Japanese submarine commanders became notorious for their almost routine brutality toward Allied merchant seamen, there is no reason to believe that the murderous trend began with Yokota and *I-26*.[15]

At this point we must pause, however, to consider an unavoidable fact: while the firing of a warning shot across *Cynthia Olson*'s bow and allowing the Laker's crew to leave their ship in lifeboats before beginning his attack could be seen as a chivalrous act on Minoru Yokota's part, it does not alter the fact that he violated international law. Japan was a signatory to the 1930 London Naval Treaty and the 1936 London Submarine Protocol—both of which came into being largely in reaction to Imperial Germany's initiation and perpetuation of unrestricted submarine warfare in World War I. As Dr. Joel Holwitt has pointed out,

> The two documents, which were identical, stated that submarines were required to remove a merchant ship's crew to a place of safety before the ship could be sunk. A place of safety, furthermore, was not

considered to be a lifeboat on the open sea. It did not matter if the merchant ship belonged to a belligerent nation or a neutral nation. It did not matter if a merchant ship was arguably in the service of a belligerent nation's war machine.[16]

Because no declared state of war existed between Japan and the United States at the time of *I-26*'s attack on *Cynthia Olson*, that attack was a clear violation of both statutes. So, of course, was Yokota's decision to let the lumber transport's two lifeboats drift. That by not machine-gunning the Laker's crew *I-26*'s skipper showed a level of restraint uncharacteristic of most Japanese submarine captains is laudable, but it does not absolve him or his crewmembers of responsibility for their violation of international law or their collective guilt with regard to the fate of the thirty-three men aboard *Cynthia Olson*.[17]

———

BEFORE WE CAN ADDRESS THE third alternative scenario—that Bert Carlsen and his men were safe when *I-26* departed but were killed by a second Japanese sub that later chanced upon the lifeboats—we have to examine what appears to be an historical error long accepted as fact.

In September 1983 Minoru Hasegawa told Bert Webber that the submarine *I-19*—which in December 1941 we know was captained by Hasegawa's acquaintance Commander Shogo Narahara—came across *Cynthia Olson*'s drifting lifeboats and provided the occupants with food before sailing on. Why Hasegawa had not mentioned the "second sub" incident to any previous interviewer remains puzzling, but a more important aspect of the story has emerged. In February 2010 Sander Kingsepp, a widely respected authority on the Imperial Japanese Navy—revealed to the author that it was *I-15*, not *I-19*, that supposedly stopped to provide humanitarian assistance to *Cynthia Olson* survivors.[18] Kingsepp, who is fluent in Japanese, said the confusion was caused by a mistranslation of Hasegawa's original account of the event and that the identification of the "second sub" as *I-15* had been confirmed by his recent review of articles written by Hayashi, Komaba, and others.

The Type B-1 *I-15* was commissioned into the IJN in September 1940 and assigned to Captain Hiroshi Imazato's Submarine Division 1 in Submarine

Squadron 1. Though Imazato was aboard when the boat departed Yoko-suka on November 21, 1941, as part of the *Kido Butai*'s Advance Expeditionary Force, the vessel's skipper was Commander Nobuo Ishikawa and her executive officer was Lieutenant Commander Zenji Orita. *I-15*'s mission was to patrol north of the Hawaiian Islands and sink any American ships that tried to escape during the attack on Pearl Harbor, though she did not encounter any enemy vessels in the immediate aftermath of the aerial assault.

Surviving records indicate that *I-15* kept up her patrols "north of Oahu" until December 10, at which point she, *I-19*, and five other boats were sent in pursuit of the "*Lexington*-class" aircraft carrier and two cruisers *I-6* had reported heading northeast from Oahu. When that fruitless hunt was called off on December 14, *I-15*, *I-19*, *I-26*, and other boats were ordered to proceed to the U.S. West Coast for the ultimately aborted gun attacks on coastal targets. Given that the attack on *Cynthia Olson* occurred some 1,200 miles northeast of Hawaii on December 7 and that both *I-15* and *I-19* were engaged from that date through December 14 in either normal patrolling or the pointless hunt for the phantom U.S. aircraft carrier to the northeast of Oahu, it is conceivable that either Japanese submarine could have encountered *Cynthia Olson*'s lifeboats.

While retranslation of Hasegawa's earliest mention of the "second sub" incident eliminates *I-19* as the boat involved and replaces her with *I-15*, we are still faced with something of a mystery. Zenji Orita, *I-15*'s executive officer at the time, went on to write a hugely popular postwar book about the IJN's submarine operations and his own part in them.[19] While he talked at length about *I-15*'s activities during the first weeks of war—including a night surfacing off San Francisco on December 24—Orita made absolutely no mention of encountering *Cynthia Olson*'s lifeboats. Such an event, had it occurred, would certainly have merited a mention in his volume, in that it would have formed a nice counterpoint to the blizzard of postwar accounts of IJN brutality toward Allied merchant seamen. In the absence of any official records documenting *I-15*'s supposed humanitarian gesture toward *Cynthia Olson*'s survivors and given that the submarine's second in command makes no mention of it, we must assume that the "second sub" event was apocryphal and *I-15* (and, for that matter, *I-19*) neither provided humanitarian aid to nor butchered the American mariners. Whether Minoru Yokota made the story up out of whole cloth

184 | DAWN OF INFAMY

in a belated attempt to depict his actions and those of other Japanese submariners in a better light, or heard the story from a fellow veteran at a
reunion or some other postwar gathering and simply passed it on, or was
simply mistaken, we will never know.

————

WHICH BRINGS US, OF COURSE, to the fourth and final scenario—that Bert
Carlsen and his men ultimately died from starvation, thirst, and exposure as their two undamaged lifeboats drifted in the vast Pacific. Existing
evidence—some of it admittedly circumstantial—points to this as being
the ultimate fate of the *Cynthia Olson* survivors.

The first and most important thing to consider here is *Prince Robert*'s
search of the area in which the Laker was attacked. The armed merchant
cruiser received COPC's order to change course and undertake the search
for *Cynthia Olson* at 9:42 p.m., GMT, (11:12 a.m., Honolulu time), just
under two hours after the transmission of Sam Ziskind's distress message. The Canadian vessel arrived at the American ship's last reported
position—33°42' north by 145°29' west—just over six hours later and
spent the following three hours systematically searching a wide swath of
ocean with eyes, lights, and radar. The sweep was absolutely fruitless, in
that the Canadians sighted no wreckage, no flotsam, no bodies, and no
lifeboats.[20]

While it is always possible that the position Sam Ziskind gave in his
distress message was incorrect, or even that Leslie Grogan somehow
recorded the position report incorrectly, both eventualities are highly
unlikely. The ship's exact position would have been updated several times
on each watch using both a sextant and by dead reckoning,[21] and Carlsen or
one of his senior officers would obviously have given Ziskind a very accurate position to pass on in his distress message, simply because the crews'
very lives would have depended on rescue forces being able to find them
quickly. Moreover, the position the young radioman transmitted—33°42'
north by 145°29' west—was exactly on the normal steamer track between
Seattle and Honolulu.

A second point to bear in mind is the amount of time *I-26* spent trying
to sink *Cynthia Olson*. Although the Japanese accounts all agree that the
submarine submerged at least once during the course of the attack, they

differ—often significantly—about how long the entire encounter lasted. Yokota, for example, told Gordon Prange in 1951 that the attack took place over a period of about five hours, from 6:30 p.m., GMT (8:00 a.m. in Honolulu), to about 11:30 p.m., GMT (1:00 p.m. in Honolulu), whereas in 1966 he told Alf Pratte the assault lasted approximately eight hours, until about 2:30 a.m., GMT (3:00 p.m. in Honolulu). While Takaji Komaba didn't specify an elapsed time, his account seemed to indicate that *I-26* spent no more than a few hours trying to sink *Cynthia Olson*. And though they disagreed on what time the attack began, Saburo Hayashi and Yukio Oka both stated that the entire event lasted just two hours. Hayashi offered additional information about the assault's chronology—albeit indirectly—in Bert Webber's *Silent Siege*. In the Japanese-language notation that appeared next to his picture of the burning Laker, Hayashi said he snapped the image at "around 4:10 a.m.," obviously meaning Japan Standard Time.

This latter point is important, because if Hayashi's recollection of the time was correct, it would mean that *Cynthia Olson* was on fire and listing heavily just forty minutes after the attack began at 3:30 a.m., JST (6:30 p.m., GMT), and just thirty-two minutes after Sam Ziskind's distress message at 6:38 p.m., GMT.

And there's another wrinkle. Each of the Japanese accounts differs on the attack's final act. Yokota told both Prange and Pratte that *I-26* did not stay around to witness the Laker's sinking (he also told the former that before departing the scene he watched the doughty freighter roll onto her port side, though Hayashi's photo clearly shows her listing so heavily to starboard that her deck rails are almost awash). Oka and Hayashi agreed that the sub had submerged, resurfaced, and fired additional deck-gun rounds, with the former saying *Cynthia Olson* then "capsized and started to sink"[22] and the latter remembering that the Laker "developed a heavy list and appeared to go down."[23] While Komaba said the "freighter remained afloat and we had to surface one more time to scuttle it,"[24] we can safely assume that he didn't actually mean that men from *I-26* went aboard the burning Laker to set scuttling charges. Such an act would have been extremely foolish given the American ship's list and the very real possibility that she would capsize at any moment, and Yokota would certainly not have risked sending across a boarding team when he was fully expecting the imminent arrival of Allied ships and aircraft.

All three of the issues mentioned above—the varying Japanese accounts of how long *I-26* remained in the vicinity of *Cynthia Olson*, Hayashi's timing of his photo, and whether the Laker had started to sink before the Japanese submarine left the area—are key to our understanding of what ultimately happened to the American crewmen.

We know that *Prince Robert* arrived at *Cynthia Olson's* last reported position at approximately 3:42 a.m., GMT, some eight hours after the Laker's distress message. We also know that the Canadian warship's three-hour search revealed no sign of either *Cynthia Olson* or *I-26*. This fact makes Minoru Yokota's assertion that his submarine remained stationary in the Laker's vicinity for five or eight hours (until either 11:30 p.m. or 2:30 a.m., GMT) extremely difficult to accept. If, as Yokota said, he took *I-26* away from the attack site before *Cynthia Olson* sank, it would most probably have meant that the Laker herself—or much of her deck cargo and other floating debris—would still have been on the ocean's surface when *Prince Robert* arrived to begin her search. This would have been especially true if we accept Yokota's assertion that he kept his sub near the American vessel until 2:30 a.m., GMT, which would have meant that the Canadian warship would have arrived on-scene just one hour and twelve minutes after *I-26's* departure.

Since we know that *Prince Robert* did not sight the burning and listing *Cynthia Olson*, any wreckage, or, more importantly, the Laker's lifeboats, logic dictates that we reject Yokota's assertion that *I-26* remained near the Laker for five to eight hours. And while it's difficult to imagine that the cycle of events described in greater or lesser detail in the other Japanese accounts—the initial surfacing, the warning shot, the American crews' abandonment of their vessel, the initial deck-gun barrage, the firing of one (or perhaps two) torpedoes, at least one resurfacing, and the firing of the final gun rounds—could all have taken place in from forty minutes to two hours, such must have been the case. If the shell-battered and burning *Cynthia Olson* was on the verge of capsizing and sinking two hours after *I-26's* first warning shot, she could well have slipped entirely beneath the waves up to six hours before *Prince Robert's* arrival. The funeral pyre of smoke from the Laker would have dissipated, and much of her deck cargo and other flotsam could well have drifted far enough from the site of the sinking that it was not seen by those aboard the Canadian warship.

In talking about the dissipation of smoke from the burning *Cynthia Olson* and the drifting away of debris, deck cargo, and, of course, the

Laker's lifeboats, we're dealing with two natural phenomena—currents in both the air and the ocean.

Though in early December the surface winds in the area in which *I-26* attacked *Cynthia Olson* can blow from virtually any direction, *Prince Robert*'s deck log (in which her bridge crew recorded wind speed, direction, and other pertinent data every four hours) tells us that throughout the day on December 7, the wind was blowing to the north-northwest at four to six knots. This means that if *Cynthia Olson* actually sank within, say, three hours after *I-26* commenced firing for effect, the smoke pillar could have entirely dissipated in the five hours before *Prince Robert*'s arrival. The flames, of course, would have been extinguished as the sinking ship began her hours-long plunge to the sea floor, some fifteen thousand feet down.[25]

While the surface winds would also have affected the direction and speed of drift of *Cynthia Olson*'s lifeboats (and debris), the prevailing ocean current was a far more direct agent of movement. The position Sam Ziskind broadcast before he and the rest of the Laker's crew abandoned their ship is, unfortunately, within the center of what's known as the North Pacific Gyre, a massive clockwise-circulating current[26] that encompasses millions of square miles of ocean.[27] At the point where *Cynthia Olson*'s lifeboats went into the water, the current flows almost directly east, before turning south, then eventually dead west, then north to begin the cycle again. Though the mean current is not fast—only a few miles per hour—in five or six hours the lifeboats and debris could well have been carried ten or more miles to the east of the position that Sam Ziskind sent out.[28]

We'll revisit the importance of the North Pacific Gyre in a moment, but we first must consider an additional fact regarding *Prince Robert*'s search. When ordered to change course and head toward *Cynthia Olson*'s last-known position, the Canadian warship was some 120 miles to the north-east on a heading of 041 degrees. Commander Hart ordered a change of heading to 206 degrees—almost directly to the south-southwest—and brought both of his ship's engines to full ahead. The vessel charged along, averaging just over twenty knots and, according to her deck log, arrived at the Laker's last reported location at 3:42 a.m., GMT. Or, more accurately, *Prince Robert* passed some five miles to the east of that spot. Hart held his ship on 206 degrees for another eight minutes, then turned to a new course of 090 degrees, back to the north-northeast. Over the next two hours and forty-two minutes *Prince Robert* undertook a standard "box" search—successively turning to 000, 270, 180 degrees and, finally, back onto 090 at the bottom, or due-south, corner of the box. Each search leg was approximately nineteen miles long, with *Cynthia Olson*'s last-known position just a few miles to the northeast of that southern corner.

Establishing a box-shaped search pattern whose southernmost corner was just a few miles from the reported site of *I-26*'s attack made sense, given that the surface winds were blowing toward the north-northwest. Hart was obviously assuming that the winds would have pushed the life-boats generally northward from the attack point, and he subsequently concentrated his search to the northeast and northwest of that position. The Canadian officer either didn't know about the prevailing currents in the area or believed that on that particular night the winds were a more important factor, and he shaped his search pattern accordingly.

Unfortunately for the men in *Cynthia Olson*'s lifeboats, Hart's deci-sion meant that the first full leg of the search box—the one established when *Prince Robert* turned from her 206 degree heading back to 090 eight minutes after passing the Laker's last reported position—was most likely already at least ten miles too far to the northwest. And by the time the Canadian warship "closed the box" by completing the fourth leg of the search and turning back to the northeast, the lifeboats most probably had moved several miles farther to the east or southeast. Though the night was clear with what Hart called a "brilliant moon," if we assume that the boats' distance from *Prince Robert*'s track was by that time twelve to fifteen miles, they would have been both over the horizon and well beyond the six-to-seven mile visibility noted in the Canadian warship's deck log.[29] At 6:42 a.m., GMT, having found no trace of *Cynthia Olson* or her lifeboats, Hart reluctantly shaped a course for Esquimalt.

———

PRINCE ROBERT'S DEPARTURE EFFECTIVELY SEALED the fate of Bert Carlsen and his crew. Trapped in the slowly rotating North Pacific Gyre, *Cynthia Olson*'s two lifeboats—which were almost certainly either lashed together or connected more loosely by ropes so as not to become separated—would have drifted upon a vast, inhospitable, and seemingly endless ocean.

Exposed in the open-top boats to the North Pacific's notoriously changeable December weather, Carlsen, Buchtele, and the rest would have been battered by the sea and baked by the sun, alternately shivering and sweating. Those who may have been injured in *I-26*'s attack—flesh torn open by shrapnel, perhaps, or limbs broken in the rush to escape their doomed ship—would have suffered more than their shipmates, but almost certainly not longer. As infection or gangrene or blood loss weakened them, the wounded or injured would have perished, their bodies committed to the deep by those who survived them. And as fresh water and emergency rations dwindled, even those who entered the boats in good health would have begun to weaken. Hoping every minute to sight a plume of smoke on the horizon or the glint of sun off a metal wing, the mariners would have died slowly of starvation or dehydration.[30] Or if they were lucky, perhaps death came suddenly in the shape of a crushing wave or, for the older men, a heart attack that ended all misery in a blessed moment.

We will never know, of course, how death finally came to the men of *Cynthia Olson*. But we do know that no trace of them was ever found—no bodies washed ashore for their loved ones to mourn over, no wreckage was spotted by passing ships. Eventually, days or weeks after Minoru Yokota fired that first warning shot across the Laker's bow, the last member of the doughty freighter's crew breathed his last. In the end, the thirty-one civilian seamen who sailed for Honolulu aboard the aging lumber ship joined the more than nine thousand U.S. merchant mariners who died as a result of enemy action during World War II. Moreover, as of early 2016 the Defense POW/MIA Accounting Agency continues to officially consider Carlsen and the members of his crew—both civilian and military—to be among the more than seventy-three thousand "service personnel not recovered following World War II." Fittingly, the names of the two young soldiers who voyaged on *Cynthia Olson* are listed among the service members killed at Pearl Harbor and now memorialized at the National Memorial Cemetery of the Pacific—the famed Punchbowl.

May we never forget their sacrifice.

AFTERWORD

THOSE OF US WHO WRITE for a living choose our subjects for a variety of reasons. More often than we'd care to admit, the first motive is a financial one. Because putting words on paper is how we fund the lives we lead, we try to pick topics we hope other people will be willing to pay to read. Having said that, I honestly believe that any professional writer—whether journalist, novelist, or dramatist—needs to care about the topic he or she is writing about if the finished work is to be both complete and worthwhile.

More importantly, I believe that to do the most thorough and accurate job of unraveling historical events and describing the actions and motivations of persons long dead, a writer has to get to know his story's participants as well as the documentary evidence will permit. And, of course, in the process of learning the details of another human being's life any writer whose soul has not been deadened by the passage of time or jaded by professional experiences must come to care, at least to some extent, about the people who appear in his narrative.

And I believe that if the writer has done a good job of depicting the story's participants as real people, readers will also develop a relationship to those whose actions have filled the pages. Further, engaged readers often want to know the rest of the story—how the lives of the people about whom they've been reading played out. It is this last point to which I now turn.

THE OLSONS

While the loss of *Cynthia Olson* was undoubtedly a personal and commercial blow to the Oliver J. Olson Company and its principals, the coming of war was something of a boon for the firm. Between 1941 and 1946 the company operated a variety of vessels on behalf of the U.S. government, and revenues remained relatively stable. However, the postwar years were not as kind to the company, which saw its core business—the coastwise transportation of lumber and wood products—massively undercut by competing rail- and truck-based firms. Slowly bled white by falling revenues, in 1975 the shipping company was swallowed by the massive Zellerbach Paper conglomerate, which the following year also acquired the Olson Ocean Towing Company.

E. Whitney Olson and George Olson both died in 1969, and Oliver J. Olson Jr. died in 1981.

THE JAPANESE

Minoru Yokota/Hasegawa taught high school until his retirement in the 1970s, after which he worked as a volunteer for both the Immanuel General Missions' Department of World Missions and the Immanuel Bible Training College. He died on October 15, 1995, at the age of ninety-two. His second wife, Matsuko Hasegawa, was in her mid-nineties and living in a Tokyo retirement home as this volume was being completed.

Saburo Hayashi, Yukio Oka, and Takaji Komaba are all believed to have passed away, though the author has been unable to confirm their dates of death.

ABOARD *LURLINE* AND *PRINCE ROBERT*

Matson's Commodore Charles A. Berndtson died in Alameda, California, on May 9, 1948. Rudolph Asplund and Leslie E. Grogan both saw sea duty during World War II and returned to regular Matson service after 1945. The former died in Menlo Park, California, on November 19, 1972, and the latter in Alameda on August 4, 1974.

HMCS *Prince Robert*'s Captain Frederick Gordon Hart served in the Royal Canadian Navy through the late 1950s and died in Saanich, British Columbia, on December 20, 1967.

THE FAMILY MEMBERS

Despite diligent effort, the author has been unable to determine what happened to the family members of most of those aboard *Cynthia Olson*. However, we do know the stories of a few.

Several years after her husband's disappearance Thyra O. Carlsen moved out of the couples' San Pedro home, most probably because she could no longer pay the mortgage. After briefly living near San Diego she settled in Hayward, not far from San Francisco. On February 10, 1959, while driving through nearby San Leandro, Mrs. Carlsen's vehicle collided with another car. The collision killed seventeen-year-old Paula Mary Hammons, a passenger in the second car. Though Mrs. Carlsen was cleared of any wrongdoing in the accident, the girl's parents sued her, unsuccessfully, for $51,300. Mrs. Carlsen died in Alameda on January 12, 1981.

Unlike the Carlsens, Konrad "Harry" Lofving and his wife, Hulda Lofving, had children. While a son, Marcel, had died in infancy, the couple's daughter, Olga, was twenty-five at the time of her father's disappearance. Mrs. Lofving died in Alameda on August 19, 1951. Her daughter, whose married name was Olga Burmester, died in San Rafael, California, on November 21, 1999.

Because of the German occupation of Denmark, First Officer William Buchtele's wife, Katherine Beck Buchtele, was unable to immediately inform her husband's family of his disappearance. During the final years of the war she exchanged messages with them through the International Red Cross but chose not to tell them of their son's fate until he'd been officially declared dead. She finally broke the news to them in 1945. Mrs. Buchtele and her daughter, Eleanor, were living in Southern California when the war ended, and in 1946 Katherine married Hans A. Lorentzen, a Danish-born merchant mariner. They ultimately moved to Fresno, where Mrs. Lorentzen died on November 1, 1984. Her third husband died in the same city on January 28, 1988. Eleanor Beck Robinson died in Sacramento, California, on April 5, 2010.

In November 1944 a letter from the Army's Office of the Quartermaster General informed Ernest "Dee" Davenport's mother, Pauline Clifton, that, because her son's remains had never been recovered and were deemed to have been "lost at sea," she was eligible to receive a "regulation burial flag." The flag was delivered to her via registered mail on January 4, 1945. Pauline died sixteen months later, on May 30, 1946. In 1991, in response to an application filed by his half-sisters, Olean Gibbs and Sabra Dineen, Dee Davenport was posthumously awarded the Pearl Harbor Commemorative Medal.

Perhaps the saddest story concerning a *Cynthia Olson* family member is that of Bernice Lerner Ziskind, the young wife of the ship's radio operator.

After her husband's disappearance Bernice moved to Los Angeles and lived with her mother, sister, and stepfather. The young woman returned to teaching, securing a job at a school for Hispanic girls. In 1950 Bernice, her sister Inez, and their mother took a nine-week joint trip to Europe, and the following year Bernice became engaged to a fellow teacher named Walter Willis. Before the marriage could take place, however, tragedy struck: on the evening of June 21, 1952, Inez walked into her sister's bedroom in the family home to discuss wedding plans, only to find Bernice's body on the bed. Sam Ziskind's widow had died of what the Los Angeles County Coroner's office termed a "spontaneous intracebral hemorrhage." She was just thirty-three years old. Inez Lerner Grover passed away in Montclair, New Jersey, on November 17, 2010.

THE JOURNALISTS

Riley H. Allen, legendary editor of the Honolulu *Star-Bulletin* and the man who almost single-handedly kept the memory of *Cynthia Olson* and her crew alive in the immediate postwar years, died of cancer on October 2, 1966. Sadly, Allen passed away just months before Alf Pratte's article series—which Allen had, of course, suggested—ran in the *Star-Bulletin*.

Tomi Knaefler, who interviewed Minoru Yokota/Hasegawa in Japan, was still living in Hawaii as this volume was being completed.

Alf Pratte stayed at the *Star-Bulletin* until September 1969, when he took a job with the Hawaii state senate. In 1978 he moved on to Sea Grant (a NOAA-administered, college-based program that sponsors marine research). In 1981, having completed a doctorate at the University of Hawaii, Pratte returned to the mainland. He taught journalism for three years at Pennsylvania's Shippensburg University, then took a position at Brigham Young University in Utah. In 2003 Dr. Paul Alfred Pratte retired as emeritus professor of journalism and was living in Salt Lake at the time this volume was being completed.

ACKNOWLEDGMENTS

THE WRITING OF HISTORY IS always, to some degree, a work of dogged investigation. That is especially true when one is writing about an event whose participants are all dead and for which the documentation is scarce or, worse, contradictory.

Fortunately, in my ferreting out of data pertaining to *Cynthia Olson*, those who sailed aboard her and those who destroyed her, I've been ably and generously assisted by a number of people both in the United States and abroad. Their help has been immensely important and is greatly appreciated. Any errors or omissions in this volume are, of course, mine alone.

First and foremost, I want to thank my wife, Margaret Spragins Harding. This book—and those that have both preceded it and will, hopefully, come after it—would not have been possible without her love, support, understanding, and willingness to patiently listen to me drone on about a ship neither of us has ever seen, people we never knew, and an event that occurred before we were born. Mari is, quite simply, the best person I have ever known, and I am the luckiest man on earth.

I would also like to acknowledge the following people:

IN CALIFORNIA:

The late Eleanor Beck Robinson, for sharing her remarkably clear—and still quite poignant—memories of her mother and stepfather, Katherine Beck Buchtele and William Buchtele.

David H. Grover, for his encyclopedic knowledge of World War II Army ships and for his friendship.

William Kooiman, former reference volunteer at the San Francisco Maritime National Historical Park, for his untiring efforts to locate obscure vessel movement cards pertaining to both *Coquina* and *Cynthia Olson*.

Joe Sanchez and Robert Glass of the National Archives and Records Administration's Pacific Region in San Bruno, California, for finding many more pertinent documents than I or anyone else believed existed.

Gary and Karen Rathburn, for allowing me the opportunity to tour Berthel Carlsen's former home in San Pedro.

Richard Dillman of the Maritime Radio Historical Society for giving me a quick education in 1940s maritime radio technology, and for providing transcripts of important radio logs for December 7 and 8, 1941.

Jeff Hull, Matson Navigation Company's director of public relations.

Steve Marconi, of *San Pedro Today*, for providing the 1941 article about Berthel Carlsen.

Liz Ruth-Abramian, archivist-librarian of the Los Angeles Maritime Museum, for her extensive research assistance.

Gordon Ghareeb, for expanding on his wonderful book *Hollywood to Honolulu* and for his guided tour of SS *Lane Victory*.

Lisa Nguyen, modern Chinese history archivist at the Hoover Institution Library and Archives, for locating the Bert Webber papers.

Dr. Jenny Fichmann, for her tireless research assistance in the Webber collection.

In Connecticut:

Arthur Allen of the U.S. Coast Guard's Office of Search and Rescue for explaining to me the immense challenges facing anyone trying to locate a drifting lifeboat, and for a sobering education about how quickly the occupants of that boat can perish.

In Hawaii:

Patty Lai, of the Hawaii State Archives, for providing a copy of Riley H. Allen's 1947 paper and a host of hugely important newspaper articles and other valuable materials.

Burl Burlingame, for expanding on the material in his book *Advance Force Pearl Harbor*.

Dore Minatodani, of the University of Hawaii's Hawaiian Collection, and university archivist James Cartwright.

Dr. John Wiltshire, of the NOAA/University of Hawaii's Hawaii Undersea Research Laboratory, and Patrick Caldwell, of NOAA's National Oceanographic Data Center, for providing wind and current data for the North Pacific Gyre.

In Maine:

Noted maritime historian Charles Dana Gibson, who shared his considerable knowledge of Army watercraft and the World War II operations of the Army Transport Service.

In Maryland:

Paul B. Brown and Timothy K. Nenninger of NARA's Archives II facility in College Park.

In Michigan:

Joel Stone, of the Detroit Historical Society, for providing Laker blueprints.

In New Jersey:

The late Inez L. Grover, sister of Bernice Lerner Ziskind and sister-in-law of Samuel Ziskind, for sharing her memories and photos of both.

In New York:

The research staff of the Franklin D. Roosevelt Presidential Library at Hyde Park.

Dr. George J. Billy, chief librarian at the U.S. Merchant Marine Academy at Kings Point.

Amy Bailin, niece of Samuel Ziskind, for sharing family history information.

In North Carolina:

Shirleyan Phelps and Linda Haas Davenport, for sharing Davenport family history and photos.

In Oregon:

Hannah Contino of the Coos Historical & Maritime Museum for her document- and photo-research assistance.

Ashly Norberg, of the Oregon State University archives, for providing a copy of Bert Webber's 1972 article.

IN UTAH:

Alf Pratte, for talking to me at length about his series on *Cynthia Olson*, and for sharing stories about Riley Allen.

IN VIRGINIA:

My colleagues David Lauterborn, Sarah Cokeley, and Jennifer Berry at World History Group's *Military History* magazine, for putting up with my distracted demeanor while writing this book.

Karen Jensen and Wendy Palitz, both of WHG's *World War II* magazine; Karen for commissioning me to write the article on which this book is based, and Wendy for doing such a wonderful job of laying out the article.

Naomi Barber and her mother, Yukiyo, for their translation help.

IN WASHINGTON:

Dorothy Laigo Cordova, executive director of the Filipino American National Historical Society in Seattle, for educating me about the important role played by Filipinos and Filipino-Americans in the World War II U.S. Merchant Marine and armed forces.

IN WASHINGTON, DC:

Archivist Mark C. Mollan, of NARA's Old Navy/Maritime Reference Division, for locating the absolutely crucial Merchant Mariner Deceased Casualty Files.

IN WEST VIRGINIA:

The staff of the Records Management Division in the U.S. Coast Guard's National Maritime Center.

IN WISCONSIN:

Susie Menk, archives assistant at the Wisconsin Maritime Museum, for locating great photos of *Coquina*.

IN CANADA:

Clare Sugrue of the Canadian Forces Base Esquimalt Naval and Military Museum.

Sarah Hurfurd, reference archivist at Library and Archives Canada, for providing copies of the COPC messages to HMCS *Prince Robert*.

Warren Sinclair, chief archivist in the National Defence Headquarters' Directorate of History and Heritage, for help in locating HMCS *Prince Robert*'s deck logs and Commander F. G. Hart's "Report of Proceedings."

IN ESTONIA:

Sander Kingsepp, for his help in understanding Imperial Japanese Navy (IJN) submarine operations and for his translation assistance.

IN ISRAEL:

Shmuel Ziskind, nephew and namesake of Samuel Ziskind, for sharing his family's history.

IN JAPAN:

Philip Z. Hirai and the Rev. Joshua T. Tsutada, sons-in-law of Minoru Hasegawa, for fleshing out family history and their memories of the former captain of *I-26*.

Isamu Maruhashi, for his research and translation assistance.

IN SWEDEN:

Ingemar Landin, for family history information on Harry Lofving.

NOTES

1. The USSB was established in September 1916 and formally organized in January of the following year. Its broad mission included the peacetime regulation of American maritime carriers, practices, and facilities and the development of a Merchant Marine service that could become a naval auxiliary should America be drawn into the Great War then raging in Europe.

2. The ships gained the appellation largely because the first vessel of the type was believed to have been built in the Norwegian port city of the same name.

3. As well as eight other vessels of different designs.

4. For a concise and complete history of these ships, see *The "Lakers" of World War I*, by Rev. Edward J. Dowling, S.J. (University of Detroit Press, 1967), from which much of the Laker data in this volume are drawn.

5. The last fifteen of which were canceled.

6. Indeed, only the World War II Liberty and T-2 tanker programs produced more vessels—3,200 and 525, respectively—than the WWI Laker program.

7. Deadweight tonnage expresses the maximum safe weight of the entire vessel and all it normally carries—structure, crew, fuel, cargo, ballast, etc. Gross tonnage is an expression of the aggregate volume of all of the ship's enclosed spaces, and net tonnage usually refers to the weight of actual cargo the ship can safely handle.

8. Two sets of bottom-hull plates separated by about twenty inches of void space for the entire length of the vessel's bottom, stem to stern. In coal-fired Lakers, these spaces were not used; in oil-fired vessels, the voids forward of the deckhouse were divided into two main, full-beam fuel-oil tanks.

9. The sleeping quarters and messroom for the ship's ordinary seamen was in the poop.

10. Like all fire-tube boilers, the Scotch type uses coal or fuel-oil fires to produce hot flue gases that are directed through a number of metal tubes immersed in a sealed water container. The heat coursing through

the tubes produces steam, which in a triple-expansion system is collected and forced successively through high-, intermediate-, and low-pressure cylinders. The drive and valve rods inside each cylinder are connected to the same crankshaft, which ultimately turns the ship's screw.

11. In his excellent book on the Lakers, Fr. Dowling pointed out that the vessels intended for Great Britain but requisitioned by the U.S. government in 1917 were initially referred to as "War" class ships, as their presumed British owners had given each a two-part name beginning with "War"—*War Fox*, *War Gull*, and *War Oak*, as examples. Most were given "Lake" prefix names following their requisitioning, and Fr. Dowling reported that the first thirty-three new-build ships were initially intended to bear "Lake" names as well. However, for some reason that has since been lost to history, thirty vessels were given names beginning with "C," two had names beginning with "G," and the last of the thirty-three was named, inexplicably, *Python*. *Coquina* may thus have initially referred to Idaho's Lake Coquina, though there is no way to prove this hypothesis.

12. A subsidiary of Manitowoc Shipbuilding that produced marine boilers and other machinery for both maritime and other uses.

13. The numbers and aggregate tonnage of ships involved in the effort are impressive. The USSB ultimately commandeered 87 German, Austrian, and Dutch ships with a total gross tonnage of 946,226; chartered 384 foreign-owned vessels totaling 1,262,669 gross tons; commandeered 402 vessels under construction in U.S. shipyards for a total of 2,709,792 gross tons; and contracted for 2,382 new-build vessels totaling more than 9 million tons. Data drawn from *America's Merchant Marine*, published by Banker's Trust Co., New York, NY, 1920, pp. 37–39.

14. Drawn from *Records of the United States Maritime Commission*, Record Group 178, National Archives, College Park, Maryland.

15. All data pertaining to the ship's titling history is drawn from the document *Abstract and Certificate of Record of Title of the Steam Screw* Cynthia Olson (*ex*-Coquina), generated by the Office of Collector of Customs in San Francisco on June 4, 1945, and currently held at NARA, San Bruno, California.

16. While at least one writer has indicated that *Coquina* made one or more post-WWI voyages carrying humanitarian-aid cargoes to Europe, the author has been unable to locate any documentation supporting this belief. Indeed, her name is not included on any of the lists recording the names of USSB-owned or chartered vessels that undertook such voyages.

17. See the article "Want Government Aid in Whisky Disposal" in the January 7, 1920, issue of the *New York Times*.

18. For accounts of the whiskey train and the Philadelphia port strike, see the articles in the January 1–4, 1920, issues of the *New York Times*.

19. This and all subsequent homeport data drawn from individual "Approval of Home Port of Vessel" documents generated between 1919 and 1940 by the Department of Commerce's Bureau of Marine Inspection and Repair, currently held at NARA, San Bruno, California.

20. See the article "Receivers for Earn Line" in the October 18, 1913, issue of the *New York Times*.

21. Sponsored by Sen. Wesly Jones of Washington, the act is still generally referred to as the "Jones Act."

22. To "lay up" a vessel means to take it out of service and put it into floating storage. The ship is closed down, either anchored out or tied to a pier, and visited periodically by a maintenance crew whose job is to keep the vessel mechanically sound in anticipation of future use.

23. Founded by Captains A. F. Pillsbury and Lebbens Curtis, both of whom had captained vessels for Matson Navigation Company.

24. Which is, of course, a continuing problem, given that *Coquina/Cynthia Olson*'s engineering and deck logs—as well as other vital documents—were lost with the ship.

25. For the complete, fascinating history of the line and its ships, see the thoroughly enjoyable *Hollywood to Honolulu: The Story of the Los Angeles Steamship Company*, by Gordon Ghareeb and Martin Cox.

26. LASSCO had originally gotten into the California-Hawaii market at the suggestion of the Los Angeles Chamber of Commerce, which felt that such a service would allow Los Angeles to reap some of the profits the city of San Francisco was realizing because it was home to Matson's corporate headquarters. Two former North German Lloyd liners that had been seized when America entered World War I in 1917—the 13,182-GRT *Grosser Kurfurst* and 10,531-GRT *Friedrich der Grosse*—were chartered from the USSB and put into LASSCO service as, respectively, *City of Los Angeles* and *City of Honolulu*. The latter was gutted by fire on her first voyage and was replaced by the former NDL liner *Princess Alice* (which had also been seized in 1917). That vessel went into LASSCO service in 1927 as *City of Honolulu* (II) and proved immediately popular. After being ravaged by fire in Honolulu in May 1930, the ship was moved back to Los Angeles under her own power. She was initially laid up there, but after it was determined she'd be too expensive to repair she was towed to Osaka, Japan, in December 1933 to be scrapped.

27. Not to be confused with the Spanish-American War–era liners-turned-auxiliary cruisers of the same names. Those vessels were the former *City of Paris* and *City of New York*, respectively, of the Inman & International Line, a subsidiary of the American-owned International Navigation Company.

28. Though she was unsuited to the service LASSCO had planned for her, *Iroquois* went on to attain a certain fame, albeit in an unexpected way.

In July 1940, the U.S. Navy purchased the vessel and converted her into the hospital ship USS *Solace*, and in that guise she was present at Pearl Harbor on December 7, 1941. The ship was undamaged in the attack, and her crew undertook heroic efforts to rescue and treat survivors.

29. As noted earlier, the complete record of title for *Coquina/Cynthia Olson* is in the author's collection.

30. Located on California's San Pedro Bay, Wilmington is part of the larger San Pedro/Los Angeles harbor complex.

31. See Fred A. Stindt's comprehensive corporate history, *Matson's Century of Ships*, p. 85.

32. See note 26, above.

33. Including Stindt's normally infallible volume, cited above.

34. To Schafer Brothers Steamship Company of San Francisco. The former *Corsicana* was sold several times over the following decades and was finally broken up in Hong Kong in August 1962.

35. Stindt, pp. 91–99. See also *Cargoes: Matson's First Century in the Pacific*, by William L. Worden, pp. 82–88.

CHAPTER TWO

1. Genealogical information courtesy of the Olson family.

2. *Ships of the Redwood Coast*, by Jack McNairn and Jerry MacMullen, p. 60.

3. "Her Captain Is a Boy," article in the *San Francisco Call* newspaper, December 1895.

4. Ibid.

5. William again made the newspapers when, in September 1898, he and a fellow Hind, Rolph & Co. master challenged each other to a race between their identical, brand-new schooners. And what a race it was to be: the ships—William Olson's *Honoipu* and *Muriel*, commanded, interestingly enough, by a Capt. Carlson—would dash from San Francisco to Tacoma, take on loads of sawn timber, then race to Sydney, Australia, where they'd exchange the timber for coal. They'd then set off for Honolulu, where they'd each swap the coal for 1,100 tons of sugar, and then speed back to San Francisco. The race and its progress were subjects of intense public interest, with newspapers in California and Hawaii providing regular updates. As it turned out, William Olson lost by mere hours and thus had to pay the agreed upon price—he bought Carlson a lavish champagne dinner in one of San Francisco's finest restaurants.

6. Born in Sweden in 1867, Lindstrom emigrated to the United States at age twenty. After working in a shipyard in Eureka, California, in 1898 he opened his own yard in Aberdeen. There he quickly made a name for himself as a builder of quality sailing vessels, steamships, and utility craft. He was ultimately elected Aberdeen's mayor and died in an accident in June 1908. (From the 1947 *American-Swedish Historical Museum Yearbook*, p. 59.)

7. One board foot is an inch thick, 12 inches wide and 12 inches long; a total of 144 cubic inches. Thus, a 10-foot-long, 1-inch-thick, and 12-inch-wide plank contains 10 board feet. *Ships of the Redwood Coast*, p. 7.

8. The particulars of this extraordinary voyage are outlined in the otherwise dry tome *The Cases of General Value and Authority Subsequent to Those Contained in the "American Decisions" and the "American Reports," Decided in the Courts of the Several States. Selected, Reported, and Annotated by A. C. Freeman*, p. 191.

9. Built by the Charles E. Fulton yards in Bellingham, Washington.

10. Direct descendants of the wooden sailing ships that initially carried lumber along the Pacific Coast, steam schooners were powered by triple-expansion steam engines and driven by a single screw. Ranging from 150 to 210 feet in length, the beamy little vessels were characterized by an aft deck house separated from a small forecastle by a large expanse of open deck topping one or two cargo holds. By making maximum use of the available space, these doughty little vessels could carry up to one million board feet of lumber, though many also saw service as haulers of general cargo and passengers. Built of wood to take advantage of the plentiful timber then still available, steam schooners were the backbone of the West Coast's varied maritime industries well into the 1920s.

11. Unfortunately, both ships ended their days on the rocks. In 1922, *Thomas L. Wand* ran hard aground on Pfeiffer Point, some seven miles south of California's Point Sur, and broke up. Five years later, *Jim Butler*, under new ownership and renamed *Crescent City*, met her fate six miles north of Santa Cruz, California.

12. Of course, in hindsight, we might question the wisdom of basing the city's rebirth on wooden construction, given that some 90 percent of the destruction was caused by the thirty major fires that ravaged the predominantly wooden-built city after the earthquake.

13. Among the gentleman's many interesting personal quirks, he blithely alternated the spelling of his last name between "Mahony" and "Mahoney" as the mood struck him. I've chosen to use the first spelling because that is the one that appears on the majority of documents relating to his partnership with Oliver J. Olson.

14. *Ships of the Redwood Coast*, p. 61.

15. Opened in 1898 and built almost entirely over water, the building survived the 1906 earthquake without serious damage. In the temblor's aftermath, the Ferry Building handled many of the vessels bringing relief and other supplies into the devastated city—including lumber shipments arriving aboard Olson & Mahony ships.

16. Harlan & Hollingsworth ultimately became part of Bethlehem Steel Company.

17. *Olson & Mahony*'s delivery difficulties were noted in the October 12, 1907, issue of the *San Francisco Call* newspaper. The vessel rendered

sterling service until 1916, when she was sold to the S.E. Slade Co. for service in South America. She went through several additional owners before being cut down into a barge in 1956, and was wrecked that year, rather ironically, in Argentina.

18. *Ships of the Redwood Coast*, pp. 61–62.

19. The firm, which operated several vessels of its own out of San Pedro in Southern California, would later play a supporting role in the *Cynthia Olson* story.

20. Olson & Mahony owned one ship incorporating both partners' names and three with names not associated with either partner—*Jim Butler*, *Thomas L. Wand*, and *J. Marhoffer*. The remaining vessels in their fleet were *Susan Olson* (1911), *Florence Olson* (1912), *Oliver J. Olson* (1913), and *Rosalie Mahony* (1913).

21. An advertisement in the August 1912 issue of the journal *Architect and Engineer of California* gives the address of the company's storage yards and planing mill as Fifth and Hooper Streets and lists, in addition to Charles F. Van Damme, Oliver J. Olson as president, F. K. McComber as vice president, and Andrew F. Mahony as treasurer.

22. The famous prison had been founded in 1852, followed seven years later by the small city of San Quentin.

23. From M. M. Snodgrass, *Memories of the Richmond–San Rafael Ferry Company*, pp. 43–45. See also *Ships of the Redwood Coast*, p. 62.

24. See Mahony's obituary in the November 9, 1933, edition of the *New York Times*.

25. Constructed by Kruse & Banks Shipbuilders of North Bend, Oregon, in 1917 and named for Oliver Olson's then-nineteen-year-old-daughter, she was 213 feet long and 1,185 gross tons. Sold out of Olson service in 1923 and renamed *Willapa* (one of several vessels on the West Coast to carry the name), she was wrecked near Port Orford, Oregon, on December 3, 1941.

26. Walter James Olson was born in 1877.

27. These ships were, respectively, the former *Ryder Hanify* (1,363 tons), *Ghislaine* (1,517 tons), *Yolande* (1,384 tons), and *Paraiso* (1,383 tons). Sadly, all four vessels were to have difficult careers and sad ends. In June 1944 *George L. Olson* was beached and wrecked near Coos Bay, Oregon. *Whitney Olson*, having been sold out of the Olson Co. fleet in 1947, was beached and burned in Hong Kong in 1949. Soon after her delivery to the company *Virginia Olson* was rammed by a Navy submarine in dense fog off Los Angeles and sank at her pier just after reaching the safety of the harbor; she was sold in 1924 and was ultimately destroyed by fire at San Pedro, California, in 1926. *Florence Olson*, sold in 1942 and renamed *Malano*, was sold for scrap in 1946.

28. And it was one of the very few to use unionized seamen. The once powerful Sailors' Union of the Pacific had been virtually broken in 1921,

following a series of coordinated attacks by a coalition of larger steamship companies, aided by reactionary elements in the city and state governments. The Olson Company nonetheless continued to use union sailors, and pay union wages, throughout the 1921–1934 period of the union's greatest weakness.

29. At the time of writing, the home, located at 540 El Camino Del Mar, belonged to the family of the late comedian, actor, and longtime San Francisco resident Robin Williams.

30. The plans were known, respectively, as War Plan Orange and War Plan Black.

31. Built by Albina Engine & Machine Works in Portland, Oregon, the vessel had an interesting life. In 1942, the War Shipping Administration acquired her from the Olson Steamship Company and commissioned her as the transport USS *Camanga* (AG-42). After providing yeoman service throughout the Pacific—including voyages to New Caledonia and New Zealand—the already elderly ship was decommissioned in December 1945, returned to the control of the WSA, and, ultimately, taken back into Olson service as *Oliver Olson*. She was wrecked at Bandon Harbor, Oregon, in March 1953.

32. The lumber carried to the Canal Zone was used to build barracks for the additional soldiers being sent to defend the vital waterway. The purpose of the voyage to Peru and Costa Rica is unclear.

CHAPTER THREE

1. *Abstract and Certificate of Record of Title of the Steam Screw* Cynthia Olson *(ex-*Coquina*).*

2. *Cynthia Olson* was named for Oliver J. Olson Jr.'s daughter.

3. The pertinent Bureau of Marine Inspection and Navigation documents, as well as George Pitt's letter requesting the name changes, are currently held at NARA, San Bruno, California. Copies are in the author's possession.

4. The three twenty-four-foot wooden boats with which the Laker had originally been equipped were replaced at some point in her early service life with two thirty-five-person boats.

5. Fort Mason is now a National Historical Landmark District and part of the Golden Gate National Recreation Area. Established in 1850 as the United States Military Reservation San Francisco, in 1906 it was renamed the San Francisco Quartermaster Depot. It officially became the SFPOE in 1932. For a fascinating contemporary look at the SFPOE's operations just before and during World War II, see *Gateway to Victory: The Wartime Story of the San Francisco Port of Embarkation* by James W. Hamilton and William J. Bolce Jr.

6. The series of letters and telegrams between Fisher and the Seattle inspectors is currently held at NARA, San Bruno, California. Copies are in the author's collection.

7. Given that the ship's logs were lost in her sinking, dates for her movements during 1941 are based on several alternate sources. These include the "steamship movements" columns in newspapers (including the *San Francisco Chronicle*, the *Seattle Post-Intelligencer*, the *Los Angeles Times*, the *Honolulu Star-Bulletin*, and the *Honolulu Advertiser*); vessel movement cards maintained by the Port of San Francisco (held at the San Francisco Maritime Museum); and vessel-specific Army charter records (now at NARA, San Bruno).

8. After the Japanese attack on Pearl Harbor the Quartermaster Corps' pier and warehouse complex at Kapalama quickly grew into a sprawling facility that supported operations throughout the Pacific. The Kapalama Military Reservation, as it was ultimately named, remained under Army control until closed down in the late 1990s as part of the Department of Defense Base Closure and Realignment (BRAC) effort.

9. The Office of Emergency Management had actually been authorized by Roosevelt's Executive Order 8428 of September 8, 1939, but was not officially created until May 25, 1940, when it was established by administrative order. See Record Group 214, NARA, College Park, Maryland.

10. Short-sea vessels carry cargoes within continental waters, while deep-sea vessels carry their cargoes across oceans.

11. Details of the August meeting and the Army's participation drawn from *Organization and Activities of the Traffic Control Branch, Transportation Division, Office of the Quartermaster General, 1941–1942*, a monograph prepared in December 1943 by Mr. Chester C. Wardlow, a historian in the Office of the Chief of Transportation. Wardlow would go on to become the acknowledged expert on the history of Army watercraft operations in World War II and authored (among other works) *The Transportation Corps: Movements, Training and Supply* in the series *United States Army in World War II*.

12. During the course of World War II the Army would bareboat charter a variety of ship types, including passenger vessels (for use as troopships or hospital ships), cargo ships of various types, and at least two refrigerated freighters. See *U.S. Army Ships and Watercraft of World War II* by David H. Grover.

13. Charter details drawn from the agreement itself, currently held at NARA, College Park, Maryland, and a copy of which is in the author's possession.

14. While some sources have cited November 21 as the date on which the contract was signed, the document itself is dated November 18. That

date is also cited in several postwar communications among the Olson Company, the Army, and family members of those lost aboard the ship.

15. Within four months the same NAS Alameda pier would host the aircraft carrier USS *Hornet* as she took aboard the USAAF B-25 bombers destined to attack Japan under the command of Lt. Col. James H. Doolittle.

16. Though if that was the case, one wonders why any Navy passengers weren't disembarked at Fort Mason and asked to simply take a cab.

17. The German raider *Orion* had been the first to enter the Pacific, and in mid-June 1940 she'd laid a series of mine barrages across the approaches to New Zealand's Auckland Harbor. Her first victim, the 13,415-ton freighter *Niagara*, hit one of the mines and sank on June 19.

18. The SS *City of Flint* was the first American merchant ship to encounter German forces on the high seas, when on September 9, 1939, she was captured (and ultimately released) by the "pocket battleship" *Deutschland*. The American Pioneer Line's 5,383-ton *City of Rayville* holds the dubious distinction of being the first US-flagged merchant ship to be sunk in World War II; she sank on November 8, 1940, after hitting a mine in the Bass Strait just off Cape Otway, 120 miles southwest of Melbourne, Australia. Third engineer Mac B. Bryan of Randleman, North Carolina, died in the sinking, becoming the first of more than nine thousand American merchant mariners who would die as the result of hostile action in World War II. Ironically, the mine that sank *City of Rayville* was laid by a former merchant ship, the 8,898-ton Norwegian tanker *Storstad*, which had been captured by the German raider *Pinguin* and turned into the auxiliary minelayer *Passat*. For a fascinating account of the American merchant mariners in the conflict, see John Bunker's *Heroes in Dungarees*.

CHAPTER FOUR

1. Some sources cite the birthplace as Sweden, an understandable error in that Norway did not gain full independence from that nation until June 1905.

2. The details of Berthel Carlsen's life have been assembled from a wide variety of sources, including genealogical records; official U.S. government documents (including merchant mariner records, documents generated both before and after December 7, 1941, by the Army Transport Service and other military agencies and legal documents submitted to those agencies by the family members of *Cynthia Olson*'s crewmen); property records; the personal recollections of Mrs. Eleanor Robinson; and the surviving records of the Olson Steamship Company and other shipping firms. For a more detailed listing, please see the bibliography.

3. The term "plank owner" refers to a crewmember of any rank who is officially assigned to a naval vessel at the time of its commissioning.

4. Mines that had become detached from their mooring cables and were floating freely in the current.

5. While remaining under USSB ownership, *Nantahala* undertook a variety of tasks until broken up in Baltimore in November 1929.

6. USSB ultimately sold *Western Spirit* to a subsidiary of France's *Compagnie Générale Transatlantique*, for whom she operated as *Verdun*. She was broken up in Baltimore in 1933.

7. *Osage* was built as *Lake Fannin* at American Shipbuilding Company's Cleveland, Ohio, yards and completed in June 1919. A Design 1093 Laker, her deadweight tonnage was slightly higher than that of the Manitowoc-built Design 1044 ships like *Coquina/Cynthia Olson*.

8. Indeed, the home is still a gem. The author is indebted to the current owners, Gary and Karen Rathburn, for a guided tour of the former Carlsen home.

9. Approximately $160,000 in 2016 dollars.

10. Given that most records for both companies were lost or destroyed in the post–World War II years, it's difficult at this point to determine their precise business relationship.

11. As indicated by arrival and departure notices in the shipping news columns of the *Los Angeles Times*, *San Francisco Chronicle*, and *Seattle Post-Intelligencer*, and from vessel movement cards maintained by each port.

12. The author is indebted to Buchtele's stepdaughter, Eleanor Robinson, for much of the information in this and following chapters pertaining to his background and later life.

13. Including the author's Swedish forebears.

14. Information on his naturalization and name change are contained in his official "Deceased Merchant Mariner File," currently held at the main National Archives facility in Washington, DC.

15. Two other children, Leon and Catherine, remained with their father in San Francisco.

16. His elevation to third mate made him eligible to join the Masters, Mates and Pilots of America, and in September 1935 Buchtele was duly initiated into that organization's Local 90.

17. Biographical information on crewmembers was drawn primarily from the "Deceased Merchant Mariner" files held by the National Archives in Washington, DC. Additional information was obtained from genealogy databases, both print and online; records held by the U.S. Merchant Marine Academy at Kings Point, New York; and, in some cases, through contact with family members.

18. Though non-ATS members of the ship's crew were listed as Olson Company employees for purposes of the Army charter, they remained union members who could be hired on a per-voyage basis.

19. Unfortunately, biographical information on many of the Filipino ATS mariners is extremely scarce, and the author apologizes for being unable to provide more complete thumbnail sketches of these men who served the United States so well.

20. The family records consist of letters, birth certificates, and other records sent by Davenport's stepsisters to the Defense Department in the early 1990s in support of a request that Davenport be posthumously awarded the Pearl Harbor Commemorative Medal. The records are currently held by the Military Personnel Records Center in St. Louis, Missouri.

21. Ibid.

22. Biographical information regarding Samuel J. Ziskind courtesy of the Ziskind family (see acknowledgments page) and Inez Lerner Grover (sister of Bernice Lerner Ziskind). While Samuel J. Ziskind's military records were destroyed in a 1973 fire at the Military Personnel Records Center in St. Louis, Missouri, the author obtained copies of some pertinent documents from family members and from the National Archives' Modern Military Branch in College Park, Maryland.

23. Biographical information on Bernice Lerner Ziskind courtesy of her sister, Inez Lerner Grover. Additional data obtained through records held by Los Angeles County and by NARA College Park.

24. Additional details on Sam Ziskind's life were provided by his niece, Amy Bailin.

CHAPTER FIVE

1. These vessels were also sometimes referred to as the *I-15* class, after the first vessel in the series.

2. These single-engine monoplanes were ultimately given the Allied codename "Glen." The two-man aircraft was twenty-eight feet long, had a wingspan of thirty-six feet one inch, and was powered by a nine-cylinder radial engine.

3. While Japanese practice is to list a person's family name first and given name second, throughout this volume we will follow the English-language practice of given name followed by family name.

4. A complete explanation of the planning and execution of the Pearl Harbor attack is beyond the scope of this volume. For further reading on the topic, please see the bibliography.

5. Information on *I-26*'s construction and Pearl Harbor–related operations is drawn from *Submarines of the Imperial Japanese Navy*, by Dorr Carpenter and Norman Polmar; *Imperial Japanese Navy Submarines 1941–1945*, by Mark Stille and Tony Bryan; and *Advance Force Pearl Harbor*, by Burl Burlingame.

6. Biographical information for Minoru Yokota was provided by his family members (see acknowledgments section) and drawn from his

typewritten memoir *I Was the Captain of a Submarine*, a copy of which was
provided to the author by his family.

7. Ibid.

8. The other institution, of course, was the *Rikugun Shikan Gakko*, or
Imperial Japanese Army Academy, in Tokyo.

9. The IJN was formally established in July 1869, following the conclusion of the 1868–1869 Boshin War. That conflict was a civil war between
the ruling Tokugawa shogunate and an alliance of reactionary hered-
itary samurai seeking a return to traditional imperial rule. Before the
IJN's creation, private domainal navies—such as those of Hiroshima and
Satsuma—were the rule.

10. Graduates left Etajima as midshipmen, with promotion to ensign
normally occurring after eighteen months of operational service.

11. *I Was the Captain of a Submarine*, p. 1.

12. Such visits were wholeheartedly endorsed by Admiral Yamamoto,
who had spent several years in the United States both as a student at Harvard University (1919–1921) and as a naval attaché.

13. In a 1966 interview with *Honolulu Star-Bulletin* reporter Tomi Knaefler done as part of the research for her colleague Alf Pratte's five-part
series in the paper about the sinking of *Cynthia Olson*.

14. A Type KRS boat completed in 1927. This class of vessel was based
on, and virtually identical to, the World War I German *U-125*-class boats.
I-22 was redesignated *I-122* in 1938 and should not be confused with the
Type C1 *I-22* that was commissioned in March 1941. *I-122* was sunk in the
Sea of Japan on June 10, 1945, by the submarine USS *Skate*.

15. These three vessels had different fates. *RO-63* and *I-154* both survived the war but were scuttled by the Allies in 1946, and *I-165* disappeared in the Mariana Islands in June 1945 and was presumed lost with
all hands.

16. On pp. 45–45 of his excellent book *Left to Die: The Tragedy of the USS
Juneau*, which covers later actions in Yokota's naval career.

17. Satô would go on to command his own submarines, *RO-62* and
RO-37, though he and his entire crew were killed when the latter vessel
was sunk in the Solomon Islands on January 22, 1944, by the destroyer
USS *Buchanan*.

18. *I-10* was a Type A1 boat built by Kawasaki at Kobe and launched in
September 1939.

19. So called because their year of introduction, 1917, was the sixth year
of Emperor Taisho's reign.

20. A submarine-launched variant of the formidable Type 93 "Long
Lance" torpedo carried by Japanese surface ships from 1933 onward, the
Type 95 was the fastest torpedo then in service anywhere in the world and
carried the largest warhead. It also had about triple the range of the most

common American torpedo of the period, the trouble-plagued and often unreliable Mark 14.

21. See *Silent Siege: Japanese Attacks Against North America in World War II*, by Bert Webber, p. 10.

22. *I-26*'s reconnaissance of Kiska and Attu provided valuable information used by Japanese military planners when mapping out the landings on both islands by the 301st Independent Infantry Battalion in June 1942. Nearly a year later, the author's father was among the American troops tasked with retaking Attu from the Japanese.

23. For details on the U.S. military presence on Unalaska at the time of *I-26*'s reconnaissance, see *The Garrisoning of Alaska, 1939–1941*, which is chapter 9 in the volume *Guarding the U.S. and Its Outposts*, in the series *The United States Army in World War II*.

24. As with several wartime incidents Yokota spoke of in later life, this one has proven impossible to verify. No surviving U.S. document mentions the presence of twin-engine U.S. military aircraft on Unalaska at the time of *I-26*'s reconnaissance, though it is entirely possible the aircraft Yokota mentioned was a B-18A medium bomber of the U.S. Army Air Forces' Anchorage-based 73rd Bombardment Squadron on detachment to the newly opened airfield on Unalaska.

25. Usually translated as "Mobile Striking Force [or Unit]."

26. Two of the destroyers were tasked with the destruction of U.S. forces at Midway Island.

27. Also sometimes translated as "Submarine Patrol Formation."

28. The sub was redesignated *I-154* in May 1942. Having survived the war, the vessel was scuttled in the Inland Sea in May 1946.

29. In 1941 Mt. Niitaka, on Formosa (now Taiwan), was the highest point in the Japanese empire.

CHAPTER SIX

1. The U.S. and Canadian governments had recognized the need for the joint defense of the Strait of Juan de Fuca as early as 1939, and in October 1940 a five-member joint American-Canadian military commission made a thorough study of how best to protect the vital waterway. The commission ultimately drafted an "International Joint Defense Plan for Strait of Juan de Fuca and Puget Sound Area," which provided for such things as coordinated patrolling and joint codes. The measures were quickly adopted (after minor modification by the defense staffs in both Washington and Ottawa), and this marked the first cooperative venture undertaken by the two nations on a tactical level in the World War II period. For a more complete discussion of U.S.-Canadian military relations, see chapter 4 of *Military Relations between the U.S. & Canada*, in the series *The U.S. Army in World War II*.

2. Figures concerning the amount and value of lumber loaded are drawn from an ATS voyage data card compiled from period records by Army-vessel historian Charles Dana Gibson, a copy of which he graciously provided to the author.

3. The sub-port was established on November 1, 1941, as a subordinate organization of the San Francisco Port of Embarkation. On January 17, 1942, the increasing importance of Seattle as a departure point for troops and equipment led the Army to redesignate the sub-port as a separate and distinct port of embarkation. See *Gateway to Victory*, p. 21.

4. The possibility of a German naval presence in the northeastern Pacific was not that farfetched; auxiliary raiders were known to be active in the waters around Australia and New Zealand, and the chance that an enterprising German captain might attempt to intercept Commonwealth vessels plying between North America and Asian ports could not be discounted.

5. *Heroes in Dungarees: The Story of the American Merchant Marine*, pp. 327–346.

6. This despite a cable sent to the State Department on January 27 by U.S. Ambassador to Japan Joseph Grew stating that Japan was planning to launch a surprise attack against Pearl Harbor. He'd heard the news from his first secretary, Edward S. Crocker, who in turn had heard it from Peruvian diplomat Ricardo Rivera-Schreiber. Because it was based entirely on what senior State Department leaders termed "hearsay," the warning was ignored. For details, see Gordon W. Prange's *At Dawn We Slept: The Untold Story of Pearl Harbor*, pp. 31–36.

7. Army Chief of Staff General George Marshall's warning, War Department Message 472, went out on November 27, and its recipients included the SFPOE and its subordinate installations. The message said, in part, "Japanese future action unpredictable but hostile action possible at any moment." Ibid., p. 402.

8. Telephone interview with Eleanor Robinson.

9. While "armed merchant cruiser" is a term that has historically referred to an oceangoing passenger vessel that is requisitioned and armed by a sovereign government for wartime use with a naval crew, other types of vessels—most notably the small and medium-sized cargo ships used by Germany in both world wars—have also provided sterling service in the role.

10. In 1938 CNS had sold *Prince Henry* to Canada's Clark Steamship Company, and she'd been renamed *North Star*. Following her requisitioning she reverted to her original name and in 1943 was converted into a Landing Ship, Infantry [LS(I)]. In 1946, she was sold to Great Britain's Ministry of Transport, renamed *Empire Parkston*, and used as a troop transport until 1961. She was scrapped in 1962. *Prince David* remained in RCN

service until 1948, when she was sold to the Charlton Steamship Company. She sailed as *Charlton Monarch* until being broken up in 1951–1952.

11. The same modifications were made to both *Prince Henry* and *Prince David*, and the three converted liners remained the RCN's most powerful individual warships until well into 1943. Ironically, they were not particularly well-suited for their appointed tasks, in that their tendency to roll heavily in even moderate seas made accurate gun-laying more than a little challenging.

12. Beard (1890–1948) is one of the legends of Canadian naval history. Over the course of his long and distinguished career he served in the British merchant marine and Royal Naval Reserve; the Canadian fisheries services; and, of course, the RCN. He was called out of retirement to command *Prince Robert*, and his capture of *Weser* made him a national hero.

13. Put into Canadian service as *Vancouver Island*, the former Norddeutscher Lloyd vessel was torpedoed and sunk with all hands by *U-558* on October 15, 1941, in the North Atlantic.

14. For the larger story of *Awatea's* World War II experiences, see *Awatea at War* by G. Huston in the summer 1991 issue of the New Zealand Ship and Marine Society's journal *Marine News*.

15. For the complete, tragic story of "C" Force, see Brereton Greenhous's *C Force to Hong Kong: A Canadian Catastrophe*.

16. All details regarding *Prince Robert's* activities between October 27 and December 10, 1941, are drawn from the ship's deck logs for the period and from Hart's "Report of Proceedings" for the month of December 1941. Copies of the pertinent deck-log pages were provided to the author by Library and Archives Canada, and a copy of Hart's report was forwarded by the Office of the Director of History and Heritage at National Defence Headquarters, Ottawa.

17. "Ill-fated," of course, because the poorly equipped Canadian force was virtually wiped out when the Japanese took Hong Kong. Though some 290 men were killed outright and the rest were captured (many of whom subsequently died in Japanese captivity), "C" Force acquitted itself well, and its members were eventually awarded more than one hundred decorations.

18. *Matson's Century of Ships*, p. 241.

19. A copy of Grogan's "Record for Posterity" (less page 3) is included in author John Toland's papers at the National Archives' Franklin D. Roosevelt Library and Museum in Hyde Park, New York.

20. And as was recounted in the article "Something Is Going to Happen," on pp. 10–11 of the Winter 1991 issue of *Amper&and*, the house magazine of Alexander and Baldwin, parent company of the Matson Line.

21. Ibid.

22. "Record for Posterity," p. 4.

23. Lieutenant Commander Philip H. Jacobsen (USN, Ret.) spent twenty-seven of his twenty-eight years in the Navy as a cryptologist and signals intelligence officer. During World War II he served at various Navy radio-intercept stations in the Pacific. He went on to become the attorney general for the U.S. territory of Guam and wrote extensively on various aspects of cryptology in World War II.

24. In an excellent, well-reasoned, and ultimately convincing article in the April 2005 issue of the scholarly journal "Cryptologia" titled "Pearl Harbor: Radio Officer Leslie Grogan of the SS *Lurline* and His Misidentified Signals."

25. Ibid., p. 103.

26. *Something Is Going to Happen*, p. 10.

27. All-around athlete Robinson had been hired to play semiprofessional football for the racially integrated Honolulu Bears, one of four teams in a nascent Hawaiian league, and was returning to California at the end of the team's season. See *Jackie Robinson: Young Sports Trailblazer*, pp. 115–119.

28. Hawaii-born Tsubota was commissioned a second lieutenant in January 1940 from the University of Hawaii's Reserve Officers Training Program, and when called to active duty in March 1941 was one of only a handful of Nisei officers in the Army. He ultimately became one of the few non-Caucasian officers in the predominantly Japanese-American 100th Infantry Battalion and saw combat in Italy. He retired from the Army as a lieutenant colonel in 1963.

29. "Record for Posterity," p. 4.

30. Collins's memories of the events surrounding the December 1941 voyage are included in his article "Rendezvous with Destiny: The SS *Lurline*'s 'Pearl Harbor' Voyage," on pp. 6–7 of the Winter 1991 issue of *Amper&and*, cited above.

31. Ibid.

32. *Silent Siege*, pp. 22–23.

33. As is often the case when dealing with veterans' memories of long-ago events, there is some confusion about exactly when *I-26* sighted *Cynthia Olson*. In his account, "My Memories of *I-26*," in the 1979 book *History of Japanese Submarines* by Kaneyoshi Sakamoto, Diving Officer Yukio Oka states that the Laker was first seen on the evening of the sixth and tracked through the night, while in a 2000 article in a Japanese military history magazine (*Gakken Pictorial*, volume 17), Chief Gunner Saburo Hayashi says *I-26* first saw *Cynthia Olson* at 3:00 a.m. local time and followed for only two hours before surfacing to begin the attack. Because Oka was on watch at the time of the first sighting, and because his account was recorded years earlier than Hayashi's (who, as we'll see later in this account had more than a little difficulty in correctly recalling key aspects of the action), the author has decided—in this instance—to use Oka's account as the narrative base.

34. "The Outbreak of the Greater East Asia War Aboard *I-26*," by Takaji Komaba, in Sakamoto's *History of Japanese Submarines*, p. 815.

35. Among the Lakers that joined Japan's merchant fleet were *Koshin Maru* (Cleveland-built in 1917 as *Lakeport*); *Toyo Maru No. 6/8* (Superior-built in 1918 as *Lake Washburn*); *Shoko Maru* (Duluth-built in 1919 as *Chamblee*); *Hozen Maru* (Wyandotte-built in 1918 as *Goodspeed*); and *Sumida Maru* (a 1918-built Manitowoc sister ship of *Cynthia Olson*). Virtually all the Japanese-operated Lakers were sunk by American submarines during World War II. See *The Lakers of World War I* for details on these vessels.

36. This will become an important point later in the narrative.

37. *Silent Siege*, Ibid.

38. *History of Japanese Submarines*, p. 193.

CHAPTER SEVEN

1. The eight major and scores of minor Hawaiian islands are located more than two thousand miles from the nearest landfall.

2. The names and destinations of the vessels are drawn from a variety of sources, including Matson's *Century of Ships*, *Advance Force Pearl Harbor*, *Gateway to Victory*, *Over Seas*, and *Army Cargo Fleet in World War II*. Many other American vessels were, of course, at sea in the Pacific, but to the west of the Hawaiian Islands. The figures cited also do not include vessels underway locally in Hawaiian or coastal U.S. waters.

3. The Matson ships were *Mauna Ala* (carrying Christmas trees), *Makaweli* (oil and molasses), *Manoa* (general cargo), *Maunalei* (general cargo), *Waimea* (cement), and *Malama* (general cargo).

4. USAFFE was created on July 26, 1941, with headquarters in Manila. MacArthur had retired from the Army in December 1937 as a four-star general, but he was recalled to active duty as a major (two-star) general to head USAFFE. He was promoted to lieutenant (three-star) general the day after USAFFE's activation.

5. Referred to as the "Pensacola Convoy," the group included the Army troopers *Willard A. Holbrook* and *Meigs*, the Navy troopers *Republic* and *Chaumont* (both formerly Army vessels), and the Army-chartered merchantmen *Admiral Halstead*, *Coast Farmer*, and *Bloemfontein*.

6. Carlsen and Buchtele each had their own staterooms on the forward part of the boat deck, the former to starboard and the latter to port. The rooms were separated by the small head reserved for Carlsen's sole use and to which he had sole access. In the original Design 1044 Lakers this "Master's Head" was equipped with a bathtub, though by the late 1930s the tubs on most surviving Lakers had been replaced by seawater showers.

7. In 1960 the measurement unit was renamed kilohertz (kHz); for clarity, we will use the terminology in use during the 1940s.

8. MF systems were the norm in the prewar years and were not consid-ered inadequate; messages intended for receivers beyond the MF unit's range would simply be relayed through a nearby vessel equipped with a high-frequency, and thus longer-range, system.

9. The call sign had been changed from WVAA at the time the ship's name was changed from *Coquina* to *Cynthia Olson*.

10. *Cynthia Olson* had two antennas, a primary and a backup.

11. "My Memories of I-26," p. 193.

12. Details of the attack and of *Cynthia Olson*'s final hours are drawn pri-marily from *Silent Siege*. Author Webber extensively interviewed Minoru Yokota and Saburo Hayashi by letter and in person in the 1970s and 1980s, and in the absence of official Imperial Japanese Navy records of World War II submarine operations (most of which were apparently destroyed either by American bombing or by the Japanese themselves), the interviews and correspondence provide virtually the only existing records of the events.

13. "My Memories of I-26," p. 193.

14. Ibid.

15. Ibid.

16. Ibid.

17. The headbands were traditional Japanese bandanas bearing, in this case, the *hinomaru* (rising sun) motif.

18. Author Dan Kurzman has an alternate, but comparable, version of Yokota's decision to allow the Americans to leave their ship before it was sent to the bottom, a decision that Kurzman says was greeted with surprise by a man he identifies as *I-26*'s "weapons officer." As quoted by Kurzman, the exchange was as follows:

"Why, sir, can't we attack right now?" the weapons officer asked Yokota.

"No," the skipper replied, "we must warn them first. You can see through the periscope that this ship is unarmed."

The weapons officer could hardly believe what he heard. But according to Tsukuo Nakano, a petty officer second class who was a torpedo man subordinate to the weapons officer, "Yokota was adamant. He would not issue the order to sink the ship until warning shots were fired over the vessel to give the men aboard a chance to escape. It sim-ply didn't seem fair to the skipper that he kill the men on the unarmed ship." (See *Left to Die: The Tragedy of the USS* Juneau, pp. 45–46.)

This information seems more than a bit hagiographic and may have had less to do with recording the facts of the case than with Nakano's postwar desire to sanitize the events of *Cynthia Olson*'s sinking.

19. "My Memories of *I-26*," p. 194.
20. *Silent Siege*, p. 23.
21. "My Memories of *I-26*," p. 194.
22. Ibid.
23. Ibid.
24. *Silent Siege*, p. 23.
25. "My Memories of *I-26*," p. 194.
26. Ibid.
27. *Silent Siege*, p. 23.
28. This statement is drawn from "Record for Posterity," from which much of the following material is also derived.
29. Ibid., p. 4.
30. Ibid.
31. This message text is included in the March 1947 document "Reports of Death of Personnel of USAT '*Cynthia Olson*,'" which was produced by the Casualty Section, Personnel Actions Branch, U.S. Army's Adjutant General Office.
32. See Riley H. Allen's *A Footnote to the History of World War II: First Shot of the War in the Pacific*, p. 8, for details on Ferrill's actions upon receiving *Lurline*'s message.
33. See *Gateway to Victory*, pp. 1–3, for more on the messages received by *Etolin* and *Will H. Point*. The authors' contention that the former vessel was only sixty-five miles from *Cynthia Olson* when she received the distress signal is not correct, however, given that *Etolin* was less than eight hundred miles from San Francisco when ordered to return to California.
34. Gilbreath commanded SFPOE until 1944, when as a major general he took command of the South Pacific Base Command in New Caledonia. He retired in 1946 and died in 1969. In April and May 1942 one of the young officers on Gilbreath's SFPOE staff was Second Lieutenant Ronald Reagan.
35. An engineer by training, in 1942 Somervell was promoted to lieutenant general and made commander of the Army's Service of Supply (later Army Service Forces). He retired as a full general in 1948 and died in 1955.
36. *Gateway to Victory*, pp. 1–3.
37. "Rendezvous with Destiny," p.6.
38. And, according to Dan Gutman, Herb Dunn, and Meryl Henderson (in "Jackie Robinson," pp. 118–119), Berndtson also made the following announcement to his passengers:

Attention! I have an important announcement to make. I just received word that Japan has launched a surprise attack on Pearl Harbor, the American naval base on the island of Oahu.

Most of the United States fleet was in that harbor. Nineteen of our ships were damaged or sunk in the attack. One hundred and eighty-eight of our planes were destroyed. They didn't even have the chance to get off the ground. There were very few Japanese casualties. More than 2,000 Americans soldiers were killed.

President Roosevelt is going to address the nation tomorrow. In the meantime, we must travel carefully. These waters are very dangerous. This ship is not armed. We are vulnerable to attack from submarines, ships and planes. Your windows are being painted black so that we can travel tonight without being seen. All lights on the deck will be turned off when the sun goes down. We will proceed to the mainland with as much caution as possible.

Thank you, and God bless the United States of America.

While the author has found various other references to a statement made by Commodore Berndtson to *Lurline*'s passengers and crew regarding the Pearl Harbor attack, none were as specific as the one quoted. Indeed, Matson historian Fred A. Stindt, in his comprehensive *Matson's Century of Ships*, says only that "the passengers were gathered together in the ship's lounge, and Commodore Berndtson briefly explained the nature of the emergency." Given that the source for the quoted statement was not provided in *Jackie Robinson*, its accuracy must remain open to question.

39. Greenwich Mean Time sets the world time zones in relation to the prime meridian (0° longitude) in Greenwich, England. In common naval and military use, time is expressed both in local time and GMT, the latter allowing units operating several time zones apart to synchronize their activities.

40. In addition to *Prince Robert*, the message went to several other vessels then at sea in the Pacific as well as to the "Naval Officers in Charge" at the shore stations in Vancouver and Prince Rupert, B.C.

41. This message is part of Library and Archives Canada's Record Group 24-D-20A, Volume 12160, "Commanding Officer Pacific Coast, 1939–1946."

42. The identity of the American submarine is not revealed in any of *Prince Robert*'s logs, though it may have been either *Pollack* or *Pampano*, both of which were en route to Pearl Harbor from Mare Island. For more on this incident, see *The Prince Ships*, p. 54.

43. Ibid.

44. All three messages to *Prince Robert* were marked as having been sent by "Signal Distributing Office, H.M.C. [His Majesty's Canadian] Dockyard, Esquimalt, B.C." and are time stamped and dated December 7, 1941.

45. See chapter 6, note 15.

46. Nautical twilight had commenced at 3:35 P.M., ship's time, and it was fully dark by 4:03.

47. Hart's "Proceedings."

CHAPTER EIGHT

1. *All the President's Spokesmen*, p. 38.

2. Ibid.

3. Without going into details that are beyond the scope of this volume, historians continue to debate the exact time that Daly broke into the broadcast, primarily because of postwar editing of the original program recordings. However, most scholars agree that Daly's mention of the attack on the unnamed lumber transport occurred during the early section of his interruption of the Philharmonic broadcast.

4. Within hours of the first news of the Pearl Harbor attack, Army and Navy bases on the West Coast began receiving telephone calls from citizens certain they'd spotted Japanese ships and aircraft, with some callers even reporting landings by enemy troops. While Japanese activity off California, Oregon, and Washington would not actually commence until the middle of December, several cities—including San Diego—imposed blackouts beginning on the night of December 7.

5. The weekly program was sponsored by the Pan American Coffee Bureau (a consortium of eight Latin American coffee-growing countries). The First Lady did twenty-six Sunday evening broadcasts, beginning in October 1941.

6. *Eleanor Roosevelt and the Media: A Public Quest for Self-Fulfillment*, p. 150.

7. While the main Japanese air assault in the Philippines, at Manila's Clark Field, did not occur until 11:35 p.m., on December 7 (EST), probing attacks on northern Luzon had already occurred by the time Mrs. Roosevelt went on the air.

8. Drawn from FDR's December 7 draft of the December 8 speech, held at the Franklin Delano Roosevelt Library and Museum.

9. Author's interview with Inez Learner Grover.

10. "Record for Posterity," p. 8.

11. The Japanese submarines involved in the actual attack on Pearl Harbor were Type A–class two-man "midgets."

12. A copy of this message was included as a supporting document in the Adjutant General Office's March 1947 "Report of Death of Personnel of USAT 'Cynthia Olson.'"

13. San Pedro *News-Pilot*, December 12, 1941. The article's reference to the Olsons as the ship's "former owners" is incorrect, in that the Olson

Company retained ownership of *Cynthia Olson* despite her bareboat charter to the Army.

14. Quoted by Alf Pratte in the first part of his "Prelude to Pearl Harbor" series in the Honolulu *Star-Bulletin*, December 3, 1966.

15. Letter from E. Whitney Olson to Katherine Buchtele, dated December 22, 1941. A copy was provided to the author by Eleanor Beck Robinson.

16. Letter from Sax to Katherine Buchtele, marked "231.8 Cynthia Olson," dated December 24, 1941. A copy was provided to the author by Eleanor Beck Robinson.

17. The Army's waterborne transportation operations were part of the Office of the Quartermaster General until March 1942, at which time they were transferred to the agency first known as the Transportation Division, Services of Supply, and which became the Transportation Corps on July 31, 1942.

18. Letter from Lt. Col. C.H. Kells to Mrs. Berthel Carlsen, marked "QM 201 T-W-C, Carlsen, Berthel, Mrs.," dated December 26, 1941. A copy was provided to the author by Eleanor Beck Robinson.

19. The 13th ND commander had jurisdiction of the matter since *Cynthia Olson* had departed for Hawaii from his operational area of responsibility.

20. This statement is quoted in the documents used to support the Navy's June 1943 rebuttal to the Olson Company's petition for a $346,000 war-risk insurance payout for the vessel. This topic is covered in greater detail in chapter 9 of this volume.

21. These memos were included as supporting documents in the AGO's March 1947 "Reports of Death of Personnel of USAT 'Cynthia Olson.'"

22. Letter included in "Reports of Death of Personnel of USAT 'Cynthia Olson.'"

23. *New York Times*, February 7, 1942.

24. Letter, Colonel J. H. Mellon to Mrs. W. P. Buchtele, marked "231.8–Cynthia Olson" and dated January 22, 1942. A copy was provided to the author by Eleanor Beck Robinson.

25. A copy of this letter was provided to the author by Eleanor Beck Robinson.

26. See *United States Government Manual*, First Edition, 1945, pp. 568–571, "United States Employees' Compensation Commission."

27. See "Reports of Death of Personnel of USAT 'Cynthia Olson.'"

28. Letter to Mrs. Katherine Buchtele from S. D. Logson, USECC chief of section, marked "File No. 859685" and dated August 25, 1942. A copy of the letter was provided to the author by Eleanor Beck Robinson.

29. Ibid.

30. Author's interview with Bernice Ziskind's sister, Inez Learner Grover.

31. The inventory of Bill Buchtele's personal items that his wife submitted to the WSA, for example, included a sextant, a portable typewriter, a

portable radio, a short-wave radio, various pieces of furniture, six complete dress uniforms, twenty-two items of casual clothing, and a gold watch. The list is contained in a letter Katherine Buchtele wrote to the WSA on February 20, 1943, a copy of which was provided to the author by Eleanor Beck Robinson.

32. "Reports of Death of Personnel of USAT 'Cynthia Olson,'" p. 8.

33. Ibid.

34. This information is contained in the May 5, 1947, judgment rendered by the U.S. Court of Federal Claims in the case of *Oliver J. Olson & Co. v. United States*.

35. A copy of the report, labeled "SPTOW 345.02: Loss of the Steamer 'Cynthia Olson,'" dated June 8, 1943, is in the author's possession.

36. A copy of this telegram, marked "WA327 June 2 1945 12477P," is in the author's possession.

37. Established in 1926, the firm went on to huge prosperity during the so-called Internet bubble years by handling the initial public offerings of hundreds of high-tech companies in the San Francisco Bay area. However, when the bubble burst the firm went bankrupt and closed its doors in 2002.

38. A copy of the court's decision, labeled "Oliver J. Olson & Co. v United States, No. 46232" and dated May 5, 1947, is in the author's possession. Discussion of the case is also included in the Department of the Army's "Military Law Review," vol. 34, 1966 Annual Index, in the chapter "Army Maritime Claims."

CHAPTER NINE

1. The other being the archrival Honolulu *Advertiser*. The two papers merged in 2010 to become the Honolulu *Star-Advertiser*.

2. In the process scooping the rival *Advertiser*, whose presses had been torn down for maintenance. See "Editor for the Islands," *Time*, August 1, 1960, p. 26.

3. *New York Times*, "Riley H. Allen," October 3, 1966.

4. This document is in the collection of the Hawaii State Archives in Honolulu. Hereafter referred to as "Footnote."

5. "Footnote," p. 2.

6. Ibid.

7. The "Roberts Commission" to which Allen referred was the first of two commissions appointed by President Franklin Roosevelt to be headed by Supreme Court Associate Justice Owen J. Roberts. The first commission was formed soon after the Pearl Harbor attack to investigate the circumstances of the assault, and in its January 1942 report to Congress the commission excoriated the Army and Navy commanders on Oahu, General

Walter Short and Admiral Husband Kimmel, accusing both of dereliction of duty. There were eight other Pearl Harbor investigations between 1941 and 1946, culminating in the Joint Congressional Committee Allen cited.

8. "Footnote," p. 5.

9. Throughout the typescript of Allen's speech, the ship's name is misspelled as "Olsen."

10. "Footnote," p. 9.

11. Allen was quick to differentiate between the first U.S. shot of the war and the first by Japan, pointing out that the former occurred more than an hour before the Japanese aerial attack, when the destroyer USS *Ward* detected, fired upon, and then depth-charged a Japanese Type A midget sub off the entrance to Pearl Harbor.

12. "Footnote," p. 10.

13. Ibid, pp. 10–12.

14. "Footnote," p. 15.

15. Ibid, p. 13.

16. "Mrs. Riley H. Allen," obituary in the *New York Times*, July 7, 1950.

17. "Editor for the Islands."

18. Riley had worked for the Seattle paper in 1905 and again from 1908 to 1910.

19. The interview was conducted in April 2008, and it is the source of all of Mr. Pratte's quotes. Hereafter referred to as "Pratte Interview."

20. And future director of naval history.

21. Letter, D. C. Allard to Alf Pratte, marked "OP-09B92/ilj" and dated June 10, 1966. A copy remains in the Hawaii State Archives.

22. A San Francisco suburb well within the bureau chief's "beat."

23. Teletype message, slugged "hon to aronson-sf" and dated June 7, 1966. A copy remains in the Hawaii State Archives.

24. Pratte Interview.

25. For many of the details of *I-26*'s later wartime activities I have relied heavily on Bob Hackett and Sander Kingsepp's excellent and exhaustive IJN website, www.combinedfleet.com. Additional details were drawn from "History of Japanese Submarines."

26. His search was fruitless because both of the U.S. Navy's *Lexington*-class carriers—*Lexington* (CV-2) and *Saratoga* (CV-3)—were elsewhere; the former was on her way to conduct a diversionary attack on the Japanese base at Jaliut Atoll in the Marshall Islands, and the latter was underway from San Diego to Pearl Harbor, which she reached unscathed on December 15. *I-6*'s Inaba had most probably sighted the *Yorktown*-class carrier *Enterprise* (CV-6) and her escorts, all of which had departed Pearl Harbor on the morning of December 9 to patrol Hawaiian waters. On December 10, SBD-2 Dauntless dive-bombers flying from *Enterprise* sighted and sank *I-70*, a Submarine Squadron 3 boat that thus achieved the dubious honor of becoming the first

Japanese fleet sub sunk by the United States in World War II. On January 11, 1942, Inaba partially redeemed himself for his December 9 mistake by putting a single torpedo into *Saratoga* some 270 northeast of Johnston Island. The carrier limped back to Pearl Harbor and was unable to return to duty for some six months.

27. "Operation K-1" was intended to disrupt ship-repair activities at Pearl Harbor, and was built around two four-engine Kawanishi H8K1 flying boats. The aircraft launched from French Frigate Shoals, some 510 miles northwest of Oahu, and managed to drop a total of four bombs on a residential district of Honolulu before returning to French Frigate Shoals. The attack did no real damage and caused no injuries.

28. See "Sub Sinks Ship Off Neah Bay; 55 Saved," in the June 10, 1942, edition of the Seattle *Post-Intelligencer*. The Seattle *Times* also reported on the attack on the same day.

29. Espíritu Santo is the largest island in what is now the nation of Vanuatu.

30. He could not fire a full spread because three of *I-26*'s six tubes had been knocked out of commission when the submarine hit a reef in mid-October as she submerged to avoid detection by American aircraft near the Indispensable Reefs in the Coral Sea.

31. Among those lost in *Juneau*'s sinking were the five Sullivan brothers.

32. While in command of *I-26*, Kusaka committed a notorious maritime war crime, the March 29, 1944, sinking of the U.S. Liberty ship *Richard Hovey*. The vessel was bound from Bombay to the United States when Kusaka sighted it in the Arabian Sea and hit it with three torpedoes. He then opened fire on the sinking ship with his deck gun as the American seamen took to their lifeboats. Kusaka pulled *Richard Hovey*'s captain and three other men from the water, then ordered *I-26*'s gunners to kill the remaining survivors using the sub's antiaircraft weapons. Four Americans were killed before the sub moved off, and twenty-five survivors were eventually rescued. After the war, Kusaka was convicted of war crimes charges and sentenced to five years in prison. See Mark Felton's *Slaughter at Sea: The Story of Japan's Naval War Crimes*, pp. 138–144, for the entire story.

33. The six Type B-2 vessels are also sometimes referred to as Type B-1 (Modified).

34. Usually translated as "Rapid Naval Armaments Supplement Program," this effort commenced in August 1941 as a way to quickly produce warships of all types in anticipation of a general Pacific war. The program ultimately produced some 290 vessels of various types for the IJN.

35. *Imperial Japanese Navy Submarines, 1941–1945*, pp. 23–24.

36. Again, thanks to Bob Hackett and Sander Kingsepp of www.combinedfleet.com for details of *I-44*'s wartime activities.

37. The diminutive monarch never actually used the word "surrender" in his radio address, saying instead that he and his people would have to "endure the unendurable." For more on the events surrounding Hirohito's decision to surrender and the final days of the war in the Pacific, see the author's 2015 book *Last to Die: A Defeated Empire, a Forgotten Mission, and the Last American Killed in World War II*.

38. *I-26* disappeared on Oct. 25, 1944, off the Philippine island of Samar, soon after attempting to torpedo the escort carrier USS *Petroff Bay*. The submarine most likely fell victim to a depth-charge attack by the destroyer USS *Coolbaugh*. *I-44* survived somewhat longer; on April 25, 1945, while running on the surface off Okinawa, she was surprised by a TBM Avenger from the escort carrier USS *Tulagi*. Though she crash-dived, the submarine suffered a near miss from a depth charge and was then hit by an acoustic homing torpedo.

39. "I Was the Captain of a Submarine," p. 1.

40. Ibid, p. 2.

41. Diligent effort has failed to reveal this woman's background, maiden name, or the exact date of her marriage to Minoru Yokota. While some members of the extended Hasegawa clan believe this first marriage took place before World War II, most cite 1951 as the most likely year.

42. "I Was the Captain of a Submarine," p. 2.

43. Ibid.

44. For more on the Tsutadas and their contributions to religious diversity in Japan, see *The House of Tsutada: The Little Man with a Big God*, by Edna K. Johnson.

45. "I Was the Captain of a Submarine," p. 2.

CHAPTER TEN

1. For more on this topic, see chapter 17 of Mark Felton's *Slaughter at Sea*.

2. Her article series ultimately formed the basis of her 1991 book, *Our House Divided: Seven Japanese-American Families in World War II*.

3. Details of Tomi Knaefler's interview with Hasegawa are drawn from the author's interview with Ms. Knaefler, hereafter cited as "Knaefler Interview."

4. Ibid.

5. Ibid.

6. This episode is recounted in part 5 of Pratte's "Prelude to Pearl Harbor" series.

7. Pratte Interview.

8. Drawn, of course, from Pratte's five-part series.

9. Pratte used the former sub commander's original last name throughout the series.

10. Hawaii dropped the extra half hour in 1947.

11. Ohmae was quite possibly the most authoritative—and credible—Japanese source Pratte could have located. Citing his time as a member of the IJN's Naval General Staff, the compilers of the U.S. Navy's section of the July 1946 U.S. Strategic Bombing Survey (Pacific) called him "a most prolific source of information on all phases of the war, both operational and planning information. His wide background of experience, together with his intelligence and insight into naval operations and planning, made him the most reliable and accurate source of information developed in Japan. He was quite eager in making available all source of information and most frank in his comments and opinions." USSBS, "Interrogations of Japanese Officials," October 30, 1945, p. 564.

12. "Some Historians Believe NW Ship Sunk by Japanese before Pearl Harbor," *Oregon Journal*, December 7, 1972, sec. 2, p. 1. Webber's editors did him no favors; the published article contains numerous misspellings and punctuation errors.

13. Webber's records are held by the Hoover Institution Library and Archives in Stanford, California.

14. Including Kujuro Nakano, Teiji Suda, Mamoru Omae, Yukio Oka, Takaji Komaba, Nobuo Shimazu, Masaaki Yanagi, and Kenji Imai. See *Silent Siege III*, p. 227.

15. *Silent Siege*, p. 28.

16. Ibid.

17. *Silent Siege III*, p. 23.

18. *At Dawn We Slept*, p. ix.

19. *Dec. 7, 1941: The Day the Japanese Attacked Pearl Harbor*, pp. 49, 136–137.

20. Ibid., p. 421.

21. In his 1991 volume *Long Day's Journey into War: December 7, 1941*, Weintraub had stuck closely to Prange's version of the story—even using the incorrect *Olsen* and calling the vessel a "little wooden freighter." However, his brief article "What Happened to the *Cynthia Olson*?" in the December 2001 issue of *Naval History* magazine noted that Yokota had given conflicting versions of the event at various times and went so far as to speculate that the sub captain had ordered his men to kill the American mariners in their lifeboats. Grover—a distinguished, thorough, and highly respected maritime historian—took a far more detailed look at the entire story in his April 2003 article, "Strange Mystery of the *Cynthia Olson*," in *Sea Classics*.

CHAPTER ELEVEN

1. This is, of course, a conservative figure. Studies conducted since the war have placed the total number of dead from all causes at somewhere between fifty-eight million and seventy-two million, though the actual figure will never be known.

2. The seventy-three thousand figure is the number most often cited by the Defense POW/MIA Accounting Agency (DPAA), the U.S. Department of Defense organization tasked with providing "the fullest possible accounting of all Americans still missing from all of the nation's past conflicts." Having observed and reported on a recovery team's search for the remains of a World War II B-24 bomber crew on Kwajalein Atoll in the Marshall Islands, the author fully understands the difficulties—both technical and bureaucratic—with which the agency's men and women must contend.

3. "Footnote," p. 9.

4. "The Mystery of *Cynthia Olson*," p. 32.

5. Ibid.

6. GMT time zones are fifteen degrees of longitude apart, and begin with the 0° prime meridian at Greenwich.

7. "The Mystery of *Cynthia Olson*," p. 32.

8. All data regarding KPH are drawn from that station's daily logs for the period December 7 to December 10, 1941, copies of which were provided to the author by Richard Dillman of the Maritime Radio Historical Society. All messages logged by KPH regarding *Cynthia Olson* were on 500 Kcs.

9. Tracking the message chronology in GMT also resolves the "local time aboard *Lurline*" issue. Grogan logged *Cynthia Olson*'s first auto alarm at 6:38 p.m., GMT, which was 8:08 a.m., local time, in Honolulu, and his notation that local time aboard the liner at that point was 9:12 a.m.—a difference of just four minutes—clearly indicates that *Lurline*'s clocks had indeed been put forward thirty minutes on each of the two midnights she'd been at sea. The four-minute disparity is easily explained by the high level of activity sparked in the liner's radio room by the receipt of that first auto-alarm message. It seems the oft-maligned Leslie Grogan was right again.

10. Including a Pearl Harbor chronology compiled by the U.S. Naval History and Heritage Command from information contained in the deck logs of Navy ships moored in the harbor on the morning of the attack. For example, the deck log of USS *Avocet*, a minesweeper docked at Pearl Harbor's Naval Air Station pier, lists the first Japanese bomb explosion as occurring at Ford Island at "about 0745 [7:45 a.m.]."

11. And in the U.S. Strategic Bombing Survey volume *Campaigns of the Pacific War*, p. 18.

12. The wreck of *I-20tou*, the Ko-Hyoteki Type A midget sub *Ward* attacked with gunfire and depth charges, was located in 2002 by the submersibles *Pisces IV* and *Pisces V* of the University of Hawaii/National Oceanic and Atmospheric Administration's Hawaii Undersea Research Laboratory (an organization universally referred to as HURL). The midget sub is intact, is lying in 1,200 feet of water some four miles off the entrance to Pearl Harbor, and still has both of her Type 97 torpedoes. Her two

crewmen, Ensign Akira Hiro-o and Petty Officer Yoshio Katayama, are assumed to have died either during *Ward's* attack or when their vessel sank, apparently as the result of flooding through two holes punched in the lower part of the small conning tower by gunfire from *Ward*.

13. As noted earlier in this volume, the "Certificate of Inspection for Steam or Motor Vessels" was signed by inspectors John P. Tibbets and Winslow D. Conn on May 28, 1940.

14. Grogan's statement is taken from "Record for Posterity," p. 4.

15. Indeed, as Mark Felton points out in *Slaughter at Sea*, on March 20, 1943, the IJN made the murder of Allied merchant seamen official when it ordered submarine crews to "not stop at the sinking of enemy ships and cargoes. At the same time carry out the complete destruction of the crews." Felton estimates that between 1941 and 1945 the IJN murdered some twenty thousand Allied merchant mariners and other civilians in cold blood. He also points out that the vast majority of IJN personnel were never charged for their crimes.

16. *"Execute Against Japan": The U.S. Decision to Conduct Unrestricted Submarine Warfare*, p. 2. Holwitt is both a historian and, at the time he wrote the book, a serving U.S. Navy submarine officer.

17. In fairness, we must also consider the fact that within five hours of the *Kido Butai's* strike against Oahu the U.S. chief of naval operations, Admiral Harold Stark, ordered the beginning of unrestricted submarine warfare against Japan. Holwitt's *Execute Against Japan* covers that policy in fascinating detail.

18. Kingsepp, cocreator of the IJN history website www.combinedfleet.com, was also a consultant on this book.

19. *I-Boat Captain*, 1976.

20. Flotsam refers to items that enter the water through shipwreck or other unintended events, while jetsam refers to items intentionally thrown into the sea.

21. The sextant—the dominant maritime navigational tool in the days before the satellite-based Global Positioning System—is highly accurate when used correctly. While less precise, dead reckoning (which estimates a vessel's current position from an initial fixed and known point as affected by course, speed, and elapsed time) is a valuable back-up navigational tool still widely in use.

22. "My Memories from *I-26*," p. 4.

23. "The First Success," in *Gakken Pictorial*, p. 176.

24. "The Outbreak of the Greater East Asia War Aboard the *I-26*," in *History of Japanese Submarines*, p. 815.

25. According to NOAA's National Oceanographic Data Center, the sea depth at the Laker's last-known location is about 4,565 meters, or 14,977 feet.

26. Which, in fact, comprises the North Pacific, California, North Equatorial, and Kuroshio currents.

27. Today, the North Pacific Gyre is home to a vast accumulation of floating man-made garbage known as the Pacific Trash Vortex. Some estimates put its size as comparable to that of the state of Texas.

28. Interestingly, in 1966, Minoru Hasegawa told Tomi Knaefler that when he last saw them, the two lifeboats were drifting "toward Honolulu," a statement that found its way into Alf Pratte's series.

29. Arthur Allen of the U.S. Coast Guard's Office of Search and Rescue pointed out to the author that virtually all mariners grossly overestimate their ability to see small objects floating on the open ocean, even at fairly close ranges and in the daylight. While the bright moonlight, relatively calm seas, and use of searchlights undoubtedly improved visibility for those aboard *Prince Robert*, the searchers would most probably not have been able to spot even something the size of a lifeboat at a range of more than a mile to either side of their ship.

30. In a study of World War II life-craft voyages they conducted for their book *Essentials of Sea Survival*, researchers Frank Golden and Michael Tipton determined that a person in a lifeboat would need to consume four to eight ounces of water per day to survive. While humans can survive roughly thirty days without food, three days without water is generally fatal.

BIBLIOGRAPHY

PRIMARY SOURCES

Official Files

Case History of the Cynthia Olson. Memorandum to Chief, Casualty Section, Personnel Actions Branch, Adjutant Generals Office. (Facts, Timeline, Time Charter Contract, Record of Radio Messages, Crew List, History of Financial Claims). Mar. 11, 1947. National Archives and Record Administration, National Personnel Records Center–Military Personnel Records, St. Louis, Missouri.

Loss of Personal Effects of the Crew of the USAT General Royal T. Frank. Memorandum for the Secretary of War from Acting Chief of Transportation (References to Payment of Cynthia Olson *Family Member Loss Claims, Oliver J. Olson Co. Loss Claims under Charter Agreement).* (No date) NARA, NPRC-MPR.

Non-Recoverable Remains Re-Examination of Records, Davenport, Ernest J., and Ziskind, Samuel J. Casualty Section, Personnel Actions Branch, Adjutant General Office (Individual Personnel/Medical Records, Crew List, Description of Known Facts, Correspondence from Families). Feb. 19, 1951. NARA, NPRC-MPR.

Pearl Harbor Commemorative Medal Application, Made on Behalf of Ernest J. Davenport by Viva Olean Clifton Webb. (Application and Supporting Documents). Feb. 26, 1991. NARA, NPRC-MPR.

Status of Personnel of USAT Cynthia Olson. *Report to Chief, Water Transport Service, Marine Casualty Division, Transportation Corps, from Adjutant General.* (Report, Crew List, Supporting Documents and Records Pertaining to Financial Claim Made by Family of Sotero V. Cabigas) Mar. 11, 1947. NARA, Modern Military Records Center, Archives II, College Park, Maryland.

Archival Sources

Abstract and Certificate of Record of Title of the Steam Screw Cynthia Olson (*Ex*-Coquina). NARA-Pacific Region, San Bruno, California.

Daily Log, Dec. 7 to Dec. 10, Station KPH, Bolinas, California. Maritime Radio Historical Society, Point Reyes Station, California.

General Arrangement Plans, Emergency Fleet Corporation Design Series 1044 Freight Vessels Lake Haresti and Lake Kyttle. Detroit Historical Society, Detroit, Michigan.

HMCS Prince Robert, *Deck Logs, November–December 1941.* Library and Archives Canada, Ottawa, Ontario.

Merchant Mariner Deceased War Casualty Files, 1939–1952. NARA, Archives I, Washington, DC.

Merchant Ship Movement Cards. MMRC, NARA, Archives II.

Papers of Bert Webber. Hoover Institution Library and Archives, Stanford, California.

Papers of John Toland. NARA Franklin D. Roosevelt Library and Museum, Hyde Park, New York.

Record Group 24-D-20A, Volume 12160, "Commanding Officer Pacific Coast, 1939–1946." Library and Archives Canada.

Record Group 32, Records of the Ship Construction Division of the Emergency Fleet Corporation. In Records of the U.S. Shipping Board, NARA, Archives II.

Record Group 92.5.4, Records of the Transportation Service/Division (1920–1942). In Records of the Office of the Quartermaster General. MMRC, NARA, Archives II.

Record Group 178, Records of the United States Maritime Commission. NARA, Archives II.

Record Group 181.2.13, Records of the 14th Naval District (Pearl Harbor, Hawaii). NARA, San Francisco, California.

Record Group 214, Records of the Office of Emergency Management, 1940–1944. NARA, Archives II.

Report of Proceedings, HMCS Prince Robert, *Dec. 1941, F.G. Hart, RCN.* Library and Archives Canada.

U.S. World War II Army Enlistment Records, 1938–1946. MMRC, NARA, Archives II.

Vessel Movement Cards, Port of San Francisco (1940–41). National Park Service, San Francisco Maritime National Park, San Francisco, California.

Interviews

Bailin, Amy (niece of Samuel J. Ziskind). October 12, 2009.

Grover, Inez Lerner (sister of Bernice Lerner Ziskind, sister-in-law of Samuel J. Ziskind). October 9, 2009.

Knaefler, Tomi (Honolulu *Star-Bulletin* reporter who interviewed Minoru Yokota and his wife in 1966). March 26, 2008.

Pratte, Alf (Honolulu *Star-Bulletin* reporter who wrote the paper's 1966 articles on *Cynthia Olson*). April 3, 2008.

Robinson, Eleanor Beck (stepdaughter of William P. Buchtele). April 10, 2008.

Unpublished Manuscripts

Allen, Riley H. "A Footnote to the History of World War II." Paper read at the meeting of the Social Science Association, Honolulu, T.H., November 3, 1947.

Yokota, Minoru. "I Was the Captain of a Submarine." n.d.

SECONDARY SOURCES

Books

————. *America's Merchant Marine*. Banker's Trust Company, 1920.

————. *American-Swedish Historical Museum Yearbook*. American-Swedish Historical Foundation, 1947.

————. *History of the Honolulu Engineer District, 1905–1965*. U.S. Army Engineer District, Honolulu, Hawaii, 1970.

————. *Merchant Vessels of the United States (years 1918, 1928–32, 1939)*. U.S. Government Printing Office, 1918, 1928–32, 1939.

————. *Ships in Gray*. Matson Navigation Company, 1946.

Allen, Gwenfread; *Hawaii's War Years, 1941–1945*. University of Hawaii Press, 1950.

Beasley, Maurine H. *Eleanor Roosevelt and the Media*. University of Illinois Press, 1987.

Benson, Richard M. *Steamships and Motorships of the West Coast*. Superior Publishing, 1968.

Boyd, Carl, and Akihiko Yoshida. *The Japanese Submarine Force and World War II*. Naval Institute Press, 1995.

Bridgland, Tony. *Waves of Hate: Naval Atrocities of the Second World War*. Naval Institute Press, 2002.

Browning, Robert M. *U.S. Merchant Vessel War Casualties of World War II*. Naval Institute Press, 1996.

Bunker, John. *Heroes in Dungarees: The Story of the American Merchant Marine in World War II*. Naval Institute Press, 1995.

Bureau of Marine Inspection and Navigation, U.S. Department of Commerce.

Burlingame, Burl. *Advance Force Pearl Harbor*. Naval Institute Press, 1992.

Bykofsky, Joseph, and Harold Larson. *The Transportation Corps: Operations Overseas*. In the series *United States Army in World War II*. U.S. Government Printing Office, 1957.

Carpenter, Dorr, and Norman Polmar. *Submarines of the Imperial Japanese Navy, 1904–1945*. HarperCollins, 1986.

Charles, Roland W. *Troopships of World War II*. Army Transportation Association, 1947.

Clephane, Lewis P. *History of the Naval Overseas Transportation Service in World War I*. U.S. Government Printing Office, 1969.

Conn, Stetson, Rose C. Engleman, and Byron Fairchild. *Guarding the United States and Its Outposts*. In the series *United States Army in World War II*. U.S. Government Printing Office, 1964.

Dorrance, William H. *Fort Kamehameha: The Story of the Harbor Defenses of Pearl Harbor*. White Mane Publishing Co., 1993.

Dowling, Rev. Edward J., S.J. *The "Lakers" of World War I*. University of Detroit Press, 1967.

———. *Know Your Lakers of World War I*. Marine Publishing Co., 1978.

Dunn, Herb, and Meryl Henderson. *Jackie Robinson: Young Sports Trailblazer*. Alladin, 1999.

Dzuiban, Stanley W. *Military Relations Between the U.S. and Canada*. In the series *United States Army in World War II (Special Studies)*. U.S. Government Printing Office, 1959.

Edwards, Bernard. *Blood and Bushido: Japanese Atrocities at Sea, 1941–1945*. Brick Tower Press, 1997.

Felton, Mark; *Slaughter at Sea: The Story of Japan's Naval War Crimes*. Naval Institute Press, 2008.

Freeman, A. C. *The Cases of General Value and Authority Subsequent to Those Contained in the "American Decisions" and the "American Reports," Decided in the Courts of the Several States. Selected, Reported, and Annotated by A. C. Freeman*. San Francisco, 1907.

Ghareeb, Gordon, and Martin Cox. *Hollywood to Honolulu: The Story of the Los Angeles Steamship Company*. Steamship Historical Society of America, 2009.

Gibson, Charles Dana, and E. Kay Gibson. *Over Seas: U.S. Army Maritime Operations, 1898 Through the Fall of the Philippines*. Ensign Press, 2002.

Golden, Frank, and Michael Tipton. *Essentials of Sea Survival*. Human Kinetics, 2002.

Greenhous, Breteton. *"C" Force to Hong Kong: A Canadian Catastrophe*. Dundurn Press, 1997.

Grover, David H. *U.S. Army Ships and Watercraft of World War II*. Naval Institute Press, 1987.

———. *The San Francisco Shipping Conspiracies of World War I*. Western Maritime Press, 1995.

Hamilton, Captain James W., and First Lieutenant William J. Bolce Jr. *Gateway to Victory: The Wartime Story of the San Francisco Port of Embarkation*. Stanford University Press, 1946.

Hashimoto, Mochitsura. *Sunk: The Story of the Japanese Submarine Fleet, 1942–45*. Avon Books, 1954.

Holwit, Joel Ira. *"Execute Against Japan": The U.S. Decision to Conduct Unrestricted Submarine Warfare*. Texas A&M University Press, 2009.

Johnson, Edna K. *The House of Tsutada: The Little Man with a Big God*. Wesley Press, 1988.

Klein, Woody. *All the President's Spokesmen*. Praeger Publishers, 2008.

Kurzman, Dan. *Left to Die: The Tragedy of the USS* Juneau. Pocket Books, 1995.

Larson, Harold. *Expansion of the Water Transport Branch, 1939–1942*. Office of the Chief of Transportation, Army Service Forces, June 1944.

———. *Water Transportation for the United States Army*. Office of the Chief of Transportation, ASF, August 1944.

———. *Troop Transports in World War II*. Office of the Chief of Transportation, ASF, March 1945.

———. *The Army's Cargo Fleet in World War II*. Office of the Chief of Transportation, ASF, May 1945.

———. *Role of the Transportation Corps in Overseas Supply*. Office of the Chief of Transportation, ASF, May 1946.

Leonard, M. K. *The Prince Ships, 1940–45*. Canadian Forces Directorate of History and Heritage, 1965.

Lucia, Ellis. *Head Rig: The Story of the West Coast Lumber Industry*. Overland West Press, 1965.

McNairn, Jack, and Jerry MacMullen. *Ships of the Redwood Coast*. Stanford University Press, 1945.

Newell, Gordon, and Joe Williamson. *Pacific Lumber Ships*. Bonanza Books, 1960.

Oka, Yukio. *Kaerazaru wakaki eiyutachi no densetsu*. Kojinsha Press, 1990.

Orita, Zenji, and Joseph Harrington. *I-Boat Captain*. Major Books, 1976.

Prados, John. *Combined Fleet Decoded: The Secret History of American Intelligence and the Japanese Navy in World War II*. Random House, 1995.

Prange, Gordon W., Donald M. Goldstein, and Katherine V. Dillon. *At Dawn We Slept: The Untold Story of Pearl Harbor*. Penguin Books, 1981.

———. *Dec. 7, 1941: The Day the Japanese Attacked Pearl Harbor*. Warner Books, 1989.

Sakamoto, Kaneyoshi. *History of Japanese Submarines (Nihon Kaigun Sensuikan-shi)*, Tokyo, 1979.

Shrader, Grahame F. *The Phantom War in the Northwest, 1941–1942*. Privately published, 1969.

Slackman, Michael. *Target: Pearl Harbor*. University of Hawaii Press, 1990.

Snodgrass, M. M. *Memories of the Richmond–San Rafael Ferry Company*. University of California, Berkeley, 1992.

Stille, Mark. *Imperial Japanese Navy Submarines, 1941–45*. Osprey Publishing, 2007.

Stindt, Fred A. *Matson's Century of Ships*. Privately published, 1982.

Stinnet, Robert B. *Day of Deceit: The Truth About FDR and Pearl Harbor*. The Free Press, 2000.

Thompson, Erwin N. *Pacific Ocean Engineers: A History of the U.S. Army Corps of Engineers in the Pacific, 1905–1980*. Pacific Ocean Division, U.S. Army Corps of Engineers, Honolulu, Hawaii, 1982.

United States Army Air Forces. *United States Strategic Bombing Survey Summary Report (Pacific), Naval Analysis Division, Interrogation of Japanese Officials*. U.S. Government Printing Office, 1946.

United States Coast Guard. *U.S. Merchant Ship Losses, December 7, 1941 to August 14, 1945*. U.S. Government Printing Office, 1948.

————. *Summary of Merchant Ship Personnel Casualties in World War II*. U.S. Government Printing Office, 1950.

United States Congress. *Joint Committee on the Investigation of the Pearl Harbor Attack, Part 22, Proceedings of the Roberts Commission*. U.S. Government Printing Office, 1946.

United States Navy. *Dictionary of American Naval Fighting Ships* (7 volumes). U.S. Government Printing Office, 1959–2008.

United States Office of War Information. *United States Government Manual, First Edition*. U.S. Government Printing Office, 1945.

Wardlow, Chester. *Organization and Activities of the Traffic Control Branch, Transportation Division, Office of the Quartermaster General, 1941–1942*. Office of the Chief of Transportation, Army Service Forces, Dec. 1943.

————. *The Transportation Corps: Responsibilities, Organization and Operations*. In the series *United States Army in World War II*. U.S. Government Printing Office, 1951.

————. *The Transportation Corps: Movements, Training and Supply*. In the series *United States Army in World War II*. U.S. Government Printing Office, 1956.

Webber, Bert. *Silent Siege III*. Webb Research Group, 1992.

Weintraub, Stanley. *Long Day's Journey into War: December 7, 1941*. Truman Talley Books/Plume, 1991.

Wenstadt, Tom. *Freighters of Manitowoc*. Author House Press, 2007.

Wisconsin Maritime Museum. *Maritime Manitowoc, 1847–1947*. Arcadia Publishing, 2006.

Worden, William L. *Cargoes: Matson's First Century in the Pacific*. The University Press of Hawaii, 1981.

Young, Donald J. *First 24 Hours of War in the Pacific*. Burd Street Press, 1998.

Newspaper Articles

Honolulu *Advertiser*:
   "Ship Movements." Aug.–Dec., 1941.

Honolulu *Star-Bulletin*:
   Pratte, Alf. "Prelude to Pearl Harbor: The Story of the Cynthia Olsen."
   Dec. 3–8, 1966.

London Times:
   "Japan Strikes." Dec. 8, 1941.

Los Angeles Times:
   "Shipping News." 1939–1941.

Manitowoc *Herald-Times* (Manitowoc, Wisconsin):
   "Manitowoc-Built Freighter Victim of Jap Submarine." Dec. 20, 1941.

New York Times:
   "Receivers for Earn Line." Oct. 18, 1913.
   "Whisky Train Arrives." Jan 1, 1920.
   "Strike Hits Whisky Export." Jan. 3, 1920.
   "Want Government Aid in Whisky Disposal." Jan. 7, 1920.
   "Andrew F. Mahony" (obituary). Nov. 9, 1933.
   "Japan Wars on U.S. and Britain." Dec. 8, 1941.
   "Army Freighter Lost with 35 Men Aboard." Feb. 7, 1942.
   "Riley H. Allen" (obituary). Oct. 3, 1966.

News-Pilot (San Pedro, California):
   "'Transport' Reported Sunk Commanded by San Pedran." Dec. 12, 1941.

Oakland *Tribune*:
   "Coasters to be Diverted." June 26, 1941.

Oregon Journal:
   "Some Historians Believe NW Ship Sunk by Japanese Before Pearl
   Harbor."
   Dec. 7, 1972

San Francisco *Call*:
   "Her Captain Is a Boy." Dec. 9, 1895.

San Francisco *Chronicle*:
   "Steamship Movements." Sept. 12–16, 1941.

Seattle *Post-Intelligencer*:
   "Shipping News." Oct.–Dec. 1941.
   "Sub Sinks Ship Off Neah Bay; 55 Saved." June 10, 1942.

Seattle *Times*:
"Survivors Safe Ashore." June 10, 1942.

Washington *Daily News* (Washington, North Carolina):
"Mother of Soldier 'Lost at Sea' Gets Confirming Letter." Feb. 13, 1942.
"Ernest J. Davenport, of Creswell, First Man from This County to Die in War." Feb. 14, 1942.
"In Memoriam." Feb. 16, 1942.
"To My Brother." Feb 16, 1942.
"Get Death Certificate for Soldier Missing Since First Day War." Mar. 7, 1942.

Magazine/Journal Articles
"Architect and Engineer of California." August, 1912.
Boyd, Carl. "American Naval Intelligence of Japanese Submarine Operations Early in the Pacific War." *The Journal of Military History*, vol. 53, no. 2, April, 1989.
"Editor for the Islands: Riley H. Allen." *Time*, Aug. 1, 1960.
Grover, David H. "Strange Mystery of the Cynthia Olson." *Sea Classics*, April, 2003.
Hayashi, Saburo. "The First Success of an I-Class Submarine on the Opening Day of the War." *Gakken Pictorial 17, IJN Submarines*, 2000.
Huston, G. "Awatea at War." *Marine News*, New Zealand Ship and Marine Society, Summer, 1991.
Jacobsen, Philip H. "Pearl Harbor: Radio Officer Leslie Grogan of the SS *Lurline* and His Misidentified Signals." *Cryptologia*, April, 2005.
McKellar, N. L. "Steel Shipbuilding Under the U.S. Shipping Board 1917–1921." *The Belgian Shiplover*, May/June, 1963.
"Rendezvous with Destiny." *Amper&and*, Alexander & Baldwin, Inc., Winter, 1991.
Shelley, C. R. "HMCS *Prince Robert*: The Career of an Armed Merchant Cruiser." *Canadian Historical Review*, vol. 7, no. 4, 1996.
"Something Is Going to Happen." *Amper&and*, Alexander & Baldwin, Inc., Winter 1991.
Weintraub, Stanley. "What Happened to the Cynthia Olson?" *Naval History*, December, 2001.

Internet Databases/Resources
University of Detroit, Mercy, Fr. Edward J. Dowling, S.J. Marine Historical Collection.

INDEX

merchant marine and mariners,
44, 51, 54, 61, 80, 117, 154,
164, 181, 189, 193
Merchant Marine Act (1920), 9
Midway, 74, 84, 138, 213n26
Mills, James Wood, 52, 78, 97, 145
death benefits for, 129
minesweepers, 37
Missing Persons Act, 128
Mito, Hisashi, 68
Montegrejo, Isidro Espejo, 53, 95
Moore, Thomas Grier, 53, 78, 95
Moore & McCormack, 47, 48
Morison, Samuel Eliot, 163
Muirhead, Thomas, Jr., 52, 78, 95
Murray (Captain of *Etolin*), 107

Nagato (battleship), 75
Nagumo, Chuichi, 72
Nantahala (cargo ship), 45–47
Narahara, Shogo, 73, 182
National Memorial Cemetery of
the Pacific, 189
Naval Overseas Transportation
Service (NOTS), 45
Newton, John H. (Rear Admiral),
74
North Pacific Gyre, 187
NOTS. *See* Naval Overseas
Transportation Service

Office of Emergency
Management, 37, 208n9
Office of Naval Intelligence
(ONI), 117–18, 122, 140
Ohmae, Toshikazu, 162, 173,
227n11
Oka, Yukio, 68, 91, 100–102, 104,
166, 178, 185, 192
Oliver J. Olson (schooner), 19–20,
26
Oliver J. Olson Steamship
Company

Army contracts (WWI), 24–5
Army contracts (WWII), 26–28,
31–36, 38–39
on the loss of *Cynthia Olson*,
116, 118–19, 162
demise of the company, 191–92
partnership with Mahoney,
21–3
payment agreement for crew of
Cynthia Olson, 124, 127
purchase of *Coquina* and
Corrales by, 1, 15, 29–30
request for reimbursement for
loss of *Cynthia Olson*, 131–34
spin-off of Richmond-San
Rafael ferry, 23
start up under Oliver Olson,
19–21
under Whit and George Olson,
26–28
Olson, Delia Lacey, 17
Olson, Edward Whitney "Whit",
27–30, 32, 38, 39, 118, 126, 192
suing for reimbursement,
131–34
Olson, George, 27–30, 32, 38, 39,
118, 192
suing for reimbursement,
131–34
Olson, Lewis (Lars Ollsen
Vastvedt), 17–19
Olson, Mary Elizabeth Whitney
(Mrs. Oliver), 23
Olson, Oliver John, 17–27
Olson, Oliver John, Jr., 23–24, 25,
27, 192
Olson, Walter, 25
Olson, William, 18–19, 25, 204n5
Olson & Mahoney (cargo ship), 22
Olson & Mahoney Steamship
Company, 21–24
Olson Company. *See* Oliver J.
Olson Steamship Company

World War I, need for shipping
and transportation in, 5–7
World War II
Allen's talk on, 137–41
casualties of, 189
civilian mariners killed during,
127
Cynthia Olson as first casualty
of, 162, 171
and Japanese Americans in
Hawaii, 158
missing service members and
merchant seamen, 127, 172
and war in the Pacific, 151

Yale (passenger-cargo steamer), 12
Yamamoto, Isoroku (Admiral),
64, 75, 101, 146
Yamazaki, Shigeaki, 68
Yokota, Minoru (Commander)
action after sinking *Cynthia
Olson*, 145–47
answering Webber's questions,
166–67, 172
assigned to IJN submarine
I–44, 150
assignment for Operation
Hawaii, 74–75, 89–90
attack on the *Cynthia Olson*,
102–5
conversion to Christianity,
153–55, 164, 165
early training and education,
64–67
on the fate of *Cynthia Olson*'s
crew, 159, 163–64
firing on Estevan Point
lighthouse, 148
firing on *Saratoga*, 149
as high school teacher, 153, 155,
157

interrogated by Allied war-
crimes investigators,
151–52
interview with Tomi Knaefler,
158–59, 172
interviewed by Prange, 169,
172, 185
later life, 192
photos, photo insert
Pratte's search for, 157–58
preparations for reconnaissance
mission, 67–69
promoted to captain, 151
reasons for altering facts of
attack, 172–73
reconnaissance in the
Aleutians, 70–72, 74
repatriation duty, 152
sighting and identifying
Cynthia Olson, 90–91, 100–101
sinking of *Coast Trader*, 147
sinking of *Juneau*, 149
training for submarine duty,
66–67
Yokota, Utako, 153

Zellerbach Paper conglomerate,
192
Ziskind, Bernice Lerner, 59–60,
116, 128, 193–94, photo insert
Ziskind, Samuel J. "Sam"
background, 58–59
with Bernice, photo insert
death notification and benefits
to family, 122–23, 128
radio signal sent by, 102, 106–9,
113, 167, 172, 174–78, 180,
184–85, 187
responsibilities on *Cynthia
Olson*, 56, 98–99
Zuikaku (aircraft carrier), 72